Let Your Light Shine

Volume II

Pioneer Women Educators of Wyoming

Editor: Priscilla McKim

Printed by: Rustler Printing and Publishing, Cody, Wyoming

Published by: Alpha Xi State, Delta Kappa Gamma

Copyright © 1985 by Alpha Xi State, Delta Kappa Gamma

All rights reserved. Except for use in a review, the reproduction or utilization of this work in any form or by an electronic, mechanical or other means, now known or hereafter invented, including xerography, photocopying and recording, and in any information storage and retrieval system, is forbidden without the written permission of the publisher.

Library of Congress Catalog Card Number: 84-063062

ISBN: 0-930535-01-4

Manufactured in the United States of America.
Second Edition, First Printing

To the people of Wyoming who have been influenced by the loving care and dedication of these fine educators.

Priscilla Fay McKim
State Chairman LYLS Committee, 1985

ALPHA XI STATE
Wyoming

Alpha	Cheyenne	April 26, 1941
Beta	Casper	October 12, 1950
Gamma	Powell	May 14, 1949
Delta	Afton	November 12, 1949
Epsilon	Goshen, Platte and Niobrara	April 22, 1950
Zeta	Albany County	April 22, 1950
Eta	Fremont County	March 21, 1953
Theta	Campbell and Crook	April 29, 1955
Iota	Hot Springs County	May 14, 1955
Kappa	Sheridan and Johnson	April 12, 1959
Lambda	Newcastle	March 17, 1962
Mu	Carbon County	October 4, 1963
Nu	Converse County	May 4, 1968
Xi	Douglas	August 1978
Omicron	Kemmerer	October 14, 1978
Pi	Cody	May 4, 1980
Rho	Big Horn County	May 4, 1980
Sigma	Washakie County	September 13, 1980
Tau	Sundance	September 25, 1980
Upsilon	Laramie County	April 1982
Phi	Laramie County	April 1982
Chi	Teton County	October 9, 1982
Psi	Rock Springs	May 17, 1983
Omega	Evanston	May 17, 1983

TABLE OF CONTENTS

BERYL AGEE

I firmly believe that the early-day school teacher deserves a place among the pioneers of Wyoming. The hardships endured, the primitive conditions that existed in the rural schools, the many tasks required of her, and the meager salary received for her services should most certainly qualify her to be listed as a true pioneer.

My parents owned a wheat farm near Beardsley, Minnesota, where I was born, August 24, 1900, the fourth child of John William and Elsie Wakefield Hoel. They moved to Idaho when I was 2 years of age, and later located in South Dakota. Because my father was successful in a land drawing, we lived on his section of land on the Rosebud Reservation during the summer months. In September, we moved back to our home in Bonesteel to attend school.

It was while living on the Indian Reservation near Dallas, South Dakota, that I first saw and made friends with Indian children. I enjoyed playing with them and soon learned of their interest in books. Together, we built a makeshift schoolroom of boxes and whatever materials we could find. We put our books on shelves made of orange crates and played school. They usually wanted me to be the teacher, a role that I enjoyed.

We left South Dakota in the spring of 1910 to make our home in Wyoming. Our farm was located three miles south of Basin on South Bench, as it was then called. That fall, my sisters and I attended the South Bench School. It was our first experience in a rural school, and we were eager to find out how one teacher could teach all the grades. Miss Lucy Federson was our teacher, and I learned later that it was her first term of teaching. Looking back on that year, I can appreciate just how she must have felt when she faced that group of children in the one-room schoolhouse with the pot-bellied stove and double desks. Little did I realize that in a few years I would find myself in a similar situation.

The following year, we were enrolled in the Basin elementary school and continued to attend school there until we finished high school.

Because of World War I, teachers were in great demand, especially in the rural schools. Mrs. Bertha K. Van Devender, my former eighth-grade teacher, recommended me for the position of a rural teacher to Mrs. Elaine Kinder, county superintendent of Big Horn County. Mrs. Kinder interviewed me and urged me to teach the first four grades at the Stringtown School between Otto and Burlington. In order to qualify, I took examinations in several elementary subjects and obtained my third-class teaching certificate.

Thus, I ventured out on my teaching career; a young girl with only a high school education, but with a strong determination to make good, if possible. I felt hopelessly unqualified and unprepared, as I struggled through the first week of teaching. Fortunately, Miss Caroline McIntosh, the upper grade teacher, was most understanding and helped me to solve many of my problems. We did our own janitor work, built our fires in the crude, old-fashioned stoves, carried coal and kindling from the coal shed, and pumped water from the well in the school yard.

It was a constant worry to me whether I was teaching the children as I should and was greatly relieved when Mrs. Kinder visited our school in the early spring. After reviewing the work and visiting my classes, she assured me that all was well and seemed pleased with my accomplishments.

That winter of 1917 and '18 was a severely cold one. Miss McIntosh and I shared a room and boarded with a family who lived one mile from the schoolhouse. For this, we each paid $20 a month out of our salary of $65. Modern conveniences were not available in farmhouses at that time and snow often blew through the cracks of the logs into our bedroom.

On April 26th of that year, we had one of the worst blizzards I have ever seen in Wyoming. On arriving at school, we filled every container we had with coal, since the storm was becoming more severe. We thought that surely no parents would allow children to come to school in that storm, but felt obligated to stay, since some child may have started before the storm became so bad. We were relieved when none appeared. We let the fire go out in my room to save fuel, and after eating our lunches, felt uneasy about returning to our boarding place, but decided to try it. That seemed the longest mile I have ever walked. The snow had drifted over the fences, and visibility was nearly zero. Fortunately, the wind was blowing toward our backs and we took hold of hands, so we couldn't become separated. Finally, we came in contact with a haystack which we knew was not far from the sheep corrals near the barn. By edging our way around the stack, we came to a board panel that we knew was on the west side of it. This helped us to get our bearings, and by going in a straight line from there, we soon reached the corrals. We followed around this to the gate and then on to the house, very cold and exhausted, but thankful that we hadn't become entirely lost or frozen.

The storm continued for another day, and on the following day one of the men at the farm took us to school in a wagon. The snow had drifted over the steps and nearly to the top of the door, so had to be shoveled away before we could get inside the schoolhouse.

There were fewer pupils at Stringtown the following year, so the school board decided to hire only one teacher. I attended the University of Wyoming at Laramie for the summer term, and was asked to teach the rural school at Bonanza for a salary of $90 a month. The closest boarding place was three miles from school, and cost $30 each month which included the use of a saddle horse to ride. I was skeptical about how this would work out in cold weather.

The pupils were very well-behaved and cooperative, but having 16 in all eight grades was indeed a challenge. By means of correlating the subjects, I finally worked out a schedule that could be followed.

Since the children lived so far from school, and their cold lunches seemed inadequate for proper nourishment, I suggested to the mothers that we arrange for a hot dish at noon. Each mother agreed to provide food each day for one week, food that could be heated on the top of our stove in the schoolroom. This plan worked very well, and the children were delighted with the idea.

As the days grew colder, I found the ride on horseback to school became too uncomfortable and endangered my health. I decided to ask permission of the school board to put up curtains in one corner of the schoolroom and set up housekeeping there. They agreed, and each family donated enough articles of furniture that I could live comfortably. However, it was a lonely life and I had no means of transportation. The stage driver brought my mail and groceries from Manderson or Hyattville, and one of the mothers did my laundry.

At the close of the term, I refused to sign a contract to return to Bonanza. I arranged to take some correspondence courses from Laramie, and earned a first-class teaching certificate.

Mr. Asa Mercer wrote and asked to see me about teaching the Mercer School near Hyattville. The salary was attractive, and I could have room and board with the Asa Mercer family who lived near the schoolhouse. That was a pleasant term and all went well. Mrs. Bertha K. Van Devender took office as county superintendent in January, and I was pleased to have her visit school that spring. At the close of the term, I was asked to return, but since a romance was coming into my life, I decided not to sign the contract.

Soon after the close of school, I was married to Ernest L. Agee and we made our home on his ranch near Burlington. I hadn't planned to teach that year, but a teacher in Burlington resigned and I was asked to finish the term.

Two sons were born to us and my time was occupied with the role of wife and mother. However, when our sons were in high school, I began taking extension courses in education and completed several subjects by correspondence from the University of Wyoming.

During the depression years, we sold our farm and moved to Basin. Both sons completed high school and went to the service in World War II.

A shortage of teachers was prevalent and I was urged to return to teaching. I attended a term of summer school at Northwest Community College at Powell to further qualify myself. Mrs. Myrtle Hunsaker was county superintendent at that time and asked me to teach at Stringtown, since that district was in need of a teacher. So I taught at the school where I had first begun my teaching career in 1917, but under very different circumstances. This time, I drove my car from Basin each day and had a janitor. At the close of the term, the Stringtown district was consolidated with the Greybull schools.

In October 1945, I received a call from Mr. J.C. Quigg, superintendent of the Greybull schools, asking me to substitute for a second-grade teacher whose mother was critically ill. The teacher did not return and I completed the term. I was asked to return the following year, and continued to teach second grade in Greybull until my retirement in 1969. This was a valuable experience for me, and I enjoyed those years in Greybull.

While teaching there, I served one term as president of the Greybull Classroom Teachers. In 1955 I was elected president of the Rebekah Assembly of Wyoming and was granted a one-year leave of absence to assume the duties pertaining to that office.

Each summer while teaching in Greybull, I attended the summer sessions at Eastern Montana College of Education in Billings, Montana, and was graduated with a B.S. degree in June 1963. This was a goal for which I had worked long and very hard.

As an active member of the Methodist church in Basin, I have taught Sunday school classes for many years; have been active in the Mission Circle of the WSCS, and the Basin Women's Club. In 1969 I served as worthy matron of Lewisia Chapter of the OES.

Since retirement, I did substitute teaching in the Basin elementary school and am grateful for the privilege of helping to teach when needed. I later moved to California to live near one of my sons. (She died there December 16, 1983.)

— Rho Chapter

JESSIE MAE AGNEW

Age above 90 and still going strong! These words describe Jessie Mae!

Illinois, California, Nebraska, Louisiana, Texas, Wisconsin and finally Casper, Wyoming! where, to put it in her own words: "I intended to stay only two years but the Casper board was so good to furnish my needs and assistants, and the teachers so fine to work with that I stayed on as supervisor of Casper and Midwest music for 25 years. When I was required to retire in 1948 because of my age, it nearly broke my heart, as I loved my work."

But she didn't repine long. Soon she was as busy as ever: directing local singing groups, selling real estate, taking dancing lessons, traveling over the world, and otherwise "having a ball." She even rode in the parade as marshal of the Central Wyoming Fair and Rodeo. Who could ask for more! As she put it, "My life has been a most happy one, with wonderful parents, a happy home life, and the successes I have had are memories to be cherished. The joys of teaching have been mine; I hope I have imparted ideals for richer living on the part of my students and those with whom I have been associated."

— Beta Chapter

LEAH MARSH BAIN

Leah Ellen Marsh was born September 14, 1894, at the Marsh Ranch, 45 miles northeast of Cheyenne on Bear Creek. She was the third of seven children born to Amanda and France Marsh.

Leah attended school through the eighth grade at the Marsh Ranch School. She attended College High School in Greeley, Colorado. Following graduation in 1912, Leah took the test for teacher certification, passed it, and taught her younger brothers and sisters and a cousin at the red schoolhouse at the ranch.

Leah married R.C. Bain and lived in Greeley and Denver for several years. When the marriage broke up, Leah and her two children returned to the Marsh Ranch. Again Leah took the test for rural teaching. She and her daughter rode horseback three and a half miles—and seven gates!—to a country school where Leah taught all grades and performed all janitorial duties—building fires in the wood stove, carrying water in a bucket, etc. Even the grain for the horses had to be carried in a sack tied onto the saddle. This was really the beginning of a remarkable career in education.

The following year Leah taught a rural school a mile from the ranch. She had only three students—her son, daughter and a neighbor's daughter.

The next three years Leah taught first and second grades at Chugwater, Wyoming. Then she and her children moved to Greeley, Colorado, where Leah attended college for a year. This was followed by teaching first grade for five years in the Greeley public schools.

Leah Marsh Bain came to Cheyenne to teach in 1934. She taught third grade at Corlett School, at the old Administration Building (on the corner of Central Avenue and 22nd Street), and at Fincher School.

In 1946 Leah became principal of the new Deming School and also taught half a day. In 1949-1950 she was principal of Deming and Clark schools. When the new Henderson School opened in 1951, Leah was appointed principal. She held this position until her retirement in 1960.

Leah's education was necessarily spread over many years of summer school, extension and correspondence courses, and one full year on campus. After 17 years she received her AB degree from Colorado State Teachers' College (now the University of Northern Colorado). Her daughter had already received her AB from the same school. Leah's undergraduate work was also from the University of Wyoming. Her graduate work was from the above-mentioned universities plus the universities of Denver and Colorado.

Leah had been reared with the premise that each person must construbute to the community. During her years in education she served three years on the Laramie County Welfare Board, eight years on the Laramie County Library Board, and on the Steering Committee for United Way. She served as president of the Laramie County Teachers' Association. For many years she was a member of the choir of the Methodist Church. Leah was an active member of the Order of Eastern Star and served as worthy matron of Oak Leaf Chapter 6.

In addition, Leah was a charter member of Alpha Chapter, Delta Kappa Gamma, an active member of AAUW, WEA and NEA. She was appointed by Governor Clifford P. Hansen to serve three years on the state School District Reorganization Committee. She was very active in the DePaul Hospital Guild, serving as co-chairman of the lunch committee for the annual bazaar in addition to other duties. She was also a member of the Memorial Hospital Auxiliary. She has been an active member and past president of Chapter C of the PEO Sisterhood.

5

Following her retirement from teaching, Leah was elected as the first active woman board member to the School District 1 board (Cheyenne). The first time she was elected, she polled the most votes of all candidates. She served eight years. During this period she was a panel member at the National School Board meeting at Houston, Texas. She also received the Golden School Bell Award from the Wyoming State School Board Association.

Since her retirement, Leah Bain has traveled extensively: 1960, NEA tour to Hawaii; 1966, tour of the Orient and a tour of Europe; a cruise to Acapulco; a cruise of the Caribbean; 1976, cruise through the Panama Canal to Buenos Aires, Argentina, with a return by air via Lima, Peru.

Before retirement Leah had traveled by automobile coast to coast and border to border in the United States plus western Canada and short trips into Mexico.

In addition to traveling, her hobbies have included bridge, handcrafts, gardening and her family. Through the years she ran an unofficial hotel and boarding house for her numerous relatives.

Her delightful sense of humor and optimistic outlook have carried her successfully through all the ups and downs—her divorce, having to make a living for herself and two children, obtaining an education, several near-fatal illnesses, culminating in the death of her son, Robert, in 1964. He had a heart condition which had caused several prolonged hospitalizations and home bed-care. He had not been able to work for a number of years and had made his home with his mother.

Leah's daughter, Enola, followed in her mother's footsteps and taught in Cheyenne and is also a member of Alpha Chapter of Delta Kappa Gamma. There was a problem with Enola's being hired in Cheyenne. At the time she applied, after acquiring the mandatory two years' experience, she was told she was too young. A year later she was told her mother was such a tradition in Cheyenne there was no point in Enola's applying, because she simply could not live up to her mother's reputation, despite the two different fields—elementary and secondary. Enola was eventually hired and taught at McCormick Junior High and Central High School. Many years later, Enola returned to Cheyenne and taught at Johnson Junior High.

Leah says her greatest satisfaction in teaching is exemplified by one incorrigible boy. She is reminded each year of her great success with him by a letter from this very successful businessman thanking her for his success as a human being. This kind of influence is one of the greatest rewards of teaching.

Perhaps the greatest of Leah's honors came after her retirement when the new school in Sun Valley was named the Leah Marsh Bain Elementary School. She is especially proud that the principal, Weldon Borgaard, continues the same ideals and principles of education she always strived for.

— Alpha Chapter

RUTH BEEBE

R uth Beebe, daughter of Stuart Joseph Sharp and Virginia Clark, was born on the Bar V Ranch, Carbon County, Wyoming, September 12, 1895.

Ruth's father came to Wyoming in 1880 after persuading a boyhood friend to go west. The young men helped moved a Texas trail herd north to Ogallala, Nebraska. It was there where Mr. Sharp's friend returned to their native home in West Virginia while Mr. Sharp came to Laramie to spend the winter working for the Union Pacific. The next nine years were spent working on the various ranches until August 7, 1889, when he acquired the Bar V Ranch on Cherry Creek at the foot of the beautiful Ferris Mountain.

In 1893 he returned to West Virginia to marry Virginia Clark and bring her to their ranch home in Wyoming. On October 20, 1894, Ruth's sister, Mary, was born and on September 12, 1895, Ruth arrived. Just as she is today, Ruth couldn't be conventional and arrive in the normal nine-month period; eager to "get with it," and not waste a precious minute of her life, Ruth arrived two months early and spent the first three months of her life in a shoe box on the oven door. Today, Ruth claims her mother was never the same after Ruth joined the family. However, her mother was a great-niece of Capt. William Clark of the Lewis and Clark Expedition, so she had true "pioneer" blood in her veins and was, therefore, ready for anything her adventuresome daughter might hand out.

Ruth's education began with Miss Irene Daley in their tiny ranch school at the Bar V that the school districts provided in those early days because of the great distances between ranches and the lack of transportation as we know it today. Her first eight years were spent at the Bar V school with the exception of her third grade, which was spent in West Virginia because of her mother's health, and the seventh grade spent in Denver because of her sister's health. She attended East Denver High School for four years where she graduated in 1914. After graduating from Denver University in 1918, she began a 30-year teaching career, starting as assistant principal at Elizabeth High School in Elizabeth, Colorado. One year of city life and work was enough for this ranch girl. She returned to Wyoming to begin teaching at the very same small ranch schools she had known and attended as a child. Her first ranch school was at the J.T. Grieve home on the Diamond Six Ranch. In 1919 she married Ed Beebe and on September 20, 1921, their daughter, Virginia, was born. In 1922, she returned to the schoolroom at the R.L. Tully Ranch where she taught for four years. The next three years were spent in the Lamont School before she returned to Muddy Gap where she taught for the next 16 years. In 1955 she returned to Lamont to teach until her retirement in 1961.

Ruth has been a member of the Sweetwater Homemakers Extension Club for 40 years. She has held every office many times in her club and in 1959 directed the three-act play "They Went That-a-Way," which her club presented in the communities of Jeffrey City, Bairoil and Sweetwater. One scene was presented as entertainment at the 1960 Wyoming Extension Homemaker Council state meeting in Powell at the Powell High School. Ruth is the past county treasurer of the Carbon County Extension Homemakers Council and has attended many state meetings. She is a member of Delta Kappa Gamma, Delta Zeta, Wyoming State Historical Society, WEA, NEA, Carbon County Cow-Belles and the Wyoming Extension Homemakers Club. She holds a life certificate in teaching and is a life member of the NEA. In 1979 she shared the honor of acting as parade marshal of the Carbon County Fair with Mr. Herring of Encampment. Ruth is an active member of France Memorial Presbyterian Church of Rawlins.

Mrs. Beebe is the author of a book, REMINISCING ALONG THE SWEETWATER, published in 1973, for which she received an award from the Wyoming Historical Society, and in 1976 complied a book entitled SKELETONS OF THE PAST, built around her collection of antique bottles and tales of her community. The latest book was published in 1980. She also keeps and maintains her own personal and private museum of beautiful antiques at her ranch home on the 47 Ranch.

Ruth resides on the family ranch, the 47, which her father purchased in 1912. Her daughter and son-in-law, Virginia and Bill McIntosh, reside nearby at the Hat Ranch and her granddaughter, Ellen, resides in Rawlins. Both Virginia and Ellen, with Ruth, are active members of the Sweetwater Homemakers Extension Club.

As we look to history today and prepare to recognize our heritage, we have only to look at women like Ruth Beebe to see what pioneering contributed to developing women. Her love of life and family is a constant beacon for the young women of today to follow. If they do, they will find the true meaning of "Women's Lib"; the feeling of love and accomplishment as they work beside their husbands to build a home and family and at the same time to have a career of their own, to be their own person. Ruth Beebe is a woman and homemaker loved and revered by all who know her.

— Mu Chapter

MARGARET LUCILLE SNOW BEEDE

On Halloween in 1881, James Andrew Snow was born to Scotch and Irish parents. On Christmas Eve of that same year, Minnie Morris Chenoweth (a descendant of Robert Morris) was born to English and German parents, and 20 years later she would become his wife. On Thanksgiving Day in 1903, a son was born to them. On July 4th, 1906, another child was due. But it was not until July 7th that Margaret Lucille Snow made her debut into this world, thus breaking the holiday chain of birthdays. The father, mother and two children were all born at Decatur, Illinois. In 1918, another son was born, and in 1926 another daughter. The father might have become a great doctor, but there was not enough money for medical school, so he settled for the meat market and grocery business after three years as an insurance agent. At home he was a gourmet cook, with a unique flair for decorating the food and table.

The mother, before her marriage, made and designed hats at Decatur's largest department store. Later, she worked with her husband in his store, as well as providing a home full of love and security for her children. She, too, was an excellent cook, and her children and grandchildren can still remember the delicious aroma of hot homemade bread or cinnamon rolls when they came home after school. Yes, they remember—they remember! They remember the father's expert and tender dressing of serious cuts, and wish he could have been the doctor he so wanted to be. They remember the mother's going from house to house during the "great flu epidemic" with kettles of hot soup, clean bed linens, and loving care. Ah, yes, they remember—they remember!

As a little girl, while attending kindergarten in Denver, Lucille would curl her father's hair at night as he read his paper and say, "Someday I'll either be a hairdresser or a kindergarten teacher." She never became a hairdresser. It took nearly a quarter of a century before her dream to become a kindergarten teacher was realized, but then she taught kindergarten for four decades. She finished high school at Torrington in 1924 as valedictorian and so earned a four-year scholarship to the University of Wyoming. She had taken a "normal training" course during her senior year in high school. That made it possible for her to secure a teaching certificate for a rural school. That fall she was hired to teach a rural school in the Torrington district, five miles south of town, for $85 per month. So began the nine-year cycle of teaching in the winter and going to school each summer until 1933 when she received her BS degree from the University of Wyoming.

That first rural school was a "gold mine" of experiences. With 27 children in all eight grades, the teacher learned a lot. She learned never to make an eighth grade arithmetic assignment until she had worked every single problem first; she learned to kill her first rattlesnake the first week of school; she learned how to deal with a boy who had seizures; she learned how to enlist the help of a big boy just two years younger than the teacher; she learned how to organize box suppers and pie socials.

At the end of the year a sign was tacked on the school that said, "Model Rural School." She has seen many of the innovations run full cycle—open classrooms (she had it then); working individually with small groups (she did it then); having older children work with younger or slower children (she did it then); parent conferences (she had them then); hot lunch program (she had it then, only she cooked in the "cloak room"); physical education and physical fitness (she had it then—the children walked two and three miles to school and from school—the teacher, too—they played baseball and activity games at recess).

Of course, there were some "new" things that they hadn't yet experienced. They had never heard of "coffee breaks"; sending a child to the nurse for band-aids or bloody noses; playground supervisors; a "noon break"; custodians; teachers' aides; or audio-visual materials; guidance counselors or vomit compound. She was a bit like the old-fashioned family doctor—she had to do it all. It was her job, so she did it the best she could. But progress has brought many wonderful things to education, and dedicated teachers have always made a contribution.

In addition to her bachelor's degree from the University of Wyoming, Lucille also received her master's degree there in 1952. She also has 32 extra semester hours—some courses from the Sorbonne at Paris, France, the University of Northern Colorado at Greeley, and Colorado University at Boulder. She taught elementary education for eight years at what is now Eastern Wyoming College. She taught extension courses for six years for the University of Wyoming. She taught for four summers at the University of Wyoming field summer schools. She operated her own private kindergarten for over 35 years, then helped to set up the kindergarten in the Torrington public schools where she taught until retirement. She has worked four years since retirement in the Torrington schools where she has set up an "Early Childhood" program and she was asked to continue her work. She has taught at **every level** during her career from "Early Childhood" and kindergarten to the college level. She has also taught in Head Start, been education director of TriCounty Head Start, and taught in the migrant program for five summers.

Lucille is a member of the United Methodist Church, is a certified kindergarten laboratory teacher, has served as church school superintendent, teacher, children's coordinator and education chairman. She is a charter member of Epsilon Chapter of Delta Kappa Gamma, a member of Delta Psi Omega and Kappa Delta Phi. She is a past worthy matron of Eastern Star, past guardian of Job's Daughters, past president of Junior Women's Club, and past president of AAUW. She has traveled in 42 states, Mexico and seven European countries. She started the Adult Basic Education classes in Torrington, and taught in their night classes at the college there for four years. She served on the Torrington Board of Education and was on the board when the college was started there.

Her hobbies are giving book reviews and doll talks. She has a doll collection of 287 dolls, which includes dolls from 27 countries. One of her favorite dolls is a character doll of Madam Schumann-Heink, who wears a dress made of the curtain from the Metropolitan Opera where she so triumphantly sang. After Schumann-Heink's death the curtain was cut and sold and the proceeds went to help struggling young artists and musicians.

Lucille was married to Richard Fields, a young doctor who was to serve his internship at the American Hospital in Paris. Soon after their arrival in Paris, he contracted pneumonia and in three days was dead. Lucille finished her work at the Sorbonne and that fall resumed her teaching in Torrington. In 1936 she married Paul Beede. She has been a widow since 1957. They have two daughters, one son and eight grandchildren. There are no words to express the love and joy they have brought. Life has not always been easy—no one ever said it would be. But always it has been filled with love and warmth and hope. There is a Biblical passage that says, "Without a vision, the people perish." And always there has been a vision of what life can be, and especially a vision of what a teacher can and should be.

— Epsilon Chapter

THE BIDDICK SISTERS

On the plains northwest of Laramie is the well-known Biddick Ranch which was established in the mid-1880s by the parents of Edna and Mary Ethel Biddick. Under the guidance of their mother, a former teacher in England, the little girls began their first years of schooling at home. Their father, who loved the ranch life, shared his pleasure with his family and taught the girls to ride the gentle horses. At no time did he ever have the women folk work in the fields.

The growing girls listened to their parents and Aunt Delia Neville as they related days with relatives they knew in their native England. Dreams came true in time when the young ladies traveled to visit the cousins.

Graduates from the University of Wyoming, Miss Edna came to teach Latin in Laramie High School in 1910 and Miss Ethel went to teach in Rock Springs. In a few years Miss Edna resigned her position to travel and to do advanced work at Columbia University in New York City, Denver University and the University of Wyoming. She gained recognition as an outstanding scholar, reader and conversationalist.

While at Columbia she was offered a splendid position in the New York schools. She declined the attractive offer, giving as her reason that Laramie was her home and the people there were her people. She returned to Laramie High School to teach social science. Her popular course was that dealing with American problems. She was adored by the students in her classroom and the senior class members through the years were pleased to have her their class sponsor. Later, young men entering military service in World War II called on her preceding their departure to pay their respects. These simple formalities touched Miss Biddick deeply.

Following her successful teaching in Rock Springs, Miss Ethel came home to advance her knowledge in the ranching business under the guidance of her father, who raised top-grade Shorthorn cattle. The family had a home in Laramie in addition to the one on the ranch. When in town she frequently helped in the Laramie elementary schools as substitute teacher for several years.

In time she took over the business. An able manager helped, continuing the successful enterprise. Carloads of cattle were shipped to out-of-state stock centers where the top market was frequently reached. The Biddick herds were well-known among the stockgrowers of the nation.

In a quiet, unassuming manner, the friendly Biddick sisters took interest in community affairs. They participated in activities of the Catholic Church and were members of the American Association of University Women. They are remembered for their principles and ideals, the examples for dedicated living, broad minds and pleasing personalities.

— Zeta Chapter

VELMA BIDDLE

"Only the brave should teach, only the men and women whose integrity cannot be shaken, whose minds are enlightened enough to understand the high calling of the teacher, whose hearts are unshakably loyal to the young. . . ."

Miss Velma Biddle was born in Trumbull, Nebraska, the daughter of Mrs. Elsie Biddle of Holyoke, Colorado, and the late Arthur Biddle. She has three brothers—Vern, Larwill and Joel, all residing in Colorado.

When Miss Velma was a small girl living on a farm, she and her brothers were especially fond of little, woolly, yellow chickens. They also found a new pastime by smashing little chickens under planks by jumping on them.

She was graduated from Phillips County High School in Colorado as valedictorian of her class and received her bachelor of arts degree from Hastings College, Hastings, Nebraska, with a major in mathematics and English.

Her teaching career began at Highland Center School in Phillips County, Colorado, where she taught third, fourth and fifth grades for one year following her graduation from college. Then, she taught mathematics for eight years in Holyoke High School, Holyoke, Colorado, her hometown.

Lieutenant Biddle served her country during World War II in the Women Accepted for Volunteer Emergency Service, the name given to the Women's Naval Reserve, better known as the WAVES in the United States Navy. She was stationed in Washington, D.C., working in office administration from 1943 to 1946.

Wheatland, Wyoming, was her home in 1946-47 when she taught math there. She was not teaching the 1947-48 school term, but was called to Powell High School in the spring of 1948 to complete a school year. She taught English and mathematics there until her retirement, with the exception of 1955-56 when she had a leave of absence to earn her master of arts degree at the University of Colorado, Boulder, Colorado, with education as her major.

Baking cookies is only one of her many diversified hobbies. Nieces, nephews and friends are fortunate at Christmastime, and other special occasions, to receive a box of cookies—beautifully decorated, delicious cookies. Reading, of course, would be a hobby of an English teacher; she has many books and reads many magazines. Stamp collecting and gardening (both flower-growing and raising vegetables) are two longtime hobbies.

Miss Biddle is a member of Powell Classroom Teachers Association, Wyoming Education Association and the National Education Association. She served as president of the Northwest District of Wyoming Education Association in 1960-61 and conducted that district meeting in Cody in October of 1962. She was a member of the executive board of WEA, and has attended the Delegate Assembly of WEA several times. She was president of the Wyoming High School Press Association in 1957-58; and she is a member of Pi Sigma Rho, an organization of FTA advisers.

She was president of Gamma Chapter of Delta Kappa Gamma for two years. This is a Big Horn Basin chapter of the International Honor Society for Women Educators. She is also a member of two national honorary educational fraternities—Pi Lambda Theta and Kappa Delta Pi.

Other outside-school organizations of which she is a member include: Business and Professional Women of which she has been the state second vice president; American Association of University Women; Eastern Star; American Legion; and the Evening Circle of the Methodist Church.

Her travels include a trip to Europe and the Holy Land in 1936. She has attended the National English Teachers Convention in Boston, New York and Minneapolis. She has toured the United Nations on two occasions. She attended the national convention of Delta Kappa Gamma in Florida in the summer of 1960. In 1961 she attended the state convention of Delta Kappa Gamma in Sheridan, Wyoming, and the regional convention in Sun Valley, Idaho, where she was a speaker at both conventions with the topic, "Best Wishes, 1961." She attended the National Education Association Convention in Atlantic City, New Jersey, in the summer of 1961, and the 1962 NEA Convention in Denver. In late

July 1962 she left the states via jet airliner for an NEA tour of South America.

Miss Biddle served two years as a member of the Legislative Committee of WEA. She flew to Cheyenne in March to attend a committee meeting. This committee of 25 educators studied educational problems and endorsed and proposed legislation which came before the state Legislature.

"A teacher affects eternity, he can never tell where his influence stops," said Henry Adams. In Powell Senior High School, Miss Velma Biddle's influence affected the lives of the members of the PANTHER yearbook staff, Quill and Scroll and the Future Teachers of America, as well as those in her classroom. At the FTA convention banquet in Laramie, spring of 1961, a jeweled key was awarded to her for having a record of one of the longest sponsorships of continuous FTA in the state of Wyoming.

So, in 1962, it gave the members of the Helen Hayes Chapter of the Future Teachers of America great pleasure to pin her with a rose corsage and to award her the "Teacher of the Year" certificate.

— Rho Chapter

KATHRYN VIDA BLACK

Alpha Xi state.

Kathryn died in Powell October 11, 1964.

K athryn Black was born in Kearney, Nebraska February 5, 1902, and received her elementary and secondary education there. She attended Nebraska Teachers' College, University of Wyoming and Colorado College of Education in Greeley, receiving her bachelor's degree in elementary education from there in 1944.

She taught kindergarten in Gering, Nebraska, and Grand Island, Nebraska, until 1929 when she came to Powell where she taught grades one and two and grade three until her retirement in the spring of 1964.

She was secretary and treasurer of the Powell Classroom Teachers several years and was assistant grade school principal. She was also a member of the Presbyterian Church.

She became a charter member of Gamma Chapter of Delta Kappa Gamma in Cody in May 1949 and served as its parliamentarian, also belonging to its Scholarship, Membership and Teacher Welfare committees. She also was state chairman of Research Committee and state chairman of Welfare and Morale Committee for

— Gamma Chapter

MAURINE CARLEY

T hrough years of work with the Wyoming Historical Society, authorship of many historical books and articles, contributions to her community and profession, and teaching the story of Wyoming to hundreds of junior high children, Maurine Carley exemplifies the impact a teacher can have on her city and state. Her life is one of action and interest in Wyoming.

Maurine was born in Chadron, Nebraska, but came to Cheyenne at the age of 3 months, held on a pillow during the train ride. Most of her life has been spent in Cheyenne, living on the block between Capitol and Central in the area of the state capitol building. She attended Central School, also located near there, and later graduated from Colorado College in Colorado Springs. She taught history, including Wyoming history, at McCormick Junior High School in Cheyenne. An MA degree was obtained after four summers attending Columbia University in New York City. Her family witnessed much of the history of Cheyenne; her father was invited by Sheriff C.J. Smalley to witness the execution of Tom Horn on November 20, 1903, although he did not attend.

A desire by Maurine to preserve the history of Cheyenne and Wyoming in the pioneer spirit has resulted in much research and publication. The young people of Wyoming have used her books co-authored with Virginia Cole Trenholm as texts and great reading about Wyoming. They are WYOMING PAGEANT and SHOSHONIS, SENTINELS OF THE ROCKIES.

For 20 years she was the secretary of the Wyoming Historical Society. Recently, they honored her by presenting her with a painting of some Indian children, done by local artist Gordon Wilson, to commemorate her interest in history, children and Indians. Ten historical trail treks were organized by her and written up in the ANNALS OF WYOMING. These treks took place in automobile trips over the Oregon Trail, Bridger Trail, parts of the Bozeman Trail, and the Overland and Cheyenne-Deadwood stage lines with some freight trails and the Lander cutoff included. On the 1974 trek she was the guest of honor. The speeches and reminiscences published from the treks have preserved a part of Wyoming lore that might have have been lost.

Maurine served on the state 75th Anniversary Committee and was the only woman to serve on the Cheyenne Centennial Celebration Committee. Working with four others, they published the history of Cheyenne, entitled "Cheyenne, Magic City of the Plains." She was also chairman of the Cheyenne Homes Committee and wrote up the history of the famous old homes in the area. She has written the history of the Congregational Church and the Young Women's Christian Association of Cheyenne.

Her perspective on Wyoming has remained true and clear, giving comparison to the world which she has sought out and learned about through travels to Europe, Spain, Portugal, the Caribbean, two trips to the Orient, eight trips to Mexico and a visit to every state except North Dakota and Alaska.

Contributions to the teaching profession have been given by Maurine through leadership in professional organizations. For two years she was president of the Cheyenne Classroom Teachers' Association and president of the Wyoming Classroom Teachers' Association (1950-1952). In 1959 the Cuban government invited one teacher from each state to be its guest for two weeks in Havana and she was privileged to represent Wyoming. She served on the state Retirement Committee and in recent years has been secretary of the state Retired Teachers Association.

In addition, Maurine has served her community. She taught the Americanization class and English for the foreign-born for 16 years and always attended the Naturalization Court. She was the first woman to give a speech to the court in Wyoming when she was invited to do this in 1973. Another first was as the first president of the Cheyenne Chapter of AAUW. She also belongs to the Pioneer Club, DAR, Delta Kappa Gamma and participates very successfully in the bridge marathon group.

Cheyenne and Wyoming are the richer for her service, writing, teaching and keen interest in life—past and present.

Works by Maurine Carley in the Wyoming State Library: "Annals of Wyoming," Wyoming State Archives, Museums and Historical Department, 1925-1974. "Oregon Trail Treks," compiled by Maurine Carley, Trek Historian—Trek No. 1, 27:2:163-194; Trek No. 2, 28:1:41-67; Trek No. 3, 28:2:166-192; Trek No. 4, 29:1:67-85; Trek No. 5, 29:2:177-194; Trek No. 6, 30:1:37-55; Trek No. 7, 30:2:193-213; Trek No. 8, 31:1:77-93; and Trek No. 9, 31:2:213-236. Gives talk, "Castle Rock and Ruts" 29:2:188-189; review of Indian summer 25:1:104-109; review of Oglala Sioux 28:2:219-220; and in picture 30:2:220.

Trenholm, Virginia Cole, and Maurine Carley, WYOMING PAGEANT, Prairie Publishing Co., Casper, Wyoming 1946.

Carley, Maurine, THE YOUNG WOMEN'S CHRISTIAN ASSOCIATION, CHEYENNE, WYOMING, Cheyenne 1969.

Trenholm, Virginia Cole, and Maurine Carley, SHOSHONIS, SENTINELS OF THE ROCKIES, University of Oklahoma Press, Norman 1964

— Alpha Chapter

Rosella Carson

Rosella Carson was born on a homestead north of Pine Bluffs, Wyoming, on November 27, 1891. She married C.K. Carson in 1916, and they have been residents of Laramie County since that time. They have one son, Dr. Charles "Kit" Carson Jr., who resides in Cheyenne; one granddaughter, Lana Carson Brown; and one great-grandson.

Her elementary schooling was in Pine Bluffs and her high school education in Cheyenne. Her advanced training was at the University of Wyoming. She taught in rural, elementary and high schools of Laramie County. Mrs. Carson was elected county superintendent of schools, from which position she retired in 1959, after serving the many people of Laramie County and the state of Wyoming in an educational capacity.

Mrs. Carson was instrumental in aiding and encouraging many high school pupils to complete their education by sharing her home with them. While working in the state Department of Education, she was privileged to spend six weeks as the "sighted companion" for a blind girl who was on an observation mission to complete her teacher training program to enable her to become a teacher of the blind. Another example of her help to young people was shown when Rosella took into her home and for several months cared for a teacher who was ill and had become a terminal case.

As a member of the Methodist Church, she participates in its many functions, especially those pertaining to the Women's Society of Christian Service.

Mrs. Carson holds memberships in several civic, educational and fraternal organizations. Among those are Women's Club, National Education Association, Wyoming Education Association, life member of Delta Kappa Gamma, American Legion Auxiliary (25-year member), past matron of the Order of Eastern Star, White Shrine, Pythian Sisters, and Wyoma Rebekah Lodge 40. In 1958 she was selected by the Business and Professional Women's Club as their "Woman of the Year."

Rosella is ever ready to "visit the sick, aid the distressed, and care for the needy," and is ever ready to recognize the capabilities of others and always speaks highly of them.

— Alpha Chapter

MARION DUGUID CLEWORTH

Marion Cleworth was born in 1902 to Dr. John and Isabella Duguid at Springfield, South Dakota. She says she began to learn by doing in the fourth grade with her first violin, then a full-sized violin by fifth grade. When she was in about eighth grade, she received a much better instrument—with it she played in a college orchestra, a string group and an orchestra of townspeople. During her high school days, Marion gave violin lessons to the local children.

In 1916 Marion worked on a ranch during harvest time, helping with food preparation, especially the noon meal, for a table full of workmen. She also did dish washing, cleaning up after the meal, then made beds and did laundry—and anything else that was requested of her!

During the summer following her junior year, she worked in a general store doing office work on Wednesday evenings until 9 or 10 and on Saturdays until midnight. During her senior year, she worked part-time and then full-time in the summer, saving toward her first year at Yankton College.

Marion continued her music at the Conservatory in piano and violin. She also was accompanist for a voice student. She was a member of a church choir. Her second year of college was at the Normal School in Springfield, South Dakota, where she continued music (violin and voice). She had charge of a church choir and sang and played in recitals.

In the fall of 1922 she began teaching seventh and eighth grade in Frankfort, South Dakota, where she taught two terms. She has kept in touch with those students through class reunions since then.

Marion married in the summer of 1924. She has a son and daughter whom she saw through college. While living in Watertown, South Dakota, as a mother and homemaker, she participated in church choir and programs.

Marion lived in Aberdeen, South Dakota, in 1928 until the end of 1952 where she was involved in church activities, choir director, Women's Club, travel department, the YWCA. From 1941-1952 she was executive director and camp director. She sponsored many activities while in the Glider School and for the Radio School in Aberdeen.

Marion was responsible for the Information Desk at the Milwaukee Depot during the World War II period.

Marion attended many colleges including: Southern Normal School, Springfield; Yankton College; Southern State College; South Dakota University, Vermillion; Northern State College; the University of Wyoming; the University of Alaska; and she also attended the Recreation Leader Camp near Minneapolis for six summers. This was a very stimulating leading situation.

Marion received her degree in 1960 by continuing college studies as she worked. Her area of study was very broad and varied. She majored in sociology, economics and speech, with minors in English, German, educational psychology, guidance and secondary education.

Marion has held a number of positions, some of which were seventh and eighth grade at Frankfort, South Dakota; seventh and eighth grade at Hot Springs, South Dakota; English and speech, Springfield High School, South Dakota; English and German, Moorcroft High School; librarian and library science, Southern State College, South Dakota; and English instructor at Southern State College.

Marion says the summer school duties and teaching at Southern State Teachers' College were very stimulating experiences in working with students who, during the school year, were teachers with a wide area of interests.

Marion belonged to many professional associations including National Education Association, Wyoming Education Association, Newcastle Education Association, Foreign Language Department of NEA, South Dakota Personnel and Guidance Association, Wyoming Foreign Language Teachers' Association, Delta Kappa Gamma and Eastern Star.

Marion has traveled extensively and has taken a number of tours abroad including tours to England and Scotland, Alaska and western Canada, Europe, Hawaii and western United States, Scandanavia and Jerusalem.

Of her travels, Marion says, "Wherever I've gone—the areas differ, climate, occupation, traditions, customs, etc., were of special interest to me. We may read about other places and other people or hear lectures, but being there in person makes the total experience alive and in reality, a fact. European history, cities, people and countries have a totally different meaning for me today, especially when I read or hear news of places where I toured."

Of teaching, Marion said, "It is important to evaluate oneself and also necessary to look at oneself in terms of better procedures, better work results, and better student reaction to one's part of the total school program. It is important to look back a year or two or even five years or more and realize there have been personal improvements and that classroom work has not slipped into a rut or a fast, tight pattern."

Since retiring from classroom teaching, Marion has been very active in senior citizens' activities. She makes a report on the center and other happenings every Friday morning on the local radio station, KASL. She is also active in the District 1 Retirement School Personnel organization.

— Lambda Chapter

LAVINIA A. COLE

Lavinia A. Cole was born in Cheyenne in the Territory of Wyoming, October 14, 1885, and has lived there all her life.

Both parents were born in the British Isles. Her father, William Cole, was reared in Glasgow, Scotland, and her mother, Catherine Colton Cole, was reared in Monehan, Ireland. Both came to the United States in their early teens in sailing ships that took from three weeks to a month to cross the ocean. Her mother pioneered in Grand Island, Nebraska, in 1867 when she was but 15 years old. She lived with an uncle and aunt who were with the crew that were building the Union Pacific Railroad tracks. Later, she returned to Cleveland where she married in 1873. They lived there until 1879 when the call of the West brought them to Denver, Laramie and in 1883 to Cheyenne.

Lavinia received her first seven years of schooling in the old Johnson School. She attended eighth grade in the old Central School where Miss Lulu McCormick was her teacher. Her first-grade teacher, Alice Hebard, taught under Lavinia when she became principal of Johnson School. Her four years of high school were spent in the building that is now the Administration Building. She attended the Colorado State Teachers' College for two years and received the bachelor of arts degree from the University of Wyoming.

Her 44 years of teaching experience were spent in Wyoming. The first year in the country she received $50 a month for eight months. She paid $15 a month for board and room. She taught in Johnson School in Cheyenne for 43 years, and taught every grade from first through eighth. Her beginning salary in Cheyenne was $65 a month for nine months. She received this salary for 11 years. Then she was promoted to principal for $75 a month.

About this time the salary went on a yearly basis. Since World War I, the salary gradually increased until her last year of teaching, 1947-48, she received $3,600 a year.

The Cole School in south Cheyenne was named for Lavinia Cole in honor of her long years of service in that community.

One of Miss Cole's hobbies was travel. She visited every state in the United States, both Eastern and Western, Canada, Alaska and Mexico. She and her sister, Cassie Cole, also traveled in Europe, Australia, New Zealand, Hawaii and South America.

— Alpha Chapter

WILLA WALES CORBITT

On January 25, 1975, Riverton, Wyoming, lost one of its foremost citizens, former Mayor Willa Wales Corbitt, 86. Mrs. Corbitt had been a teacher and state president of Wyoming Classroom Teachers. After her retirement she served as Riverton's mayor, Wyoming state senator, voting delegate to the 38th American Municipal Congress in Seattle, school board member, one of 50 delegates to the 1960 Inter-American Congress in San Diego, and was one of 30 selected by President Eisenhower in 1959 for a people-to-people program to visit Russia.

She was a member of Alpha Chi Omega and won its Award of Achievement. She belonged to Kappa Delta Pi and Delta Kappa Gamma, education honoraries. She also had affiliations with the Order of Eastern Star, Riverton Chautauqua Club and the Business and Professional Women.

Her outstanding achievements in her eight years as mayor included a paving program, installation of an adequate water system and sewage plant and paying off of all city debts, some of which dated back to 1927. Her business acumen reorganized finances so that the city became solvent.

Mrs. Corbitt was recognized as a great civic leader and articles about her appeared in the *Denver Post, Omaha World Herald, The Milwaukee Journal, The Billing's Gazette, The Wyoming Club Woman* and the *Riverton Ranger*.

The following article was written quite some time ago and approved by Willa Wales Corbitt:

HER HONOR, THE MAYOR OF RIVERTON

Riverton, the "Uranium Capital of Wyoming," oil center, farmers' and ranchers' town, founded in 1906 in connection with a reclamation project, this real he-man town went to the polls and elected a woman mayor in 1955. The people knew what they were doing for they did not bestow this high office upon a weakling. They elected a person with vision, mathematical precision and drive who could assuage the growing pains of their city by finding out the cause thereof and then doing the logical thing.

Willa Wales Corbitt, mathematician and educator, was always known as a practical person. Her associates recognized her ability to think clearly and to penetrate to the heart of things. Many students from her advanced mathematics classes found themselves extremely well qualified for college courses and subsequent success as engineers or doctors.

Wyoming may well be proud that Willa Wales was born in its capital city. Her parents had come to this state in 1884 and were engaged in the cattle industry. Her mother, Sally Faye Lewis of Kentucky, imbued with Southern charm and hospitality, had seen no other white woman during her first six months in Wyoming. Her father, George Lincoln Wales, had come from Illinois where his family had been closely associated with the Lincoln family.

Willa Wales attended Cheyenne public schools and Bethany College in Topeka, Kansas. Her bachelor's degree was earned at the University of Colorado at Boulder. Here she became a member of Alpha Chi Omega Sorority and later served as Wyoming president of its alumnae groups from 1949 to 1953. She was a staunch member of the Episcopal Church and the "Daughters of the King," which group she served as president. She was also a charter member of Cheyenne's Mizpah Chapter of the Order of the Eastern Star.

Willa Wales was married to William T. Corbitt of Au Sable Forks, New York, and had two sons, Claude, an engineer for Phillip's Petroleum Company, recently sent to Stavanger, Norway, and Lieutenant Colonel Gilland, lost in Vietnam.

At Elk Mountain, Wyoming, Willa had her first teaching experience. Even then she realized that this was her field though subsequently she served as vacation director of Knight Hall at Laramie and NYA supervisor for Colorado with headquarters at Colorado Springs. Later teaching positions brought her to the schools of Cheyenne, Evanston, Dubois and Riverton. At first she taught mathematics and English but her complete absorption into the field of mathematics was inevitable. The concept of geometrical figures was made not only understandable but also vivid as she had her charges construct models. At the instigation of her colleagues who felt that this was the unique and practicable approach, she prepared an article which was printed in the *WEA News* and reviewed in the December 1952 *Clearing House.*

While Mrs. Corbitt was studying for her master's degree, which she received from the University of Wyoming in 1946, she was initiated into Kappa Delta Pi, an education honorary society. Because of her outstanding work in the field of education in 1951 she was invited to join the Alpha Xi Wyoming state chapter of Delta Kappa Gamma. Later she became a charter member of Eta Chapter in Riverton. She was elected state president of Classroom Teachers in 1953 for a two-year term after previous service as treasurer and president of local groups, and membership on the executive committee of the WEA. Later she served on the National Advisory Council in the Department of Classroom Teachers in the NEA.

To keep herself a well-rounded person, Willa was an active member of the Business and Professional Women's Club, president of the Riverton club in 1950 and later state corresponding secretary. She also served for three years as Fremont County chairman for TB Christmas Seal sales. This roster of Willa's activities and accomplishments makes her appear rather formidable, but that was not the case. Once a group of teenage boys gave her membership in their hot-rod club.

Willa was a delightful traveling companion. In 1951 it was my privilege to accompany her to a B&PW regional conference at Seaside, Oregon. We drove across a corner of Yellowstone Park, through Montana, Idaho, Washington and British Columbia before reaching Seaside. We did not miss any point of interest. To watch Willa with her mathematical mind glorying in Grand Coulee Dam was an unforgettable experience. She looked perfectly at home on the deck of a steamship, too. Whenever she entered a city she wanted to know what made it successful. Its raison d'etre and industries intrigued her. Thus, she proved to be a mayor par excellence. She inquired into causes and never stopped until she got results.

I would like to append to this article excerpts from a tribute paid Mayor Corbitt at a Delta Kappa Gamma meeting. This was written by Pearl and Ivin Gee of Lander, Wyoming, and expresses well her manifold accomplishments and the impact of her personality.

"Willa Wales Corbitt, we salute you.

"To enumerate and give proper credit to the multitude of accomplishments and honors that are yours would take more than our allotted time, and would serve little purpose, for your life has enriched the lives of thousands, and therein lies your tribute—tribute far greater than any words of the most gifted poet.

"A daughter of the West, yours is the strength of the hills. The beauty of the forest is in your soul and the calm of the quiet mountain lake is in your life.

"A mother, you have given your sons the vision of far horizons, the desire to reach the heights.

"An educator, you have unlocked the mysteries of mathematics for thousands of the youth of our state and taught a few to think. Your counsel has been sought and given in hundreds of meetings of the educators of this state, this region and the nation. . . .

"Not to sit back and rest on your laurels, you have now perhaps the most thankless job of all—mayor of a thriving community, beset with growing pains and plaqued with knotty problems.

"To this office you bring the enthusiasm of youth, the wisdom of age and the determination of your Western heritage to do an outstanding job, not for the salary, which is nil, nor for the glory, for that never comes to a prophet in his own country, but for the satisfaction of a job well done, and to leave behind something good in the lives of your townsmen."

As Mayor Corbitt was about to leave for the people-to-people journey to Russia on July 7, 1957, she was given a bon voyage dinner and the following tribute:

BON VOYAGE, MAYOR CORBITT

All the people of Riverton
Are proud of their paving sewers.
And proud of their woman mayor, too,
Who soon will go forth with the viewers
Of cities and places across the Atlantic.
Thirty dignitaries soon travel
To see what is good in the "Old World"
And come back with tall tales to unravel.
Our Mayor is one of these chosen
(From the housetops above let us shout it!)
Who will look and hear and evaluate
Then come back to tell us about it.
Just think of our Mayor in Paris,
Prague, Berlin, and even Helsinki!
She'll find spots exceedingly lovely
(And probably some a bit stinky).
Even Leningrad, Moscow and Stockholm
Are on her itinerary;
Amsterdam, London and Brussels,
With sights varied and extraordinary.
Many famed places renowned
With history filled and imbued,
Are waiting for our thirty
Primed to be reviewed.
Wonders of science and building
For them to see are in store;
So Bon Voyage, Mayor Willa,
Auf Wedersehen, Au Revoir.

—Josephine Irby Lester, Eta Chapter

EDITH RECH CRIBBS

I was born in Shell, Wyoming, on September 24, 1893. My parents were Mr. and Mrs. Jacob Rech. They were typical pioneer people, diligent, hard-working and fine parents.

After graduation from Big Horn County High School at Basin, in the fall of 1912, I started my career as a "schoolmarm." At that time a high school graduate was given a third-grade teacher's certificate if she wished to take up that vocation.

My school was a one-room log building located about half way between the ML Ranch and Five Springs Ranch on the east side of the Big Horn River near Kane, Wyoming.

My pupils numbered 14, with grades one through eight, a few grades were missing. We had good textbooks and plenty of them. At that time I had to prepare tests every six weeks, administer them and grade them.

We went to Basin to a teachers' convention in November. Mr. A.F. Fillerup was county superintendent and visited once a month.

After a day of many classes, I cleaned the schoolroom; teachers had to be janitors, too. We had a wood-burning heater which I had to keep putting wood into when it was cold. Water for drinking came in a five-gallon milk can from Five Springs Ranch. Wood was furnished by parents of the school children. I had to walk a good mile to and from school.

When I arrived at the home where it was understood I was to board, they weren't ready for me; so, Mrs. Brosious, at that time a member of the school board, took me to a couple who had no children in school. She hesitated quite a while before she said "yes." Then she rode five miles horseback to get a cot from a neighbor for me to sleep on. When the other family was ready for me, Mrs. Hixson didn't want me to go, so I was there the full eight months.

The Hixsons had a watch dog who wouldn't let me come to the door without Mrs. Hixson's sanction; after six weeks he met me out on the trail and escorted me home.

On holiday observances we had programs which the children loved. The parents came and made it a very gala occasion; often times we had eats, such as cookies or cake. On Friday after recess we nearly always had a "spelling bee," or I read to them.

We had no playground equipment then, so we played games—touch tag, batter ball or "sock 'em" with everyone participating.

In those days range fences were unheard of. One evening when I was ready to go home, ML cattle were all around the schoolhouse, and even though I was ranch raised, I wasn't brave enough to go out among them afoot, so waited for a chance to run to the nearest fence, duck under and through the woods to one of the closest homes. We were just sitting down to supper when my folks came looking for me.

One morning I saw a man on foot coming into the draw as I was coming down the opposite end; it was unusual to see anyone afoot. When we met he tapped his ragged hat and said, "Mornin' Ma'am"; I just barely made a noise. When I arrived at school the stove was still red hot and about six cans of steaming water on it, so I knew this character had spent the night there. Had I found him in the house I am sure I would have either run; or been too petrified to move.

Those homesteads along the Big Horn River are just a memory now, as is the little town of Kane. The little log schoolhouse is no more, also; my memories of my first school are for the most part all happy ones. The only living pupil I have that I am sure of is Mrs. Rose Hoffman of Lovell.

— Rho Chapter

BERNICE MORROW DAVIDSON

A row of small red brick houses owned by the coal company provided homes for the employees in Glencoe, Wyoming. I was born in one of those houses on February 3, 1907. I was christened Bernice. My parents, Andrew and Selina Howard Morrow, had moved there from Evanston, Wyoming, some months earlier. Father worked in the company store. He delivered groceries in a wagon in summer and by sleigh in winter. Glencoe is no longer in existence. When the coal vein was mined out, people moved away to find employment elsewhere. We located in Diamondville, Wyoming, where Father worked for the Mountain Trading Company. We lived on "paper collar" row in a house provided for the men who worked in the store or the mine offices. My brother, Howard, was born in Diamondville.

Before we were old enough to go to school, we moved to Kemmerer, Wyoming. Father and Mr. McKay owned a grocery store. Kemmerer has a triangular park in the center of the business district. McKay and Morrow Store was located on the north side of the triangle. JCPenney Store was on the south side. This was not the original location of the Mother Store, however.

My sister, Ethel, and my younger brother, Dale, were both born in Kemmerer. All four of us attended school there from first grade through high school.

During summers, when I was in high school, I worked in the county assessor's office. Late in August in 1923 I went to Evanston to visit my grandmother. While there I became ill with a ruptured appendix. There was no hospital in Evanston so my parents took me to Salt Lake City for the surgery. I rode on a stretcher in the baggage car. I spent six weeks in the hospital there. It was a happy day for me when I walked up the hill to school for the first time that school year, the day after the Thanksgiving vacation. That was the only serious illness I have experienced. I am truly grateful for my good health.

After graduating from Kemmerer High School, I attended the University of Wyoming where I was awarded a diploma from the Normal School.

My teaching career began with a position in the rural school 35 miles north of Kemmerer on Fontenelle Creek. As was the custom of the times, I did the janitorial tasks in addition to teaching. There were three Larson children in the school. Edgar Herschler, now widely and affectionately known as "Ed, Governor or Wyoming," was the other student. In winter we went ice-skating on the creek at recess and during the noon hour. We made hot cocoa on top of the heating stove.

The first winter was an open one in Fontenelle. The second year we had winter with a vengeance. The Larson children lived within walking distance. Edgar often rode horseback. The highlight of my week was Wednesday when I went home with the Herschlers for dinner and overnight after having given Edgar a piano lesson.

Christmas vacation came and with it snow-blocked roads. The ranchers took two other teachers and me to the highway where we hoped to ride to Kemmerer in the mail truck. The Big Piney teachers were traveling the same day, so there was no room in the cab. We rode in the back of the truck. It was COLD, COLD!

In 1929 I was assigned to teach a first grade in the Frontier School. Sometimes we thought of the situation as the "League of Nations." There were many children whose parents were born in Europe. They were delightful children and eager to learn. Twice a year the school put on operettas for the parents—at Christmas and April First. That day was celebrated to mark the beginning of the labor law that limited the number of hours the miners could work.

Catherine Rousche, our beloved first-grade teacher, had died while on vacation at her home in New Jersey. She had taught all four Morrows and many other Kemmerer children over the years. Superintendent Bloom assigned me to fill the vacancy. I accepted with humility and trepidation. There were 48 children enrolled that year. It was the greatest challenge of my life.

In 1942 I accepted a position in the Lead, South Dakota, schools. The Homestake Gold Mine is located there. One day when I was on playground duty, a little boy fell and scraped his knees. I started to take him into the building when he ran the other way. He was going to the hospital to have his injuries cared for. The company took care of all health problems, even the minor ones.

While teaching in Lead I rented a room with the Davidson family. They lived on Miner's Avenue. There were wooden steps from Main Street to the streets above. I climbed and descended many steps each day as I went to school and the restaurant. Occasionally, the Davidsons were unable to get a babysitter for 4-year-old Henry. I sometimes stayed with him and we became friends. He and his toy bulldog "Butch" visited me often.

In the summer of 1942 I earned the BA degree in elementary education. That year I started to teach in the Cheyenne school system. I taught in Churchill, Fincher and Eastridge elementary schools. I worked there 24 years.

My father came to live with me in Cheyenne after Mother died. He had retired after serving as Kemmerer postmaster for many years. He sold the home in Kemmerer, and we bought the little brick home on the corner of Richardson Court. I bought my first car soon after he came to live with me. He was not able to walk very well.

On Sunday, August 21, 1966, in the Chapel of Transfiguration at Moose, Wyoming, Dr. Henry E. Davidson, little Henry's father, and I were married. Like magic I had acquired a husband, a son, a daughter-in-law, a 14-year-old daughter, a granddaughter, a grandson and later another granddaughter and grandson. Our first home was in Sioux Falls, South Dakota. The next year we moved to Fort Meade in the Black Hills of South Dakota. "Dave" was on the staff of the veterans' hospital in psychiatric service. The 7th United States Cavalry has been stationed there during the Civil War.

When we planned for retirement, we decided we wanted to live in a warmer climate. We made reservations to visit Sun City, Arizona. In January 1974 "Dave" collapsed while on duty at the hospital. He died in April of that year of lung cancer and was buried in the Black Hills National Cemetery. In November I moved to Sun City to begin a new life and adjust to living alone.

There are many widows living here in the community developed by Del Webb. Rocking chairs are in storage and the residents are active in community projects, church activities, clubs and organizations. Our Alpha Xi Chapter of Delta Kappa Gamma has over 160 members—all transfers.

My poor vision prohibits my driving a car. My only transportation is the Adultrike (three-wheeler). It is good exercise. My hobbies are gardening, trying new recipes and travel. .

Education—I received the BA in elementary education in 1942. I earned an MA in elementary education in 1961.

Organizations—Past matron of OES, Kappa Delta Pi, president of Alpha Chapter (Wyoming) and president of Alpha Xi State (Wyoming) of Delta Kappa Gamma, National Retired Teachers' Association, National Association of Retired Persons, American Association of University Women, Wyoming Education Association (life member), Lakeview United Methodist Church, United Methodist Women and Martha Circle of Lakeview United Methodist Church.

Travel—Christmas in Mexico in 1964; history tour to eastern U.S. and the Maritime Provinces in Canada in 1965; Europe in 1966 where we visited 10 countries; New Zealand, Australia, Tahiti in 1971; Hawaii in 1973; Caribbean cruise in 1978; and Scandinavia/North Cape in 1979.

— Alpha Chapter

LETHA FARLEY DICKINSON

Born at the farm home north of Agra, Phillips County, Kansas, on Good Friday, April 1, 1904 (April Fool's Day!), I, Letha Leola Farley, at the age of 4, moved with my parents, Mr. and Mrs. William Howard Farley, to our new homestead 18 miles south of Akron, Washington County, Colorado. This was the era of the open cattle range, the advent of barbed wire fences, the hauling of water in barrels until the completion of a drilled water well, and the period of the one-room rural school.

When I was 5 years of age I walked one and a half miles with two brothers and a sister to begin school in a room of the home of the West family. During the year the district transferred the classroom to the Blair home, only one mile distant. The homemade desks and benches were so high that my feet did not touch the floor, and my hands, when placed on top of the desk, were in line with my chin. The following year the school authorities acquired a country store and cut it in two. One half became the District 22 schoolhouse two and a half miles south of the Howard Farley homestead. The other half became the school building in the district to the west. The old store-schoolhouse burned in 1916. I finished the eighth grade in a new one-room building one-half mile south of my home.

Following my graduation from the eighth grade in 1917, the family sold the homestead and freighted the household goods and farm animals to Oxford, La Plata County, Colorado, February 1918. This was an irrigated farm region with no high school. There was no opportunity to attend high school unless I rode horseback about seven miles each way.

With each passing year my desire to continue in education became stronger and in the autumn of 1921, when I should have been graduated from high school, I was enrolling in the Washington County High School, Akron, as a freshman.

I graduated in 1925 as valedictorian and received scholarships to Colorado State Teachers' College, Greeley, to Colorado College in Colorado Springs, and to Colorado Women's College in Denver. With no funds to help pay for clothing, books, room or board, I relinquished the scholarships, and with two years of normal training in high school and a second-grade teacher's certificate, I taught 17 pupils in a rural school, "Columbine," for $100 per month for eight months. From this I saved enough to attend summer school at Greeley. The day college closed for the summer, the Akron bank shut its door, leaving me with approximately $2 in my purse. During the next two years I taught in two more rural schools, one of which was a summer school at 8,250 elevation, in Routt County. I also enrolled at Western State College, Gunnison, for winter and spring quarters and passed the examination in the spring for a first-grade teacher's certificate—good for three years. The following year, 1928-29, at Greeley, was the one full year I attended college. The rest of my education came through summers, extension and correspondence. In the spring of 1929 I graduated from Colorado State Teachers' College, Greeley, with a two-year Colorado life certificate in intermediate education.

At the Larimer County Teachers' Association meeting that September of 1929, in the courthouse in Fort Collins, Colorado, I met Norman R. Dickinson, principal of school District 35, where I was to teach grades five and six and music. The following year I accepted the principalship of the elementary school in Wellington, Colorado. There were six teachers and approximately 220 pupils. On May 31, 1931, Norman and I were married. That summer we attended Colorado A&M (now CSU). The next summer we were at the university in Boulder.

The depression years were lean times. The salaries were at $75 per month for nine months, and would have gone lower if there had not been a minimum salary law in Colorado. To improve my skills and my understanding as a teacher and a mother, without college credit because money was too scarce to pay for credit, I studied for two summers under 10 Red Cross nurses, and took additional training in penmanship to receive certification. I hold teacher's certificates from the A.N. Palmer Company and from the Zaner-Bloser Company, besides having studied the Kittle Method.

After transferring credits to Greeley from the University of Wyoming, Colorado State University, Colorado University and Western State College, I returned to Greeley during the summer of 1954 to complete study for a degree in elementary education. My two-year life had been in intermediate education. For a new outlook, in 1957, my husband and I spent seven weeks at the University of British Columbia, Vancouver. Doleta, our daughter, studied voice there.

My energies have shifted direction depending upon what seemed more important or crucial at the time. I asststed with Sunday school, Girl Scouts and other groups at the time our daughter was in these groups. I have been active in the Order of the Eastern Star, the Daughters of the Nile, the International Federation of Business and Professional Women's Clubs, the American Red Cross and numerous organizations in the United Methodist Church. I belong to the Wyoming State Historical Society and its Fremont County branch. My husband and I hold memberships in the National Retired Teachers' Association.

Participating in community affairs and initiating action programs always have presented a challenge. Some of these have included instituting the Riverton Community Scholarship for Prospective Teachers, which, after paying $5,000 in scholarships, was phased out to direct funds to CWC; the introduction of the International Reading Association into Wyoming through memberships and local councils; the campaigning for an association for the accreditation of elementary schools with accrediting agencies comparable to North Central for high schools or NCATE for colleges; the speaking for a nuclear-age school, grades 11, 12, 13 and 14, tuition free; introducing into Wyoming and directing of "An Action Course in Practical Politics"; writing and directing a pioneer pageant with 60 people; directing 40 adults in a PTA radio series which ran for 10 weeks; compiling a PTA Parents' Handbook for Music in the Home; chairing panels concerning youth, crime and delinquency. My teaching certificates have included secondary social studies and elementary education in Wyoming and a two-year intermediate and graduate life certificate in Colorado and Palmer and Zaner penmanship certificate.

One of the high points of my educational experiences has been that as state president of Alpha Xi of Wyoming, the Delta Kappa Gamma Society, International Honorary Organization for Women Educators during 1961-63. Of course, many responsibilities on the local and state level preceded this honor. Included in this training and contribution period were the regional conference in Sun Valley, Idaho, 1961, and the international convention in Philadelphia, 1962. I served on the Alpha Xi State and International Scholarship Special Committee and the International Professional Affairs Committee.

Prior to retirement in 1969, I carried memberships in the National Education Association, the Wyoming Education Association, the Riverton Education Association, the Riverton Department of Classroom Teachers, the International Reading Association, and the Parent-Teacher Association and was active in all of these organizations. I was named as a finalist in the national "Teacher of the Year" selection for 1963-64.

Expressed, or otherwise, every teacher has a philosophy. Briefly, this partially states mine: "Pride in Teaching" walks side-by-side with "Pride in Learning." These are the fine arts of the classroom. No diamonds ever shone with more beautiful luster than that of the sparkling eyes of an eager, interested pupil who suddenly grasped a new idea! We, the adult world of parents, teachers, administrators and board of education, must provide the climate for learning. In our streamlining of education and challenging of pupils let us use caution against pushing children too quickly into adulthood. Each segment of education is important in its own right—elementary, secondary and college.

I believe every child has a right to mental growth within his own capabilities, as well as personal dignity, no matter what his mental capacity may be. I have looked with disfavor upon acts which are not acceptable to the school, the home and the community. I believe in firm discipline for those who insist upon going their own willful ways, but relaxed guidance for those pupils who are striving to form habits of right conduct and achievement. In my opinion, children must be given a basis of understanding. They must be made to recognize that there are many things beyond their sphere of knowledge. If they are willful and arrogant, they must be faced with their ignorance if they are to be receptive to learning. Conversely, if they are anxious to learn, they will be willing to recognize their lack of education.

Activities since retirement, 1969 to 1982: parliamentarian, Alpha Xi, the Delta Kappa Gamma Society, International; representative of city of Riverton to five-county Resources, Conservation and Development Council; president, Fremont County Retired Teachers' Association (FCRTA); member Wyoming Joint State Legislative Committee (WRTA-AARP); representative of Western Wyoming Retired Teachers to Coalition of Senior Citizens Organizations; Riverton Wildlife Association secretary.

For the United Methodist Church, I was a delegate to the 200th anniversary of the reopening dedication of Wesley's Chapel, London, in 1978; a delegate to the 100th anniversary, World Methodist Council, Honolulu, 1981; lay member of Yellowstone Conference UMC and of Wyoming Church Coalition (nine denominations); Billings District Mission coordinator for Christian Personhood and Christian social involvement.

On the local level, I served as president of the United Methodist Women's Unit; was superintendent of study areas; on the administrative board for the Council on Ministries, Finance, Parsonage and Pastor-Parish Relations committees; and was a judge on the election board.

— Eta Chapter

GLADYS ELLIOTT DONALDSON

G ladys was born near Charleston, Illinois, in 1903. Her early schooling began in rural schools in Illinois. The family moved to Wyoming in 1915 to establish residence on a homestead about 12 miles southwest of Gillette. A school was established for the pupils in the community, for all grades through eighth.

When students were ready for high school, it was necessary to stay in Gillette during the school week—that was long before the use of a school bus for transportation.

She graduated from Campbell County High School in May 1922, and received her normal training teaching certificate. Then she taught in a rural school for one term. Marriage ended the teaching career for awhile.

In the early 1930s Gladys found it necessary to return to teaching, so through residence study and correspondence lessons with the University of Wyoming, she was able to qualify for certification.

Thus, in 1937, a new start was made—a longer teaching career was on the way. In the fall of 1937 Gladys opened school at the Hunter-Alison School above Weston, on the Little Powder River. Trips to Gillette were made only when supplies were needed, because of the long distance to travel and the lack of surfaced roads at that time. The teacher could always find plenty to do during the weekend—a good time to do catch up on all janitor work, and preparation of work for the following week. She taught this same school for two terms, then moved to another school in the same district where she taught the next two years. This school was northeast of Recluse in District 12. It was a little closer to town, with better roads to travel. In spite of the long distances to travel, poor road conditions, no janitorial services, and $65 per month salary (plus a bonus), teachers did keep moving on.

During the summer of 1941, Gladys worked as bookkeeper in the office of Dr. McHenry in Gillette, and held this position until September 1942, when she married Cecil Donaldson and moved to a small ranch in Weston County, near Newcastle—another interruption to her teaching career.

In 1943, when there was such a shortage of teachers, she again took a school near Clifton, eight to 10 miles from town. It was necessary for her to drive from the ranch to school, and as gas was rationed during World War II, extra gas stamps were provided if needed to get to school. She taught at this school for four years. The last two years at this school her husband had taken over as bus driver to bring high school students to Newcastle from that school neighborhood, and during the school week they lived in a small house at the end of the bus route. That way Cecil could keep the ranch going during the day and both could spend the weekends at the ranch. By the end of her fourth term at this school the enrollment had dwindled to just a few lower grade students. Since a school bus was already bringing the high school students to town, it was deemed more economical to close the Clifton School and transport all students to town. Another interruption in her teaching career—and she did not plan to teach any longer.

Then in 1949, with the oil boom and influx of people to Newcastle, the school enrollment increased and it was necessary to divide some of the grades. She took a group of first-graders from Blanche Kelly's room and began the first-grade section in a basement room of the old school building on the hill. This building was later destroyed by fire. After some time her room was moved to the Weston County Library basement where it remained until they were able to move into the newly completed first-grade room at the Gertrude Burns School in Newcastle. It was a pleasure to teach in a brand new room, and not in a basement.

She retired from teaching in 1968, never getting away from first grade. Her bachelor of arts degree was received from Black Hills State Teachers' College in Spearfish in 1961.

"The pleasant memories far out-number the unpleasant ones of my teaching years," is the way Gladys summed up her teaching career.

— Lambda Chapter

EMMA W. DUIS

My early years were spent in a small rural village in eastern Nebraska where my father owned "The Brick Store—Gen'l Mdse." His store had everything from kerosene to fine millinery. Each spring and fall a "trimmer" came from St. Joseph, Missouri, to trim and sell hats. I have pictures that show that some of these hats were real creations. When I was about 10 years old I was allowed to "help" in the store. My father let me stick small potatoes on the spouts of filled kerosene cans. Later, I was promoted to filling egg cases with candled eggs. When I showed I could be trusted not to skip spaces in the egg trays, I was permitted to do the candling also. One day after a real dirt-raiser of a dust storm, I was drafted to wash all the dishes in the china department. Some of these things were lovely and fragile and protected by "Do Not Handle" signs. I liked cleaning these things with slow, loving care. In fact, my care was so slow that after the second day, my father said someone else could finish.

Other memories crowd in—cold winters with hot stoves and chilblains; bowls of apples and dishpans full of popped corn; summers with ripe cherries and grape arbors heavy with purple grapes; a haymow half full of dusty hay with a trapeze swinging above; grade school; high school with homework and parties; college in Ohio; teaching in Colorado; then Casper, Wyoming.

My first impression of Casper was wind. As I came down the steps of the Burlington train early that September morning, the wind snatched my black satin cherry-trimmed poke bonnet from my head and sent it scudding along the tracks. Forgetful of luggage, I raced after it to catch it before it spun under the wheels of the train.

My first year was in Mills. The next year I went to Jefferson School where I taught fifth grade and music for many years before going to junior high school where I remained as librarian until I retired from Morgan Junior High School—a total span of 40 years.

In 1941 while I was still at Jefferson I became interested in retirement legislation for teachers. For many years some of the ablest teachers in Wyoming had been working to pass a bill establishing retirement for teachers but were up against legislatures that refused to act. The following quotes from my scrapbook of newspaper clippings show the attitude prevalent in the 1941 Legislature:

Headline (quote) Cheyenne, Feb. 11, 1941, "Teacher's Retirement Bill Faces Death in the Senate. Upper Chamber Refuses to Accept Conference Report On Legislation."

Statement by a senator speaking against the bill (quote)! ". . . The bill doesn't go far enough . . . when you bring a bill in here that will provide for the dry farmer, the sheepherder and the cowboy, I'll favor it. . . ."

Headline (quote) Cheyenne, Feb. 13, 1941. "Supporters Continue Fight To Revive Teachers' Bill. Measure Appears To Have Died But May Reach Definite Vote."

Headline (quote) Cheyenne, Feb. 19, 1941. "Teachers' Measure Passed."

Headline (quote) Cheyenne, March 8, 1941. "Governor . . . Vetoes Teachers' Bill."

The first retirement bill submitted in 1937 was a 4% cash-reserve plan. The 1941 bill was a cash-disbursement (pay-as-you-go) plan. The 1945 Legislature passed a bill which was virtually the same as the one in 1941. This bill was signed by the governor (not the same governor who twice before had vetoed teacher retirement bills). The law became effective in 1945. In 1949 I was a member of the legislative committee and chairman of the retirement committee of the Wyoming Education Association.

In 1950 an actuarial report made of the retirement system showed an accrued liability of $17,-000,000. In 1951 the WEA sponsored legislation and a bill was introduced in the Legislature to change the teacher retirement law from a cash-disbursement to a cash-reserve plan. After hard-fought battles and some crippling amendments, which teachers had to accept or lose everything, the bill was passed and became law. But our opponents were not through with us.

The members of the Governor's Interim Committee of 1952 focused much of its time and energy to abrogate the new teacher retirement law. They reportedly were making a thorough study of retirement through their executive secretary. They were very secretive about their activities but rumors indicated that the committee had plans that would settle all difficulties. In 1951 the federal government made Social Security available to teachers, but in order to qualify for coverage, states were required to repeal existing retirement laws before enacting legislation to cover teachers under Social Security.

After covering teachers under Social Security, **then** the state could enact or re-enact existing teacher retirement plans as they saw fit. So far, by 1952, only one state, Virginia, had covered its teachers under Social Security and it immediately re-enacted its previous teacher retirement plan. The Wyoming Interim Committee gave no indication of what they had in mind, but an article appeared in a Cheyenne paper September 21, 1952, under the headline "Legislators fail to decide on pension switch." From the text of the article (quote): "The 12-member Legislative Interim Committee tonight adjourned its executive session until tomorrow without reaching a decision on plans to substitute Social Security for the present state retirement programs . . . Today the Interim Committee heard representatives of teachers throughout Wyoming denounce the proposal to liquidate their present retirement plan. . . ."

The Interim Committee continued to keep silent about retirement legislation. As the time drew near for the Legislature to convene, we heard rumors that the committee had a bill to submit to the Legislature, but when members were questioned, they refused to answer or comment. In 1953, soon after the Legislature convened, an open meeting was held in the Senate Chambers to discuss legislation that was to be brought before the Legislature in the coming session.

When retirement legislation was brought up, the chairman of this meeting said the Interim Committee's plans for retirement legislation would not be discussed. When the Interim Committee's bill was introduced, it proposed to abolish existing retirement plans and cover the members under Social Security instead.

Teachers all over Wyoming were unified in their opposition to this measure and lost no time in letting their legislators feel the impact of their resentment and indignation. A bitter, bitter fight followed. When the 1953 Legislature adjourned, teachers and state employees had Social Security but they did retain a restricted retirement plan. Teachers lost 40% of their retirement benefits for service prior to 1953. Teachers did not submit to this cut but continued to work locally with their legislators, the WEA and the Wyoming Retirement Board until, in 1957, the Legislature repealed the 40% cut and restored full benefits to teachers.

The Wyoming Retirement System has made sound progress. Payments into the fund, benefits and interest rates have been increased. The accrued liability has been paid.

I shall miss serving on the Wyoming Retirement Board of which I had been a member from 1951 to June 1964. In October 1964 the WEA conferred upon me the Wyoming Education Association's Gold Key Award. I am proud and grateful to have received this award but it makes me humble, too, because there are many teachers who dedicate their lives to education and to the welfare of the profession often without thanks or recognition.

— Beta Chapter

ELLA ADELINE TRUAX ELLSBURY

April 27, 1882, Ella Adeline Truax was born at Amirst, Minnesota, the youngest child of Samuel and Adeline Truax. She spent the first 18 years of her life in the Amirst-Tracy area where she received her education.

On May 30, 1900, Ella and her mother arrived by train in Deadwood, South Dakota. From there they traveled by stagecoach to Spearfish, South Dakota, where they were met by Ella's brother-in-law, Dick Morgan. The journey from Spearfish to the Morgan ranch, three miles northwest of Sundance, Wyoming, was made by team and buggy.

After a year's residence in Wyoming, Ella prepared herself to teach. She took an examination in Sundance to determine her qualifications. She was granted a certificate to teach elementary grades that term. In January of 1902 she again took a test certifying her to teach until July 1905.

Her first teaching position was in 1901 at the Ellsbury School located on Deer Creek in the Bearlodge Mountain area near the center of Section 21, Township 53 North, Range 63 West. This location, in the heart of the wilderness, was about the same distance from each of the four homes from which the pupils came. The Selliez family lived about a mile northeast of the school, on Beaver Creek; the four Selliez pupils were Henry, Leon, Leontime and Lottie.

The Lanning family lived about a mile to the southeast on the Stuart place. Joe, Jenny and Ned Lanning attended from there. Vernie Taylor, the oldest pupil, lived on Taylor Divide, about one-half mile northwest.

Ella boarded at the home of Dave and Clarenda "Pet" Ellsbury while teaching in the Ellsbury School. Walter, son of the Dave Ellsburys, was a first-grade pupil that year. The Ellsburys lived about one mile south of the school. The school was called a summer school as it was in session from April to September. The snow made it difficult to keep school during the winter.

During the fall of 1902 and the spring of 1903, Ella taught at the Hutchins School and stayed at the home of the Ed Sanford family. This was on Houston Creek and was referred to as the Houston Creek School. The fall term was from August to December and April through June. Ella recalled, however, riding horseback to school when the snow was too deep for walking. She also taught the fall term of 1903 there. Among the students at this school were Mamie Sanford, Florence and Bernice Belshe and Gertrude and Uhlig Danielson.

Wages for teaching this school at this time were $12 a month. Ella bought cattle with her money. She later sold them to purchase an organ which she had wanted for some time. The organ is now in the home of one of her daughters, Juanita McElroy.

On February 10, 1904, Ella was married to Merton Ellsbury in a ceremony performed at the Dick Morgan home. Following the ceremony they traveled by team and buggy to their home on the Ellsbury Ranch on North Redwater, where Merton worked for his father, Lyman Henry, and uncle Dave Ellsbury until 1914 when Dave sold his interest in the ranch to Lyman Henry. Mert and his father then set up a partnership which continued until 1929 when Mert purchased his father's interest.

Ella became the mother of three daughters and four sons. Busy with her family and home, she still found time to take an active interest in school and community affairs. She was a member of the school board from her district for 12 years, 1929-1941. Her main interest was to promote interest in acquiring the best teachers and having the best schools the district could afford.

In 1941 Mert and Ella turned over the main operation of the ranch to their sons and moved to Spearfish where they lived until purchasing a home in Belle Fourche in 1947. They lived there until their deaths, Mert in 1951 and Ella in 1970.

— Theta Chapter

FRANCES EMMETT

Frances Emmett was born June 22, 1907, to Henry Thomas and Etta Frances Emmett in Pardeville, Wisconsin.

By the time Frances was 6 years of age, her family had moved to Casper, Wyoming, where she attended school from 1913 to 1915. Her family then moved to Worland where her father, H.T., or better known as "Pop" Emmett, was superintendent of schools from 1916 to 1929. He was very active in all phases of education. He organized and coached five to six boys each year to play basketball. They were state champions for five consecutive years.

Frances spent the rest of her elementary and high school years in the Worland system, graduating with honors in 1925. She took all the advanced classes available. These included advanced algebra and calculus in mathematics and through Cicero in Latin.

As Frances' father was superintendent of the school, he did not want to show favoritism toward his children in any way. When it became time to decide upon valedictorian for the senior class, when Frances was a senior, he asked the teachers and school board to make the choice. Of course, they found Frances' grades to be superior so told him that she was certainly the one worthy of the honor.

Raised in a family where education was a priority, for her mother, too, had been a teacher, Frances gravitated toward teaching and worked many years toward a bachelor's degree which she received in 1962. She sought continuously to become a better teacher.

Her teaching career began at Neiber, a school about nine miles south of Worland. It was here that she made her first decision concerning the welfare of a child—that did not meet with the approval of a parent. One nice day she took the children on a picnic. One of the small boys fell into the river. She hurriedly rescued him and took him home to get into dry clothing. His parents weren't at home when they arrived, so she decided she'd better get him out of the wet garments before he became further chilled. When they got down to underclothes, she found he had been sewn in for the winter. As he was drenched and shivering, she cut the stitching and got him out and into dry clothes. When his mother returned she was furious because it was not yet time to be taken out of winter underwear. Frances was supposed to let him wear them until he dried out.

Later teaching years were spent at Big Trails, a school on the Nowood River in southeast Washakie County, and at Durkee, a school about midway between Worland and Manderson. She also taught at the Gould School in Big Horn County and at Sunlight Basin School in Park County.

In 1937 Frances' mother died and she came back to Worland where she taught until her accidental death in 1967.

Frances often told of one unusual experience while teaching in Worland that called for somewhat drastic measures to be taken by another teacher and herself. They discovered that many of the children in their rooms had become infested with head lice. The only remedy they knew of at the time was to take every child and rub their heads with kerosene and then shampoo thoroughly. This had to be done twice to get both lice and eggs.

Frances taught in the Spanish School for several years and found it a real challenge as she had to teach English to the Spanish-speaking children as well as prepare them well in reading, writing, arithmetic and spelling for a well-rounded education. She also taught at Eastside and Westside schools in Worland.

Wages were low, though she did receive up to $7,000 in her last years of teaching.

Frances was a charter member of Delta Kappa Gamma when Iota Chapter was organized in May 1955. She was the first Iota Chapter president. She also served on the Delta Kappa Gamma State Executive Board Committee.

Frances was involved with church, community and school affairs throughout her years. She was a member of the Methodist Church, active in Wesleyan Guild and Mary and Martha circles. School organizations included National and Wyoming Education Associations, Classroom Teachers, Washakie County Education Association and the International Reading Association. She was very active in many clubs, among which were the American Association of University Women, Business and Professional Women, where she served as president, the Cancer Society, where she was secretary. She also belonged to the Order of the Eastern Star, Chapter 24. She had several hobbies including reading, sewing, bridge, photography and the Little Theater Group.

Frances met with an untimely death in an automobile accident May 5, 1967.

— Sigma Chapter

MARY BLANCHE ENGLISH

A very talented person, a lady of many achievements, and a teacher of wide experience was Miss Mary Blanche English, who was born at Gunnison, Utah, on January 22, 1901.

Her parents were Mr. and Mrs. William English. The family consisted of eight children, four sons and four daughters.

Her elementary education was secured at Otto, Wyoming, Big Horn County. She was valedictorian of the eighth-grade class. Following the eighth-grade graduation, she attended high school in Basin, Wyoming, where she was valedictorian of her high school class. She then secured a normal diploma and elementary life certificate from the University of Wyoming. In 1919 her name was placed in the Honor Book in Education, Department of Rural Education, at the University of Wyoming.

In 1938 Blanche received her bachelor's degree from Ottawa University, where she received first honors every quarter in the years 1936-1938. In 1949 she received a master's degree in fine arts from the Colorado State College of Education at Greeley, Colorado. her major field was English, and her minor was art.

She had a very wide experience in teaching, beginning at Stringtown, Big Horn County, Wyoming, in 1919, where she taught grades one through five. In 1920 she went to Lovell, Wyoming, where she taught in the grade schools, in the junior high school and in the senior high school. In 1954 she went to Greybull, where she accepted a position as English and art instructor and librarian in the senior high school. She passed away September 28, 1964.

College teaching was also a part of her experience. In 1954 she conducted an art workshop for Colorado teachers at Fort Collins. For three summer sessions, Blanche taught art at Northwest Community College in Powell, Wyoming. In addition to this, she taught through extension courses at Lovell, Deaver, Greybull, Basin and Worland. She also taught community credit courses in painting.

Poetry was also one of her many interests. She was a member of five poetry clubs and had a poem, "Petaldown," published in *National Anthology* in 1955.

Blanche joined Delta Kappa Gamme Society in 1950 at Cody, Wyoming. She was a very active member, having served as recording secretary, on chapter and state music committees, and served on program and nomination committees in the chapter. She also served the chapter as second vice president and first vice president and was president during the years 1958-1960. She attended the international Delta Kappa Gamma Society convention in Minneapolis and the Northwest District convention in Glacier National Park.

Church and community work were not neglected. She was an active member of the Baptist churches in Lovell and Greybull. She served as chairman of the board of education in both churches and acted as adult Sunday school teacher in both places. She served as teacher of the eighth grade and church clerk in the First Baptist Church of Greybull. She has worked with the young people of the church at Camp Wyoba, Baptist Youth Camp, acting as teacher and dean of girls for several summers.

Blanche had many interesting hobbies. Among them were flower raising, poetry collecting, cake decorating, song writing for special occasions in church, school and other organizations. Some of her original fingerpainting songs have been published in the "Wyoming Art Manual."

Gamma (later Rho) Chapter members are very proud of Miss Mary Blanche English, their lady of "many achievements."

— Rho Chapter

AMY F. KRUEGER ERWIN

Amy F. Krueger was born to Virginia and Otto F. Krueger at Sundance, Wyoming, July 16, 1888.

In 1907 she graduated from the Appleton City Academy at Appleton, Missouri. She taught one year at Montrose where her family was living, but moved with the family to DuBois, Nebraska. She taught in Violet, Lewistown and Burchard. In 1912 the family moved to Beatrice, Nebraska, where Amy taught for two years.

Wishing to further her education, she attended the state Normal School at Peru, Nebraska. Following her graduation, she taught commercial subjects in the high school of Burlington and Ottaway, Kansas.

In 1921 Amy decided to return to her native state of Wyoming where she taught in the commerce department of the Basin High School. In 1922 she moved to Powell and remained in the commerce department of Powell High School for eight years. She was able to see the results of her work in observing successful young men and women in business who had obtained their commercial training in her department.

During these years she was instrumental in organizing Chapter P of the PEO Sisterhood, which became an active and progressive group. She served in local offices and later served as state president of the group. At one time when she was in office she had the misfortune to slip on the ice, breaking her hip. This did not deter her from attending the state convention. She went in a wheelchair.

In 1930 she married S.N. Erwin, former school superintendent of Powell, who had been left with three children after the death of his wife. They moved to Glenrock where he was active in education for a number of years.

Mr. Erwin owned a farm on the west end of the Powell Flat and he had hoped to retire to this farm some day and eventually did so while he was able to participate in farming activity. Several years followed with successful crop production. Amy assisted by cultivating a good garden. She said at one time that she always hoed her favorite vegetables first. The tomatoes had very good care.

In 1944 Mr. Erwin died and Amy was left alone as the children had grown and married. At this time she leased the farm and moved to an apartment in Powell where she worked in the printing office of *The Powell Tribune*.

Later, she ran for the office of county superintendent of schools and was defeated by only a vote or two. She declined a recount, but a year later was appointed to the office by the county commissioners when a vacancy occurred. She served the remainder of the term and was in the race for reelection, running unopposed, when she was stricken with a massive embolism.

Her life was one of education in one form or another. She loved the state of Wyoming and was proud to be one of the pioneers of the state. She loved the West and its beauty. At the time of her death in 1950, the administrator of her estate found the following poem in her file case:

> When the last free trail is a prim fenced lane
> And our graves grow green with forgotten Mays,
> Rich and statelier, then you'll reign,
> Mother of men whom the world will praise.
> And your sons will love you and sigh for you,
> Labor, and battle, and die for you,
> But never the fondest will understand
> The way we loved you, young, young land.
>
> Author Unknown

— Gamma Chapter

39

HELEN FAWCETT

"If I don't get a job teaching school," I told my mother that spring of 1928, "I'll take in fine washing." I had been doing the laundry for the family, starting it in nice hot water, then hurrying off to a 7:45 class at Yankton College in my hometown, Yankton, South Dakota. Since we lived only a block from the college, I finished the laundry later in cold water before a later class.

Jobs were scarce that year. My father had died two years before, leaving just enough insurance to clear the mortgage and help us get oriented. I was 20, and wanted to be a teacher; it "ran in the family." Mother had taught four years before marriage and her father had had a number of country schools in the 1880s and 1890s.

Really, I had gotten a head start at it as I had been teaching a Sunday school class of second-graders, starting when I was 14. I must have done all right at it, as one of my pupils told her brother, "You're not s'posed to hit me. Helen said so." Her mother asked, "Is that what Helen said?" "Well, that's what she meant."

I did get my teaching job, at $90 a month, teaching 18 second-graders in the small town of Wessington, South Dakota. What a lot one learns from teaching! I did well enough to be rehired, with 11 pupils the second year. Remember October 1929? Uh-huh, the big stock market crash. It affected little towns, too; and I was to have a combined class of first- and second-graders the next year. That scared me, as I didn't know how to start 6-year-olds in reading. No doubt I could have learned how. But Mother and I got me back to finish college.

After that I became a high school teacher in the little town of Viborg, not far away. That seemed like a more glamorous job. The first week all those Danes looked alike to me. I taught Latin, English, typing and chorus. At the last part of the Irish operetta that we put on, the principal announced, "Now we'll have the grand FIN-alee." My thoughts often strayed from Viborg, for I was in love and dreaming of marriage; so, I stayed at that job only one year. Then I went off to Kansas with my husband and helped him with his business struggles through those hard depression years. After seven years we had a baby boy. Four years later my husband left me, and I went back to being a teacher. I reviewed my studies, and taught Latin and English in high school at Belle Fourche, South Dakota, for two years.

Finally I came to Wyoming and taught in Gillette Grade School for 27 years, from 1946 until I was required to retire in 1973. I cringe when I think of some mistakes I've made. But I haven't known any perfect teachers, have you? I worked hard at it. Whenever possible I got music into my teaching, and I conducted several operettas. I traded subjects with other teachers while I rehearsed these. They would teach my second-grade arithmetic or reading while I taught songs to their pupils.

One year we made a little Wyoming in our sand table, with mountains in the right places, cattle and oil wells and a Devil's Tower, made of corrugated brown paper. Another year we made a house and yard of construction paper, and the furniture inside, flowers and vegetables outside. One boy made a white picket fence around it all, of paper.

I invented a way to make my reading classes more meaningful. The words within quotation marks were read by the different assigned "characters" and other words, such as "said Billy," by those designated, and we acted out the actions. I demonstrated this method at a workshop of NEA in Denver. I got extra reading out of my pupils by having two groups going at once, with a good reader acting as "teacher" of the extra group. Those reading aloud faced away from each other in far corners of the room so they didn't bother each other. Friday afternoons during the last period we sang from music books, thus doing more reading.

We had Christmas programs in our room, with the children sitting up front on the floor between times of standing to speak or sing, and sometimes poking each other. Mothers and little visitors sat on or at the children's desks.

As the town grew, I was moved from Central School to teach in a mobile schoolhouse. The new room fit the class a little snugly around the hips. Emotional problems and discipline problems increased, no doubt helped by tensions in their homes. One year we taught in split sessions. What had been my second-grade room was occupied from 7:30 a.m. until noon by a third grade. Then I taught there from 12:30 until 5 p.m. In winter the kids came to school or returned home in the dark. Pencils disappeared; tempers flared. Tired minds in tired bodies learned less. But we kept trying; and the next year we had regular scheduling.

In my last year before retirement I got a commendation for bringing some lagging, discouraged kids up to better reading and writing. And when the princial brought in a few certificates of perfect attendance, he brought me one, too.

Now I'm not really retired. At age 71 I teach up to 18 music lessons a week and love it. I play music at church and other places. I'm happy and thankful that I'm still a teacher.

— Theta Chapter

FRANCES FERIS

S tate and national awards came to Casper through the competence and ability of Frances Feris, debate and speech teacher at NCHS.

Born in Cass County, Missouri, on August 3, 1899, Miss Feris came to Wyoming with her parents in 1907, settling in Riverton. Awarded her BA degree from the University of Wyoming in 1921, she taught for two years at Rock Springs and moved to Casper in 1923 to teach high school English.

She received an MA degree from the University of Iowa in 1931 and the same year became head of the NCHS English Department, a position she held until her retirement in 1965.

Under her direction, NCHS debate teams won 17 national championships between 1935 and 1965, an achievement recognized when the Tau Kappa Alpha national championship trophy was permanently retired in Casper in 1966.

During her career as a debate coach, she achieved the top number of points in the nation, being awarded a double diamond National Forensic League pin in recognition of an honor shared by less than a dozen speech coaches in the nation. She organized the first forensic league in the state of Wyoming in 1929 and her students were perennial winners in state and national contests in oratory and debate.

She was five times named the outstanding speech coach in the Rocky Mountain region.

Miss Feris was the first president of the Wyoming Classroom Teachers' Association and also served as president of the Wyoming Education Association. She was a Golden Arrow member of Pi Beta Phi social sorority and a member of numerous educational organizations.

After her retirement she was active in the Wyoming Retired Teachers' Association, working in support of legislation sought by that group.

She was a member of St. Mark's Episcopal Church and the American Association of University Women.

She strove always toward perfection, and the results of her efforts will live in her pupils, among whom are outstanding lawyers, doctors and other professional people in Wyoming.

— Beta Chapter

NELLIE G. FLETCHER

Nellie G. Fletcher was born July 29, 1903, in Pawnee County, Nebraska. Her elementary education was secured in the rural schools of the county. She graduated from high school in Pawnee City, Nebraska, and received her bachelor's degree from Nebraska Wesleyan University in 1925 with a major in chemistry. In 1928 she was awarded a master's degree from Kansas State University.

Miss Fletcher has held the following positions in the field of education: principal and science teacher at Cordova, Nebraska; chemistry instructor at Nebraska Wesleyan; science and mathematics instructor at Breckenridge High School, Breckenridge, Colorado; teacher of science in Park City High School, Park City, Utah. She accepted the position of science and mathematics teacher in Greybull High School in Greybull, Wyoming, in 1944, and is currently employed there at the time of this writing.

She was affiliated with Phi Kappa Phi in 1925. The following fellowships from the National Science Foundation have been awarded to her: University of Washington, mathematics, 1954; Montana State, chemistry, 1956; Shell Fellowship, Stanford University, physics, 1958; Reed College, Portland, Oregon, chemistry, 1960.

She received the American Chemical Society Award at the University of Wyoming and was chosen chemistry teacher for the state in 1958. She received the James Bryant Conant Award in high school chemistry teaching March 29, 1971. November 5, 1971, she was presented the Alumni Achievement Award by Nebraska Wesleyan University.

Elected to membership in Gamma Chapter of Delta Kappa Gamma at Cody, Wyoming, in 1955, she has served on these committees: membership, history, scholarship and personal growth and services.

Miss Fletcher was state director of National Science Teachers' Association from 1951 until 1973 and was secretary-treasurer of the Wyoming Mathematics and Science Teachers' Association. She had memberships in many other societies and organizations including American Chemical Society, Wyoming Education Association, National Education Association, American Association for the Advancement of Science, Mathematical Society of America, National Association of Biology Teachers, National Science Teachers' Association and National Council of Teachers of Mathematics.

In addition to her duties in the classroom, Miss Fletcher had served as junior and senior class sponsor for 16 years, had sponsored the high school annual for 25 years, and was sponsor of the Jet's Club. Her junior high Sunday school class of the Presbyterian Church, which she taught from 1944, held her in high esteem.

Although she was a very busy person professionally she found time for many hobbies among which were books, reading, football games and, of course, science fairs and projects.

Nellie died July 17, 1979, and her body was taken back to Nebraska.

— by Edith Scott, Gamma (Rho) Chapter
— Rho Chapter

ALO FOSSEY

I was born January 3, 1902, in Lander, Wyoming. My parents were William T. and Anna Aldenburg Jones. My father was mayor of Lander for 12 years in the late '30s and early '40s. My paternal grandparents were William and Martha Jones, who came to South Pass before 1870. They moved to Fort Washakie in 1872 where my grandfather had the beef contract for ration days. My maternal grandparents were Wilhelm and Wilhelmina Aldenburg. My grandfather came to Fort Washakie as post blacksmith in 1886, later moving to Lander.

Growing up in Lander, my first remembrance is that of Lander having alternating mud and dust streets, outdoor facilities, tin washtubs for baths, kerosene lamps, dug wells, wooden sidewalks and picket fences. There were horses, cows, chickens and sometimes hogs in every alley. The streets were lighted with lamps requiring a man to light them each evening. I attended the old red brick grade school and high school, and graduated with the first class to graduate from Fremont County Vocational High School—the name having just been changed from Lander High. I received one of the early tuition scholarships from the University of Wyoming, and attended the university for four years, graduating in 1923 with enough credits for an MA, but I did not receive it because my thesis was incomplete. I planned to return soon, but didn't do so until 1953; by that time the graduate credits were worthless. I'm still just a BA.

I taught high school Spanish, Latin, English and history in Ajo (meaning garlic), Arizona, and Holyoke, Colorado. Wanting to be back near the magnificent Wind River Mountains, I became the first high school teacher in Dubois, Wyoming. Except for having textbooks and desks, this school approximated the old pioneer schools. I had a ball in the wild West village. There were plenty of young people about my age. The last day of school a very tall young man and I eloped to Thermopolis where I became Mrs. Daniel J. Fossey. We returned to Dubois and lived there for 10 years. During that time six children were born, one of them dying at age 6.

These were the depression years, and life was a little hard. Dubois had no water system and no electricity, so our mode of life was quite primitive. I did all sorts of work, scrubbing clothes on a washboard, chopping wood and carrying water and coal when Dan was away, churning butter and using all those forgotten household arts. Also, I was editor of the Dubois *Frontier* for several years. In 1937 we moved to Lander where we still live. Four children were born in Lander, one dying at birth.

In 1952 Dan became seriously ill, and I was obliged to hunt for work. I applied at the Wyoming State Training School, where Mr. J.M. Wilson kindly supplied a job immediately. I liked the work very much, but the salary was too small for one to support the family still left at home. I then found a teaching position at Lower Mill Creek School, where conditions were almost as primitive as those in Dubois 30 years before.

In 1953 I attended summer school at the University of Wyoming and ran for county superintendent that fall. I was defeated by Helen Petersdorf, the incumbent. St. Michael's Mission needed a teacher, so I taught there one spring and the next fall resigned to campaign.

After that Dan was much better and we thought we could manage without my working. However, he became worse again. In 1954 I was hired at Lander Grade School to replace a teacher who did not return after Christmas and I taught until the North Grade School was built. I then taught there as a fourth-grade teacher until my retirement in the spring of 1969. I still substitute occasionally.

I have enjoyed teaching immensely—trying to teach children how to learn and why and also to teach them that self-respect and respect for others are interrelated. I maintained the necessary discipline to facilitate learning. Most of my pupils have done quite well as they continued their schooling.

My greatest pride is in my own children. They are good parents, good church men and women. I am enjoying my retirement as it gives me time to do things I want to do after years of doing what had to be done. Also, I can travel when I please to see my children who are located all over the United States. It's nice to rest and relax—although it has been an interesting and busy life.

— Eta Chapter

Mary Jane Franklin

Before the time of my beginning, my mother, Anna Kiskila Davis, made the long journey to America from Lemingo, Finland, by herself at the age of 18. My father, John A. Davis, also an immigrant, came from Cardiff, Wales.

My story began on June 5, 1905, at the family homestead near Inyan Kara in Crook County, Wyoming. As time passed, I shared my parents with five brothers and four sisters. Five of them now reside in the Newcastle area. One of my few regrets is that with such a rich linguistic background, we were not permitted to learn the languages of our parents. We were taught that good Americans spoke only English.

My grade school years were spent in rural schools, walking when the weather was warm. When winter began in earnest, a team of horses hitched to the sled provided our transportation. When the snow was more than belly-deep on the horses, the going became very difficult.

Summer school came along after the sixth grade. Tempted by the nice weather, I tried playing a game called "hookey" several times but gave it up when news of it reached my father's ears.

Country school came to an end with the completion of the eighth grade and I attended normal school in Spearfish, South Dakota. Then came high school at Deadwood, South Dakota, where I remained until graduation. Thanks to my height and long arms I became a very good center on the Deadwood High School girls' basketball team. I also participated in swimming competition. The summer after high school graduation, I competed in swimming meets and basketball at Black Hills Teachers College.

The next year I taught the Holwell School on Skull Creek and the following summer at the Nels Smith School. That fall, I returned to Black Hills Teachers College to continue my education.

That was the winter the normal school library burned. To save the dormitory a brigade was formed using the slop jars from the commodes in our rooms as buckets.

The next year at summer school I taught swimming at the new recreation center in Deadwood. At the dedication swimming meet, I took first place—the prize being a coral neckpiece trimmed with ostrich feathers—winning the South Dakota diving championship.

In the fall I returned to teach again at the Nels Smith School. The following year brought about some great changes in my life. I went to teach in Cambria, a wonderful, close-knit community where I enjoyed my work tremendously. After the coach resigned I was drafted to take his place, becoming the first woman in the United States to coach boys' basketball. I had a championship team, too!

It was there that I met George Franklin. Meeting George was so memorable, that we were married in 1927! I worked as assistant postmistress until the mine closed at Cambria in 1928. Engaged by the Union, I ended my Cambria days by producing an eight-hour day farewell program which touched off all the tears in town.

My memories of the move to Sheridan, where George found employment at the iron works, are both sad and happy ones. In July George was blinded in one eye by a piece of flying metal, was hospitalized and unable to work for several months. On the bright side, our only son, Kenneth Jorgen, was born in November.

Not long after that, we moved to Newcastle and George found work at the Clayspur Bentonite Plant. I worked as postmistress, fastening the mail bag to a pole for the train to pluck off as it sped by.

45

The Great Depression hit and George's job was phased out. We turned to the thing we thought we knew best—farming—and over the next 10 years leased farms in Crook and Weston counties. Each year the crop we raised seemed to be wrong. While there three daughters were born—Barbara, Shirley and Georgia.

While we shared adversities with others across America, we also shared many happy times with friends and neighbors and enjoyed our children.

In 1941 George became custodian for Newcastle High School, so we sold the livestock and moved to town. I was active in the war effort. As a Girl Scout leader I worked with 36 girls in the Girl Scout Victory Garden, hauling them eight miles to the LAK and back in a trailer and then selling the produce as it was ready.

We were a close family, camping, fishing and gardening together. When the two older children joined a dance band, guess where they practiced—that's right. Right here at the Franklins'.

A shortage of teachers resulted in my completing a year in a rural school after the teacher resigned. My two youngest daughters stayed with me at the teacherage at Knobby Knoll and they consider this experience one of the highlights of their lives.

This was the start of many years of teaching, first in rural schools, then elementary and finally junior high social studies in Newcastle.

By attending summer school and extension classes, I earned my degree in 1958 and taught until my retirement in 1970.

Since retiring, I've certainly been busy. We have traveled, visited our children, worked in the garden, hunted and fished. I belong to a homemakers' club, VFW, senior citizens, Eastern Star, Delta Kappa Gamma and the retired teachers' organization.

In 1977 George and I celebrated our 50th year together. People refer to one's later years as the golden years. When I look back I know I have had 74 golden years. Throughout all the difficulties, sorrows and joys, I have had George, and this is the greatest gift God has given me. Along with my children, grandchildren and great-grandchildren, life has been so good to me.

(This is a poem to Mary Jane, written by Frances Mosley.)

MARY JANE

Mary Jane is drinking tea.
Her cup is near full the brim with joys,
Spiced with a pinch or two of sorrows;
Poured from the teapot of past tomorrows.
Yes, Mary Jane is drinking tea.
She rocks to a comfortable, rhythmic squeak,
As even her rocking chair sings a remembered tune.
Her recollections of times past will be presented soon.

— Lambda Chapter

Elizabeth Anne Gilbert

No one could have been more fortunate in her choice of parents than I. My father, Hon. William L. Carss, was 6-feet-2, red of hair and blue of eye, with a keen sense of humor, a love of the classics, an eidetic memory, and a great love of nature and mankind. His father, James Carss, was born in Morpeth, England, sailed to Atlanta, Georgia, in 1850, went by packet to New Orleans, hiked up the Mississippi towpaths, working at odd jobs along the way, to Keokuk, Iowa, where his first steady job was building a dam there. He was a civil engineer and later surveyed the right-of-way for the first railroad to enter Des Moines.

My mother, Lilian Burnside, was of Scotch parentage, born in Des Moines, Iowa, and educated there at Hawthorne School and took painting and music lessons from the sisters at St. Ursules School. She was an accomplished pianist and artist, and with her great grey eyes and jet black hair, was considered one of Iowa's prettiest girls.

When the Merritt brothers discovered the iron ore deposits on the Minnesota Mesabi Iron Range, my father came to Prostorknott, the railroad center for the Messabe Railroad, as a locomotive engineer. My parents were married in Des Moines in 1898 and I was born in the little town of Proctor in 1899. I entered school at 6 and graduated from the eighth grade at 13. I graduated from Duluth Central High School in 1917.

Because two of my favorite high school teachers had graduated from Carleton College in Northfield, Minnesota, and it was a Christian oriented college, I entered there, graduating in 1921 with a BA in English and a minor in biology and Latin. I made many friends and am now class president and class agent.

My first year of teaching was in a rural consolidated school in Bruno, Minnesota, later being high school principal and teacher of English, history and music. In 1922-24 I taught English in the Proctor High School, attending summer school to earn credits for teaching physical education.

In 1924 I obtained a job in Spokane, Washington, where I was assistant girls' physical education teacher for some 1,500 girls in Lewis and Clark High School. Since my students competed in diving and tennis, I lost no time in getting further coaching in those areas. It kept me in physical trim!

I had driven from Minnesota to Spokane with my mother in a Model T Ford, and later, on vacations, drove back to Minnesota via California, Arizona and Colorado with another teacher from the Iron Range. In those days that was considered quite a feat for two young women, only one of whom drove!

I became head of the PE Department at Lewis and Clark in 1925 and resigned to be married in 1927. I had one daughter, Mrs. Jean Peterson of Lander, Wyoming, born in 1928. I lost my husband and father in 1930 and 1931. The Depression was just beginning to hit Minnesota and I could not get a regular teaching job, but through the PTA in which I was active as vice president of the Duluth Council, I was in contact with the St. Louis County rural schools and from 1934 to 1936 taught rural adult education. We held classes from 7 to 9 p.m. in the 92 schools for six-week periods during the year. I was also a supervisor and worked from 8 a.m. to 4 p.m. as well as in the field. We prepared people for U.S. citizenship, helped college students get extension credits, and conducted athletic meets, square dance contests and choral concerts, in addition to regular classes.

I became principal of the high school in Grand Marais, Minnesota, a fishing village on the shores of Lake Superior, in 1936. In January 1939 I took a leave of absence to earn an MA in guidance and education at the University of California at Berkeley, and in the fall of 1939 began teaching at the Ventura Junior College in California.

I married James C. Gilbert, a petroleum geologist and engineer, in 1941 and moved to Los Angeles. Since we lived near UCLA, I began work on a doctorate in education, having only six more credits and a year in residence when my husband was sent to Cody on an oil deal, so in 1944 we moved there. In Los Angeles I had been active in the League of Women Voters, the Cap and Gown Society of USC and was a member of the LA Teachers' Honorary Society and was on the Council for Job's Daughters, Bethel 91.

When the Cody High principal went off to war in 1944, I took over his position, teaching English and heading the guidance department. In 1948 I was elected president of the Classroom Teachers of WEA. I resigned in 1949 when my husband was transferred to Calgary, Alberta.

I helped organize the Cody branch of AAUW and have served as state parliamentarian. I was arts and crafts chairman in 1961 and persuaded the portrait artist Adolph Spohr to teach 10 of us the rudiments of oil painting. From that class developed the Cody Country Art League. I was a charter member of Delta Kappa Gamma but gave up my membership when I went to Calgary. I have served as president of the GOP Women's Study Group in Cody and am an active member of the Cody Music Club and the Cody Senior Play-readers. I am a member of the PEO and a 50-year member of the OES. I have taught Sunday school classes for 27 years. For six years I served as president of the board of the Highland View Manor, the HUD housing unit in Cody.

One of the greatest honors I have received has been the woman of the year award in 1976 from Beta Sigma Phi. The Cody branch of the AAUW named their scholarship after me in 1978. My greatest joy is in my daughter, three grandchildren and three great-grandchildren. My hobby is painting Wyoming wildflowers, and I am an indifferent gardener and avid reader. I am known in my neighborhood as Grandma Gilbert, the jelly bean lady.

I have traveled to the West Indies and Panama, Alaska, western Europe and Spain, England, Wales, Scotland and Ireland. I spent six months in the Holy Land, and have driven throughout Canada and most of the United States. I am still eager to visit China and am saving my money for that. In October 1979 I celebrated my 80th birthday and continually thank God for the long and wonderful life He has given me.

In retrospect, I think I was of the generation of "dedicated teachers." I began teaching younger children in the neighborhood in Proctor in our woodshed while still in the lower grades myself. My father made me a makeshift blackboard and my mother provided a wash basin and roller towel and her old school books. (Cleanliness was a prime requisite.) Years later when the shed was torn down, on the wall in scraggly writing appeared the statement, "Never twist or turn in your seat." Did my family ever rib me about that!

It never occurred to me that there was any other profession than teaching. In my first contract I agreed "not to cut my hair, not to go to any dances except on Friday or Saturday evenings and then only until midnight." I didn't feel discriminated against! I believed that one taught not only by precept but also by example. When woman suffrage was the burning question, I marched in parades carrying banners and was very proud of my father when he voted for the amendment. Working with young people has been the most thrilling thing in my life— even now I keep active in several study groups of the AAUW to keep in contact with young minds. I admit that when people talk of senior citizens I always feel they are speaking of someone else. Truly, the most rewarding of professions is that of teaching.

Reminiscences:

It was my second day, a warm September in northern Minnesota with all school windows flung wide open. That morning the teachers had taken a shortcut from their boarding house to the school and encountered a garter snake in the path, with much squealing and jumping about. That afternoon as I, the high school principal, called the assembled students to order to start the afternoon session, a young lad stepped forward, one hand behind his back and said, "Here's something for you." He handed me a garter snake. I took the loathesome thing in my hand and in one movement sent it hurtling out the window. Then in my most dignified voice said, "Take your seat, Frederick Ball, and the school will come to order." There was one sigh of deflation.

Strangely enough, the next year when I was teaching in my hometown, who should appear at my doorstep, suitcase in hand, but young Frederick. "I've come to go to school here because Miss Carss understands boys." After a good meal we put him on the next train home.

Two young teachers are driving home in a Model T Ford from Spokane to Duluth via Oregon, California, Arizona, New Mexico, Colorado, Nebraska and Iowa. It is late June and the desert between Riverside and Indio, California, is warm. After two flat tires, which the girls repair themselves, it is late and dark when they see lights of a town ahead. A rundown building with a faintly illuminated sign, "HOTEL," looms up in the darkness. The lobby, dusty and shabby, has one light bulb hanging over the dusty desk which bears a bell and the sign, "Ring for Service." They ring and in time a hard-looking woman, clutching a purple satin robe, appears on the stairway. Yes, there is a room, but they will have to carry their own baggage.

The girls, carrying their suitcases, follow the woman up the stairs to a plain but clean bedroom furnished with a double bed with sagging springs, a large dresser, two straight chairs and a washstand outfitted with the usual bowl and pitcher. After the woman leaves, the girls discover there is no key to the door so they move the heavy dresser in front of it, undress, fling the one window wide open and fall into bed.

At early dawn one wakens the other by shaking her shoulder and motioning for silence, pointing to the screenless window. Instead of opening to the outside, the window opens onto a long porch on which on a half dozen cots are stretched as many Mexican workmen!

With speed the window is closed, the girls dress, carry their bags and quietly creep downstairs. Once in the safety of the car they collapse in hysterical laughter. (They had to wait until the sun came up to find a restaurant and breakfast before bidding farewell to Indio.)

— Pi Chapter

49

GRACE GREGORY

M rs. Gregory was born in Shenandoah, Iowa, on January 11, 1910. Her family of six included her father, Jasper E. Holmes; her mother, Frances Annie, an immigrant from England; one brother, two sisters and Grace. She was the youngest member of the family. At the age of 2, Grace's family left Iowa, moving west for her mother's health. They traveled by passenger coach, but their possessions were loaded into a boxcar called an emigrant train. The livestock had stalls in one end and the furniture and machinery filled the other end. Somewhere along the route the boxcar was side-tracked and arrived a week later. Grace's parents bought land from the Wyoming Development Company which had opened up a new irrigation district called the Wheatland Flats.

For her first six years of school, Grace attended a large rural school one and a half miles from her home. Most of the time she rode her pony to school. When an older sister started to high school in Wheatland, Grace enrolled in the Wheatland school, too. She traveled with her sister to school. They drove a horse and buggy the five and a half miles. Sometimes it was quite a cold journey. One morning they threw a big tanned horse-hide robe over their heads to keep warm, and didn't peek out to watch the road often enough. The horse strayed off the road into a telephone pole and broke the wheel off the buggy. They were very glad that they were not far from home!

Normal training was then included in the high school curriculum, so when Grace graduated in 1927, she qualified for a Class C teacher's certificate. At the age of 17 she began teaching in a small rural school east of Wheatland. The salary at that time was $80 a month. There were seven pupils in five different grades. Grace was just two years older than her oldest eighth-grade pupil. Having attended a rural school was a great help to her in setting up a workable system in her new assignment. As usual, the teacher built the fires and was the janitor. The children carried their own drinking water. Extra-curricular activities provided for the small school included programs, box suppers, dances and parties.

Since she enjoyed teaching so much, after two years in rural schools Grace attended the University of Wyoming for one year. Through correspondence courses and summer school classes, she received a teacher's life certificate in 1933. An omnibus trip for teachers in 1932, which toured 35 states and two Canadian provinces, also provided some of her college credits. Grace specialized in primary education. Throughout her teaching career, she earned further credits from the University of Wyoming and classes she attended in Torrington. In 1964 Grace was initiated into an honorary educational society called the Kappa Delta Phi at the University of Wyoming.

LaGrange needed a primary teacher for the first and second grades. Grace took the position and stayed for three years, 1930-1933. It was quite a challenge with 36 pupils. At mid-winter the class was divided. The depression years struck the school very hard. The 1932-1933 term was reduced to eight months to cut down on expenses. Also, the wages were cut to $80 per month. No workbooks or supplies were provided for the students. Grace got the ends of newsprint rolls from the Torrington Printing Office to use for construction paper.

During her third term in LaGrange, Grace married Clifford Gregory. They had to keep their marriage a secret because married women were not allowed to teach then. After her third term, they moved to Wheatland to start the farming enterprise. They stayed for 12 years, and then moved to Meriden where they lived for 14 years.

By 1955 their youngest child had started school, so Grace went back to the schoolroom again. She started with a short term of kindergarten in Hawk Springs, then returned to her former classroom in LaGrange where she continued for 17 years.

Their farm was sold in 1960. After a year in Glendo, Wyoming, the Gregorys settled permanently in LaGrange.

They had five children. Donald, who has a master's degree in special education and is program coordinator for severely handicapped persons, lives in Dickinson, North Dakota. Carolyn, Mrs. Tom Laycock, who lives on a farm, is a 4-H leader, a school bus driver and also cooks for the senior citizens' center in LaGrange. Robert J., who is a Washington representative for Teledyne-Ryan Aeronautical Company, lives in Washington, D.C. James W. is deceased. Richard, who is district mechanic for Halliburton Enterprises in Indonesia, lives in Jakarta on the Island of Java.

Teaching was a very rewarding experience for Grace. She loved primary children. She found them so eager to learn, so responsive and so loving. It was always thrilling to her to lead them into their first reading steps, and also see them learn so many skills in the second grade. She encouraged doing a lot of independent reading on their individual levels which strengthened their reading skills greatly. Grace is a firm believer in drills on fundamentals. The new math she had to teach in the '60s frustrated her. She was glad to see it modified. She was glad to see phonics again stressed in primary education. When Grace first started teaching, she used the sentence method to introduce reading.

Grace found parents very cooperative in helping their children if she sent home materials and explained the specific needs. There were no teacher's aides in the schools until the mid- or late-'60s.

There was a close relationship with her pupils in a small school and many shared experiences. There is one Grace especially cherishes. At a parent-teacher chat once, a mother shared with her an incident about her first-grade son's comment at home one evening. It was when the country was tense as the three astronauts on Apollo II were struggling back to Earth with a faulty craft. He hurried home and said to his mother, boastingly, "Mother, I was the first one to tell Mrs. Gregory that Apostle Paul was in trouble." His mother replied, "Oh, what trouble is he in?"

Grace's summary of her teaching experience is: "I think teaching is a wonderful profession for anyone who loves children. I've found it so rewarding as I have watched my little beginners progress through the grades and high school and become fine men and women. Small schools have a warmth and family feeling. I really liked it!"

Mrs. Gregory was honored by an open house on April 30, 1972, after teaching 20 years in primary grades and two in rural schools. All friends and former students were invited.

Since Grace prefers doing useful things, she spends lots of time now sewing for herself and her family. She and her husband work hard to have a pretty yard and a large garden. She stores away lots of the food he raises.

The Gregorys have gone on a number of big game hunting excursions and many fishing trips within the state of Wyoming. They have seen a lot of the United States as they have traveled about visiting their children. Grace finds many pleasures in retirement.

— Epsilon Chapter

AMELIA LYON HALL

S arah Amelia Lyon was born December 22, 1849, at Rodman, New York, where she finished grade school and high school. Later she completed the teacher training course at a normal school at Oswego, New York. She then taught 23 terms of school at Rodman, Waterton and Sackett's Harbor, all in New York; she also taught at Springfield, Massachusetts, and Hartford, Connecticut. The terms were called summer school and winter school and included all grades. At Sackett's Harbor in the winter term the pupils were mostly boys, a rough lot who worked on boats during the summer. If they did not like the teacher, they "ran him off"; however, Miss Lyon taught several terms there and never had any trouble.

Amelia Lyon and Robert H. Hall were married April 3, 1878, in New York state and traveled 2,000 miles on their wedding trip by train and stage to make their new home at Camp Stambaugh, Wyoming. There Mr. Hall was a telegraph operator for five years. It was he who sent to the outside world the tragic message of Custer's massacre. He was elected to the first Wyoming State Legislature and served for over 30 years in the House and the Senate. Two daughters were born to them.

Mrs. Hall became the third teacher in Lander, Wyoming, The pupils in this school were mostly half-breed Indians, and no power on earth could make them talk when they did not want to. This was a trying situation and took much patience and understanding on the part of the teacher. Of this school, Mrs. Hall wrote, "I had 40 pupils between the ages of 5 and 16. The school was so different from any I had ever taught—an old building with a dirt roof, a few homemade desks and benches on three sides of the room and a table and a chair were the only equipment. The books were odds and ends gathered from somewhere; no two were alike. The school fund was raised from the sale of mavericks. They were called 'schoolma'ams' and were sold at auction to the highest bidder.

"We also had the first Sunday school in this part of the country. On Christmas 1878 we gave the first entertainment ever given in Lander. Only a few of the children had ever seen a Christmas tree. Some of the older girls in the school collected money to get materials to trim the tree and to buy presents for the children. So much money was contributed that we hardly knew how to spend it all. We trimmed two trees, bought a present for every child and baby, and then to spend the rest of the money we gave a present to every bachelor and a bag of candy to every married man. Anyone could put presents on the tree for his friends. The presents on those two trees were worth hundreds of dollars and included silver-mounted spurs, bridles, riding gloves, jewelry and dozens of silk handkerchiefs. These handkerchiefs were each a yard square and had cost six to eight dollars each. The entertainment for the occasion was Madam Jarley's Waxworks which was so popular at that time."

Two of the pupils, Mrs. Dora Lamoreaux Robertson and Mrs. Emma Dickenson Johnson, still live in Lander. They were too young to recall much about that early school, but Mrs. Johnson says she can remember seeing Mrs. Hall riding horseback into town, side saddle, of course. In later years they remember her with much affection and esteem. Mrs. Johnson says, "She was one of the finest persons I have ever known."

Mrs. Hall was appointed one of the trustees for the state agricultural college which was to be built in Fremont County. This, however, was finally located at Laramie, Wyoming, and is now the state university.

What probably endeared Mrs. Hall to her many friends was her ability to write. Her letters were a joy to all who received them, and the recipients were numerous. As a girl she kept a diary which her daughters say is more interesting than fiction. The reader can relive the past with her from day to day. She wrote history of the West for newspapers and clubs. In May 1935, Mrs. Hall was awarded a prize by the Daughters of the American Revolution for her story "Autobiography of a Pioneer Woman."

Mrs. Hall loved poetry and could quote it by the hour. She always knew a quotation or poem to fit every occasion. When she found a verse that she liked, she put it into a scrapbook and usually memorized it. As she made pie or doughnuts in her kitchen, she told wonderful stories to her two little girls. They memorized many of the fairy stories and Bible stories. When she had read a book, she could tell the story in such detail that her listeners felt they had read it themselves.

When she left New York state on her honeymoon, an aunt told Mrs. Hall, "If you were only going to California, it wouldn't be so bad, for people do come back from there." In her autobiography she wrote, "Was I lonesome? Perhaps. But I never saw the time when I would say, 'Let us go back,' but if I were to live my life over and walk in the same footsteps, I am afraid I would not have the courage to live over again the hardships of those first few years in a new country."

The first of the trips back to New York had to be made by stage to the railroad at Rawlins, Wyoming, about 150 miles away. At one time she made the trip by wagon in the winter. (Going to Rawlins over Beaver Hill is not an easy trip even today with graded highways and warm comfortable cars.) Then, it was fraught with danger with the wind blowing up snow like a blizzard. Many times the driver gave the reins to Mrs. Hall while he got out to locate the road. Later, he admitted that there were times when he thought they were lost. The driver, a Dutchman, at intervals would call back to Mrs. Hall, "Be you comfortable?" Mrs. Hall, being a pioneer, knew how to keep warm. Style did not mean much in those days. Besides being warmly dressed, she wore a man's buffalo fur coat over her coat, tightly belted with a man's wide leather belt to keep it snug and warm about her, a pair of German wool socks over her overshoes, and a fur parka over her hood. Imagine climbing into a wagon box thus attired and then being tucked in with blankets and robes!

When the girls were 5 and 7 years old, Mrs. Hall took her daughters by train to New York. One would think that two lively little girls who had never been away from home would have shown some excitement or asked a million questions. But they took everything as a matter of course until they passed a cemetery which really aroused their curiosity. Their mother explained to them about a cemetery. An old gentleman who was sitting behind them leaned over and said, "Madam, will you tell me where your daughters have been raised that they have never seen a cemetery?" She replied, "They were raised in Wyoming where people never die."

Mrs. Hall passed away November 12, 1936. Once in a humorous mood she had said that her epitaph should be:

> Here lies a woman who was always tired
> For she lived in a house where no help was hired.
> But now, dear people, I am going
> Where there is no cooking, washing, or sewing;
> Where everything will be to my wishes,
> Where there is no eating nor washing of dishes.
> And though the anthems are constantly ringing,
> I, having no voice, can get rid of the singing.
> So don't mourn for me now and don't mourn for me ever,
> For I'm going to do nothing for ever and ever."

— by Myrtle Sagen McFarlane, Eta Chapter
— Eta Chapter

Ruby Fern Allison Hanson

One September morn in 1909, Ruby Fern Allison, two months shy of her fifth birthday, climbed high to sit beside the country school teacher in the one-horse buggy. She was on her way to Schuyler School. Her parents, Forest and Amanda Allison, had been asked to let Ruby enroll so that there would be more than one first-grader. Because she was so young and small, she was to ride with the teacher. After classes, she "got to" dust the erasers after standing on a box to clean the blackboard, but soon learned that the big kids had more fun as they walked the one mile, carrying their tin lunch buckets that had sat on the shelf next to the water pail with the one dipper used by all.

School furnishings were minimal: a pot-bellied coal stove, a four-shelf bookcase about five feet long, which held all the library books for eight grades, a teacher's desk, and the wide desks for two pupils each, on and in which there was an invisible center line and no trespassing was tolerated. Not to be forgotten were two high-backed board benches, each long enough for 10 or more pupils, when called up to recite.

"It seemed special to be allowed on the one-step-up platform to speak a poem or write on the board. There, too, the bad kids were punished, as I was once, after being caught eating an apple. The family had overslept and we hustled off to school without breakfast. It was awful to be tardy; the card with your name written in gold glitter was taken from the wire rack, not to be put back until the next month. I was hungry and sneaked an apple in my dress, lay down in the long seat, and got only one bite before being pulled upright by my collar and put in the corner . . . still hungry," she recalled.

Outside, two-hole toilets were at the back corners, the coal shed and horse barn at one side, and a well-pump at the other. To enter the school yard, children walked up and over a stile. Inside this stile was a favorite playhouse. Only occasionally were the boys invited.

Parents, required to furnish textbooks, bought, sold or traded within the neighborhood. Only the well-to-do had new books. Beacon Readers were used in Missouri then; words were memorized; going to a new page only after every word was learned.

September 1915 found Ruby and her brother going by buggy three miles to attend Garden City Public School. As a seventh-grader, she was two years younger than most of the class, very shy and insecure and in different surroundings; "For then," she added, "town and country were different places. There I had my very worst teacher. I withdrew into my loneliness as a turtle in its shell. A kind, capable eighth-grade teacher cracked that shell. By year's end, I was happy and recognized as a capable student and leader." Other students entering town school as freshmen were spared their country-kid embarrassments because Ruby was there as a friend.

In the spring of 1921 some of the seniors went by car to the county seat to take written examinations in the basic subjects (and PEDAGOGY), and hoping to become certificated for teaching in rural schools. If one failed any or all subjects, there was a second chance in June; a third in July. Ruby did not fail.

"Teaching at 16 and 17 . . . some pupils 14 . . . how could I have been capable?" she pondered. This eight-month term at Latour, Missouri, paid $75 per month, which seemed a great deal.

Next, Ruby enrolled at Kansas City College of Pharmacy. After one year, she married and came to Wyoming to live on a ranch near Worland.

Soon thereafter, the local teacher gave notice of resignation, because she was eloping with her brother-in-law. Board members contacted Ruby to fill her position, and the county superintendent endorsed her for temporary certification.

Four years later, the Depression of the '30s was in full sway. School trustees decided to give the position to a single man rather than a married woman with other means of livelihood.

It was 1945 before Mrs. Hanson went back to the classroom; this time during the Korean War. Booming war industries with high pay had lured many teachers from their low salaries. Once again Ruby was willing to help, "For one year," she said, "because of family and home." However, that year lasted from 1945 to 1970.

Ruby was asked to serve on numerous committees, chairing some—curriculum K-3 and evaluation K-3. Her rapport with parents, fellow teachers and administrators was admirable. She was elected a delegate to district and state WEA meetings many times, and as director of classroom teachers, northwest district, and president of that district in 1957. She was no stranger on state committees either. The most productive, she feels, was with the WEA Legislative Commission, when, after being told that it was too political to get involved in state legislative finance, she responded, "Should we ask the butcher, the baker and the candlestick maker to take time from **their** businesses to solve **our** problems? We know the needs: they control the means; let's ask to work with them." Other members agreed. Subsequent action led to an interim study and ultimately state reorganization toward more adequate and equal financing.

In 1958 Ruby attended an NEA conference at Bowling Green, Ohio. "I was shocked," she said, "that many from the liberal arts colleges considered the colleges of education as 'dumping grounds' for the less capable degree candidates. Then and there I set two goals: to help raise the status of the teaching profession through improved teacher training; and to help the low achievers."

She became active in local and state Teacher Education and Professional Standards committees. Her associations in other groups offered opportunity to further her interests. She encouraged others by pointing out that her own BA with honors in 1956, at the age of 52, proved that "it's never too late."

Ruby's guidance was used for several student teachers from the University of Wyoming. Although she tried not to take the twinkle from their eyes, she insisted on quality preparation and performance: "Know more subject matter than you expect to teach; have more materials and methods than time will allow using; then choose the best; be ready to use a back-up if advisable." There were individual differences to be recognized and dealt with; self-worth to be instilled in each child, yet a unified class group was to be maintained.

These new teachers were challenged not to teach by simply going through the books, but to do so with creative variety.

She shared with them techniques for developing bulletin boards that were attractive and educational: displaying pupil work in special ways; developing units; grouping on ability levels; and pupil evaluation and reporting. Under her supervision, they learned to be flexible. "Remember," she said to her young teachers, "you have the opportunity to give each, no matter his status or ability, something with which to grow. Future leaders may come from the humblest of homes or be the shyest of pupils."

Parents were often impressed by what they observed in Mrs. Hanson's class. Once, after a school visit, a mother arranged for the local radio station to interview each of Mrs. Hanson's students and record their rendition of "The Twelve Days of Christmas," after airing a description of their bulletin board about the song. The recording was aired later.

On other occasions, her class appeared on local television to present unrehearsed music and mathematics classes.

Realizing that many pupils were not quite ready for second grade upon completion of a year in first grade, she petitioned for a transition class to follow first grade, "to take pupils 'from where they is to where they're goin',' to use the old axiom." This idea was never approved, but later she was asked to set up and direct a remedial reading center for grades three, four and five. "Not my preference," she said, "it's too late, but still worthwhile." She accepted the challenge and served in that capacity for four years before her retirement in 1970.

Delta Kappa Gamma became a part of Ruby's life in 1952, with initiation during state convention in Laramie, as a state member. Plans to start a local chapter were dropped when the county superintendent refused to disclose the number of women teachers in the county (at that time, membership was limited to 20%), her reason being that such an organization would lead to jealousy, envy, etc.

However, in 1955 Ruby and Mary Hanssen, who had taught in Washakie County, selected charter members for Iota Chapter which was organized on May 14, 1955. Declining nomination for president, Ruby volunteered to be chairman of the program committee, feeling that she could best contribute in that area. Nearly every year since, she has served on committees or as treasurer and corresponding secretary, on state levels as recording secretary, treasurer, second vice president and president of Alpha Xi (1965-1967). While on the Professional Affairs Committee of International, she made two trips to headquarters in Austin. She keeps herself informed about society matters through many, many conventions and workshops within Wyoming. The conference in Rapid City, South Dakota, gave the first look at the society in action. Later, in Cleveland, Ohio, the vision widened. At both Vancouver, B.C., and Portland, Oregon, she took part in the program.

Ruby sees the society as a means of inspiration for involvement, not only for herself, but for fellow women educators. She willingly gives from her heart and hands with programs, decorations, such as 125 pairs of pheasant feather earrings at a DKG luncheon and 150 silk rose corsages at Sun Valley. It seems fitting that this dedicated lady was recognized as one of 5,000 Outstanding Educators in America, in its 1970 volume. Ruby was a Kappa Delta Pi during college days.

When, in 1967, Ruby was voted Hot Springs Teacher of the Year, her principal wrote, "Ruby is a complete teacher, within the classroom, the profession and the community." Appropriate, to be sure, for as a member of the Federated Women's Club, she contributed in many ways and served as president. Membership in the Methodist-Presbyterian Church was enriched through teaching Sunday school, being on the official board and delegate to conference. She held various offices in Chapter K, PEO.

Mrs. Hanson's hobbies are many and varied: perhaps her first love is growing roses and hybrid lilies. In 1976 the U.S. Bicentennial Committee of Thermopolis sought ideas. Ruby suggested a red, white and blue flower garden at the center of town. "Who would design it?" they asked. "I will," said she, and she not only did, but planted and tended it. Many tourists got a good impression of Thermopolis. Businessmen were pleased along with other citizens.

All this seemed natural for the lady who, in 1975, was one of the five international finalists, after receiving the local and state Diana Award given by Epsilon Sigma Alpha Sorority, "to recognize an outstanding woman, who has unselfishly given of herself to a remarkable degree in some area of service to benefit others."

— Iota Chapter

GRACE TRUMAN HARRIS

Grace Truman Fisher Harris is the daughter of George Taylor Fisher and Mary Harriet Sellars Fisher. Grace was born in Palo Pinto, Benton County, Missouri, July 9, 1892. She was named after the book, GRACE TRUMAN. She is one of six children—Archie, September 8, 1886-July 1908; Allie Mae, January 6, 1890-December 30, 1976; Grace; Shirley Glenn, October 3, 1984; Guy Kimball, May 10, 1896-June 3, 1958; and Susie Lee, July 24, 1899-November 2, 1966.

She attended grade schools, Union and National in Benton County, and schools in Morgan and Henry County, Missouri. She attended high school in Warsaw, Benton County. She studied English, algebra and agriculture her freshman year.

At the age of 19 she passed the county examination for teachers and began her teaching career of 39 years in the elementary schools. She attended summer school at Warrensburg, Missouri, and took her teacher training in Lander, Wyoming, and the University of Wyoming.

Grace taught in Cooper School, National and Union schools in Benton County, Missouri, for a total of four years.

Her hobbies are collecting plates, quilting, gardening and bread and jelly making. She also enjoys reading and writing poetry and plays.

Her salary for her first year of teaching in 1911 was $30 per month. There were 15 students in her one-room school, ranging in age from 6 to 14, in grades first through eighth.

She married Fred Theodore Harris, son of George Thomas Harris and Laura Jones Harris, December 29, 1914. They had one son, George Frederick, who died in 1981. Her husband of 66 years passed away December 17, 1981.

Grace and Fred moved to Wind River, Wyoming, in April 1920, after Grace's parents and two sisters had moved to that state in 1918.

Schools that Grace taught in Fremont County, Wyoming, are Mill Creek, Iiams, Borner's Garden, Upper Willow Creek and Pavillion. She taught at Green River, Wyoming, in Sweetwater County from which she retired in 1958. After retirement, due to a scarcity of teachers, she taught one year at Mill Creek and two years at Bar Gee.

The students and teacher walked as far as three miles to school in weather that was sometimes 40 degrees below zero. After arriving at school, Mrs. Harris started a wood- and coal-burning stove. The drinking water was frozen solid on cold mornings. Mrs. Harris and the students huddled around the stove after school started on cold mornings. After school dismissed the teacher did the janitor work.

Some of the things that stand out most vividly in her mind about her students are that some are ministers, some millionaires, a minor league baseball player, a member of the Navy Band and, unfortunately, two went to the penitentiary.

— Mu Chapter

MARY SMITH HATFIELD

Mary L. Smith was born at Lancaster, Wisconsin, on December 14, 1877. She appears to have obtained her education there and taught school there prior to 1909. She came to Wyoming that year and taught the Lost Cabin School. She also taught at Big Trails, then after her marriage and later in life she taught a school near the Frison Ranch on Ten Sleep Creek.

The Big Horn County records show that she was issued a second-grade certificate, which was to expire September 1, 1912.

Big Horn County Clerk's marriage records reveal that she was married to William Ellis Hatfield of Ten Sleep on June 22, 1910. The marriage was performed at the Methodist parsonage in Worland by the Rev. L.C. Thompson. Witnesses were Mayor and Mrs. C.F. Robertson. The front page of the *Worland Grit* for June 30, 1910, carries a lively account of the affair. The article says the ceremony was attended by only a few close friends but goes on to say, "His host of friends around town who were debarred from attending the nuptial ceremonies were more than recompensed for their absence by the delightful reception, ball and banquet that succeeded, and to which all were invited with a cordiality and hospitality truly western in its spirit, and the joyous time that was afforded by the happy couple. The Worland Cornet Band in full uniform turned out and gave the newly married pair a pleasing serenade of several of its most inspiring numbers and then everyone in town so disposed—for no one was barred—went to the spacious town hall, on Coburn Avenue, and the merry hours were lightly passed in dancing to excellent music." The account goes on to state that the evening closed with a banquet at the hotel provided by Mr. Hatfield, who could truly be classed as an "old-timer" in the county.

Mrs. Hatfield was elected the first county superintendent of schools for newly organized Washakie County on November 14, 1912. She defeated her Democratic opponent, Stella Collier, by a margin of 520 to 146 votes. She took office in January 1913 and served the one four-year term until 1917.

The Hatfields owned the ranch in Ten Sleep Canyon which is presently the Methodist Church "Circle J" Ranch. They lived there until their deaths and it was always a center of activity and hospitality.

Mrs. Hatfield died in a nursing home in Billings, Montana, in February 1950, at the age of 72. She is buried in the Ten Sleep cemetery.

— Sigma Chapter

GENEVIEVE PETERSON HAVELY

My father, John Nestanda Peterson, immigrated to America from Norway when he was 16 years old. He sailed in an old sailing ship that had been equipped with a steam engine, which was only used as an emergency device. It used the St. Lawrence River to arrive at its dock.

Because he had brothers in Fairfax, Minnesota, he spent his first year there. Later, while working on the railroad in Iowa, he got "gold fever" and joined an oxen freight train headed for Deadwood, South Dakota. When they were just a few days from their destination a rider told them the news of Custer's massacre at the Little Big Horn.

My father worked for the Homestake Mining Company from the time the mill started on May 1, 1878, until May 1, 1918. He was also involved in the early days' settling of Lead City and active in both city and county politics.

My mother, Sophia Matson, was 22 years old when she immigrated from Stockholm, Sweden, to Deadwood. (The last portion of her journey was made by stagecoach from Sydney, Nebraska.) Her brother, Ole, was the registrar of deeds at the courthouse there. His friendship with my father was the basis for my parents' meeting.

They were married in 1891. My father, then a widower, had a daughter who was 13 years old and a son who was 8. (The daughter was one of the first children born in Lead City in 1878.)

I was born April 12, 1906, in Lead, South Dakota. My half-sister and half-brother had left home by that time. So, in my childhood days my position in the family was that of the youngest child with three older brothers. They were three, eight and 12 years older than I.

Basic Education

I attended the Hearst Free Kindergarten and most of the first grade in Lead. In April of 1913, the end of my first-grade year, my family moved to a homestead 15 miles south of Van Tassell, Wyoming. Because homesteaders did not own the land they paid no taxes. The ranchers who preceded them were reluctant to provide schools for them and so we had no formal school for the next two years.

In the summer of 1915, my mother and three neighbors persuaded two ranchers, who were members of the school board, that a school was needed. They agreed to hire and pay a teacher's salary if the parents would supply the schoolhouse and equipment.

A homesteader's house was moved to a central location on a small hill and became known as Highland School. The building was constructed of wide boards over two-by-fours and covered with tar paper. The inside was unfinished with the rafters, studdings and outside boards showing. Because it was difficult to keep warm, we wore our coats inside on cold and windy days. There was never a fence around the school and so the cattle would use it for shade on sunny days and shelter against wintry winds. It had no foundation so rabbits and mice burrowed under it, and occasionally "came calling" inside the building. Coal had to be hauled 15 miles from Van Tassell. Each of the four families involved was to take its turn obtaining the coal.

The first two years we sat on chairs around tables brought from home. In 1917 our parents were able to buy school desks. My, were we happy and proud of them! Except for teachers' salaries and a few books, the parents of the children furnished everything for this school.

The first teacher put me in the third grade. I thus missed one grade by not being in school for two years. I think that had I not had the excellent beginning in Lead, that I would have had a greater setback. The rest of my elementary education was in this school. I was the only one in my grade for the six years. In the last half of my eighth grade I was the only pupil in the school.

In 1921, after completing the eighth grade, I did not want my schooling to stop as it had with the older boys and girls of the community. All summer I coaxed my family to let me go to high school. Finally, just about a week before school started, my father arranged to rent two rooms where a neighbor girl and I could stay. We had a small bedroom and another room for cooking, eating and studying. Many students from the country came to town to go to school and rented rooms under similar circumstances.

My home was 35 miles north of Torrington. The roads were poor and the cars those days were not the most dependable. I did not get home until Thanksgiving vacation. Before the Christmas vacation there was a heavy snow storm and it was very cold. It was impossible for anyone to come after us so my roommate and I got railroad tickets from Torrington to Van Tassell. It was a long way around —east to North Platte, north to Chadron, and then west to Van Tassell. We traveled all night and half of the next day. We arrived in Van Tassell just before the mailman was ready to leave. He let us ride with him in his sleigh. The snow was so deep that after we had gone about 10 miles the horses "played out." We walked about a mile to a rancher's home where we remained the night. He took us to my home the next day where we arrived in time for Christmas dinner.

The next three years of high school I roomed alone each year and had one room for cooking, sleeping and studying. I took the normal training courses and graduated in 1925. During my high school years I played guard on the girls' basketball team the last three years, served as a reporter for the paper for my class and participated in both the junior and senior class plays.

Teaching Experience

In the fall of 1925 I taught at a rural school. I remained at home and drove seven miles in the family Ford each day. I had five pupils the first year and only three the second year. In 1927 I taught a school nearer home. It was an abandoned homestead house which had been used as a school for about 12 years. The building was in great need of repair. Early in the school year the school district purchased a very small house to replace it. The crowded conditions during those two years are my most vivid memory.

In 1928 I received a contract for $90 per month (a $15 per month raise) to teach in a school about five miles north of Van Tassell in Niobrara County. I stayed in an old homestead house and walked about one mile to school each day. In contrast to the crowded conditions of the previous school, I had room to spare.

I returned to my home the following year. The district had built a new building with better facilities and it had a shield signifying that it was a "Model Rural School." I taught there for four years. For three of those four years, I had ninth-graders as well as elementary students. My final salary was $50 per month.

In 1934 I decided to accept an offer of Mr. Share, the superintendent of schools in Lingle, Wyoming. I taught second grade there for three years. I married Otis Havely in 1937 and because of a ruling against married women teaching I was unable to teach for the next eight years. Because of a great teacher shortage in 1945, the schools were happy to get married women as teachers. I taught second grade one and a half years and first grade one year in Lingle. We moved to Torrington in 1947 and I taught first grade there until my retirement in 1971.

Family

My husband, Otis, was a semi-invalid for five years prior to his death in 1957. Our only child, a daughter Beverly, is a speech pathologist with a bachelor's degree from the University of Northern Colorado in Greeley, Colorado, and a master's degree from Portland State University in Portland, Oregon. Her husband, Jim, holds a doctorate in education from the University of Northern Colorado and is a school administrator at David Douglas High School in Portland. They have one son, John, born in 1972. I spend much of my retirement with them and am now enjoying the privilege of occasionally assisting in my grandson's 3-year-old cooperative nursery school.

Education

Torrington High School normal training; summer terms at the University of Wyoming beginning 1926 and culminating with a BA degree the summer of 1952; some summer terms at Chadron, Nebraska, 1927-1935.

Organizations

Charter member of Epsilon Chapter, Delta Kappa Gamma, Alpha Xi State, president 1955-1968; initiated in Kappa Delta Pi in 1952; Lingle chapter of Order of Eastern Star 40, matron 1948; member and past president of Reed Gobble Unit 63, American Legion Auxiliary, Lingle; member of the United Presbyterian Church of Torrington, Wyoming; and life member of Wyoming Retired Teachers' Association.

— Epsilon Chapter

LEXIE F. HAWKEY

M ary Alexandria "Lexie" Fowler Hawkey was born March 28, 1883, in Indian Creek, Missouri. Her parents were Charles Peter and Sarah Virginia Fowler. The rest of this account is in her own words, taken from a story she wrote about her teaching, titled "There Will Always Be Tomorrow."

"My life as a teacher in Missouri began soon after I finished high school in Hunniwell in the year 1900. I was the usual country girl. I had never been far from home. I would have liked to go to college, but in my case I must earn before I learn. I have no memory of making an application for a school, but the good fairies who have always seemed to be near when I needed help must have gotten busy; for one afternoon my father came home with the news that I had been employed to teach the PeeDee School north of us. I could drive from home. There were 22 pupils, a six months' term, for which I was paid $30 a month.

"I made my program as I thought it should be after I had talked things over with the children. There was no course of study available at that time for rural schools. But there I was that first morning, a wisp of a girl, weighing a hundred pounds, 5-feet-3-inches tall, surrounded by all those children, some of the boys taller than I. On the playground I was a great success. Later, I learned that I gave in too easily to the plea, 'Please, Miss Lexie, just one more game.'

"That school, being only for six months, was out in March. I was not asked to teach there again. I knew why. I did not have what those people thought they needed in a teacher. Only time could supply that. I was happy just to be alive. It was no wonder that the school board felt that some other district could have me. I taught one more short term in Missouri. It was a few miles north of the PeeDee School, known as the Davis School. It was only a three-month term. I do not remember making an application. Someone from the district must have recommended me. I never tried to find out. In those days I took what was offered and hoped I could make good.

"Teachers in the country schools were paid $30 per month. Even at that small amount there were plenty of teachers, that is, persons as I was then, who thought of themselves as teachers. It is a wonder that young teachers did not give up after the first try. But in spite of the low salary, I managed to save enough to attend a six-week session at the Chillicothe Normal after I finished teaching at the Davis School.

"We came to Wyoming in the spring. Coming with me were my parents, two brothers and a sister. It may not have been all gain for Wyoming, but for me it was the realization of a dream and the beginning of adventure. I knew what I wanted to do—teach school.

"In looking back on teaching as it was done in the early days in Wyoming there were many things not mentioned when one took a school. If one felt that teaching was a good life, one went to the county seat and took an examination to show how good an educational background the applicant had. If the results were satisfactory, one went out with a paper stating that the holder of said paper was qualified. But the paper said nothing about so many things one needed to know—how to keep a fire going with wood and coal. The coal was often dug from surface mines and was far from the best. The teacher was expected to be clean and cheerful even after the bout she was bound to have with the stove on Monday morning. The ugly black devil would be cold and full of cinders and dust. The teacher herself would be cold from a horseback ride of several miles. If she were a good manager, and Heaven help her if she was not, she would have paper and kindling ready. When the room warmed and the children got there, the teacher set the mood of the school.

"On a beautiful day in April 1906 I was on my way to my heart's desire, my first school in the new land. I rode on the mail stage from Buffalo to Kaycee. It was a high point in my life, the first lap of a journey to a country school on Powder River, 12 miles below Kaycee. The day was one of the kind that have made Wyoming famous. Air like wine, the sun gentle in its warmth. The stage driver told me many stories that day. No story that he told me could have frightened me that day! But it may have been the cause of something I did after I had been teaching for a while. One day some three or four of the fellows who worked for Mr. Sutton, in whose home the school was located in the extra room, decided to visit my school. I did not want them because I was not too sure of myself. There they were, the big brutes, filling the room to overflowing, grinning at the thought of the fun they were going to have with the schoolma'am. It would have been all they were anticipating if my eye had not fallen upon the gun that someone had left standing in the corner. I picked it up and turned toward those boys. They almost knocked the door down getting away!

"During this time I had been teaching on the authority granted me in the certificate I had earned in Missouri. When I got back to Buffalo I asked permission to take an examination for a certificate good in Wyoming. It was granted and I used it until I married. It was much the same as the one I had taken in Missouri, an attempt to measure my general education with a few questions on methods. But I felt much better with a Wyoming certificate. During my years as a teacher, I was qualified by the requirements of the state for the type of school I was teaching. Most of us in the profession tried to develop any worthwhile method that we found to work well. If the children came happily to school and the parents thought the children were learning, why worry?

"That fall I received a letter from a school board across the Big Horns offering me a school in Germania. How such good fortune came my way I never knew, but it was a chance I had been wishing for. I taught there two years and became well acquainted with the German people and the parents of my pupils. As a fine example of "fools rush in where angels fear to tread," I told the German peopl' that their children should be learning to live with Americans. (There were parents in the community who had a far better education than I had!) After having so much to say, I offered to have the German children come to school on Friday and Saturday. The Saturday teaching was strictly my own idea as I was so homesick that teaching on Saturday helped to make the time go faster.

"My father, after looking over considerable country, decided on 460 acres on the Piney side of the divide between Piney and Dutch creeks as a homestead. My husband filed on an acreage a short distance away.

"One day a visitor told me a teacher was needed on Box Elder Creek. That school was a gift from Heaven. Money was almost non-existent for me then. I spent three most pleasant months.

"The winter was particularly hard. Before the snow was gone I was offered another short term of teaching on Dutch Creek. I had such a time finding a place where I could start. I knew not a word of Polish; they, very little English.

"About this time my husband came home. There was no serious trouble between us. He did not want to be a rancher but that was the only kind of work he could get.

"We sold the ranch and my mother took the older children while I taught at various times in Ulm, Powder River and at the Box Elder School near Ucross.

"I taught two more schools in Johnson County before the Great Depression reared its ugly head. I did not always have much choice. I was too much afraid that the wolf would come scratching at the door in the winter."

This is the end of the quotations from Mrs. Hawkey's book. The rest has been added by her daughter.

Mother's teaching career was not over. She went on to teach for several years in southern Montana, including a year of teaching a day school for the Cheyenne Indians near Kirby, Montana. She had many interesting experiences at this school and cooked a noon meal for the students every day. For some time she stayed in Sheridan and worked for the WPA there when there were no schools to be had. About the time of World War II she taught near Sheridan. The last school she had was a small one near Birney, Montana.

From then on she lived in her own home in Sheridan and enjoyed her children, friends and grandchildren. Early in February she passed away.

— Theta Chapter

KATHLEEN HEMRY

A pioneer is defined as "one who goes before to prepare the way for another." Aptly, this describes this Beta Chapter member who started her pioneering by being born in Casper, Wyoming in 1904—a time when few were so venturesome. She considers her outstanding achievement in her 43 years of teaching as founding and sponsoring the NCHS Newcomers Club which was a vital part of NCHS for nearly 30 years.

Mrs. Richard Burge well described her career up to retirement in 1969. We quote:

"Born on St. Patrick's Day, with the Irish name Kathleen, might just have something to do with her personality. Over 10,000 students had as their teacher Miss Kathleen Hemry since she began teaching at Natrona County High School in 1927.

"Her retirement from teaching was effective in 1969, but retirement from life—never. She is responsible for numerous building stones of our community where no job has been too big or too small to warrant her boundless energies.

"In 1941 she organized the 'Newcomers Club' for out-of-town young people who came to NCHS as strangers and uncertain of themselves. In 1968-69, 30 states and many foreign countries had representatives in the club, some from Peru, Sweden, Mexico, Yugoslavia, Canada and others. Many, many students have returned to Miss Hemry's room over the years, amazed to admit that they have achieved what she has told them they could achieve in their lives if they only tried.

"Her community activities are numerous. She was a charter member of the Natrona County Association for Mental Health and has held all offices. She has been Volunteer Services chairman for the state hospital at Evanston, and the past 10 years have seen "packing parties" in the clubroom of gifts, for the benefit of the patients of the hospital. Miss Hemry has served on the state board of Wyoming Association for Mental Health, and she received the state's Mental Health Bell Award for service.

"She has been a working member of the Memorial Hospital Auxiliary, charter member of the board of directors of the Central Wyoming Counseling Center, is presently vice president of the Natrona County Safety Council. Years ago she helped to start the car safety check. With the help of the Junior Chamber of Commerce, she organized and executed a bicycle safety program, printing her own little booklet of traffic laws, given to all bicycle riders and entitled 'My Bike and I.'

"Miss Hemry was the director of high school summer school driver-education where her list of students grew from one small class to over 200 per summer. According to police records, graduates of summer school driver education have an outstanding safety record.

"She is a charter member of the American Association of University Women, a charter member of the Wyoming State Historical Society and the Natrona County Historical Society. She was in charge of the Pony Express celebration, with 1,000 people in attendance, at old Fort Caspar. She was awarded the Wyoming State Historical Society's Honorable Mention Award for this activity.

"During World War II she saved Natrona County newspapers and later made scrapbooks from all of the clippings of boys from this county. There are over 3,000 names, all alphabetized, with gold stars on casualties. These beautifully leather-bound books were presented to the Natrona County Public Library. CASPER BOYS IN WORLD WAR II won the Wyoming State Historical Society Award, also.

"She is a member and past president of the Daughters of Union Veterans and has been decorating veterans' graves for over 30 years.

"Miss Hemry joined the First Christian Church in 1922. In honor of her parents, Mr. and Mrs.

C.D. Hemry, and her aunt, Mrs. Etta Smith, and her brother, Howard Hemry, Miss Hemry donated the Hemry Memorial Carillon Bells to First Christian Church. She has served on the church executive board for many years.

"She has been an active member of 'Citizenship Day' planning committee since its inception. This activity is to honor new citizens who have recently been naturalized. She makes a special hand-painted cup for each new citizen.

"A recent event was the memorial service held on March 9, 1969, for the boys who lost their lives in Vietnam. She contacted 15 community leaders, and arranged for presentation of memorials to NCHS, to Natrona County, and to Casper College. She provided engraved brass plaques with each boy's name.

"She is an active member of Kappa Kappa Gamma, of Delta Kappa Gamma, and a charter member of Kappa Delta Pi.

"She grew up in the Wolton area, attending the Sagebrush School, moving to Casper to attend NCHS, and was class salutatorian in 1921-1922. She received her BA degree from the University of Wyoming in 1926, and her master's in 1942, and has taken summer classes at several universities. Her areas of teaching include business education, English, science, social studies, foreign language, mathematics, physical education and driver's training."

Since retirement she has continued as a community leader in volunteer services. She was chosen as retired teacher of the year for the state of Wyoming in 1972. We quote from the Delta Kappa Gamma state publication:

"A former Casper teacher, Kathleen Hemry of Beta Chapter, who has taught 'everything but band and auto mechanics,' was named Wyoming's 'Retired Teacher of the Year.'

"Active involvement was Miss Hemry's lifestyle throughout her 43 years of teaching. This award recognizes her outstanding contributions to the community and state in meaningful programs and service to others.

"One of her top priority projects was to work for legislation to improve Wyoming's deplorable pensions. She lobbied for implied consent and other safety laws at the 1973 session of the state Legislature. As state president of the Wyoming Retired Teachers Association, she was influential in the passage of an improved pension plan for the older state employees.

"She was secretary of the counseling center board, president of the Natrona County Historical Society, active in two church women's groups, a driver for 'Meals-on-Wheels,' secretary of the Suicide Prevention League, and a volunteer services chairman for the Mental Health Association. She has received her 2,000-hour pin from Natrona County Memorial Hospital for volunteer services."

For many years she has worked tirelessly sorting and pricing and arranging books for the annual Friends of the Library book sales. The first year this sale gleaned $1,700 for the library program. Recently, the income has exceeded $8,000.

As a member of the Blue Envelope Health Fund Board, she has charge of the Memorial Books in which all activities of the project are preserved, as well as obituaries of all those receiving Blue Envelope Memorials.

She is on the board of directors of Natrona County Senior Citizens, Inc., a government-subsidized project which serves meals to seniors.

She is chairman of the advisory board for the Recreation Center for Senior Citizens, a locally sponsored program for the elderly. Ever active in the "Meals-on-Wheels" program, she is a driver chairman, taking responsibility for recruiting volunteer drivers every week.

Miss Hemry organized the local retired teachers chapter and was president for many years. She is still active in their legislative program.

In 1975 she was awarded the local Diana Award from Beta Sigma Phi for outstanding community service. Then she won first in the state and third in the nation.

— Beta Chapter

RUTH HILGENFELD

I was born Ruth Ptacek on November 21, 1905, in Kearney, Nebraska. I attended the city schools through the eighth grade, after which I attended high school in Kearney State Teachers' College training school. I remained here for two years of college work.

In 1925 I accepted a job at Bayard, Nebraska, supervising music in the city schools. Two years later I returned to Kearney College for two more years and received my bachelor of arts degree.

I returned to western Nebraska and taught music in Bridgeport and Gering where I met my husband, Herbert Hilgenfeld, who also was in educational work.

When our son, Bob, was born in 1943, I retired briefly from school work, but as in most of my life, I continued training church choirs.

In 1945 I filled in teaching music in the Huntley, Wyoming, schools. Herb was superintendent there at the time. For several years I took the music pupils to musical festivals where we won mostly superior ratings. It was during this time that Viola Shepherd, then county superintendent, saw my work producing Christmas programs and recommended me for Delta Kappa Gamma. I was taken into the organization in Cheyenne, Wyoming.

I continued doing part-time teaching until Bob was older and later took the position of vocal instructor for Scottsbluff College where I remained for eight years.

By this time Herb and I both needed a change and came to western Wyoming, Rock Springs, to remain, we thought, for one year. Herb was teaching English and I expected to rest from school work. However, Sam Boucher knew I had a minor in English and finally I consented to replace a man who came here from Denver. He took one look at the town and went back to Colorado. I "substituted" in his job for 10 years until Herb retired in 1968.

I "filled in" again when Herb took the job as superintendent in the Farson, Wyoming, schools.

Last year I received a diploma type of recognition from Kearney College reading, ". . . whose life has benefited mankind and whose contributions for 50 years have brought honor to the College with this Honorary Life Membership in the Kearney State Alumni Association on the occasion of the Golden Anniversary Class Reunion."

Herb and I are both retired now in Rock Springs where our son is teaching in the same building where we both worked.

— Delta Chapter

NELLIE G. HODGSON

At her mother's knee, as she shelled peas, broke beans or knitted black wool stockings for her three children, Nellie, the 5-year-old, decided to be a teacher when she grew up, and she would "write arithmetic" on Saturdays. Before she was 18, Nellie did become a teacher but for some reason, no "arithmetic" was written.

Before Nellie Gladys Smith was born, the family doctor explained to the father, John Madison Smith, and the mother, Mary Cynthia Merrill Smith, that the mother's physical condition and the baby's positioning would prevent the child's being born, and that both mother and baby would die. Friends of the family, Mr. and Mrs. Henry Sites, living near Eagleville, Missouri, offered a peaceful home where the mother would be surrounded by loving care until the sad hour would arrive. The father took care of the brother, Lyman Beecher, about 2 years of age, and the sister, Mary Louise, about 4, in a small, rented house in Lamoni, Iowa. On February 10, 1895, six weeks before the time set by the doctor, Nellie must have decided that she would change the expected hour by changing her position to the correct one for delivery, with no professional help, and entered the world with only the assistance of "Aunt Jane" (as she was later lovingly called). Neither mother nor daughter suffered any ill effects as a result of the unpredictable birth, returning in due time to the family home. (As Nellie grew up, throughout her life, and even today, she has surprised many people with her determination to accomplish what she sets out to do.)

When she was 10 years old, her father, who had been in ill health, passed away. Her mother, who had previous normal school training and was certified, realized that now, of necessity, she must seek a teaching position. She picked Pella, Iowa. Nellie was placed in a home where she could earn her board and room and the two older children were responsible for themselves while the mother was at school. At this time Nellie was in the seventh grade while her brother and sister were in the eighth. At the end of the school year, Nellie was given the eighth-grade examination and entered high school in the fall at the age of 11. After one year she continued to work for her board and room plus 25 cents a week, so that her mother could go back to school. Following this, she went back to high school and completed her fourth year in 1911, at the age of 16. She then attended Iowa State Teachers' College for two periods and two summer sessions, working all the while and not returning home for the entire period of time. When she did return home, she obtained a job in a drug store where her responsibility was the operation of the fountain, plus the ordering of novelties. It was at this time she met her future husband who was the operator of the theater adjacent to the drug store. The owner of the store was a very fine doctor whose brother was inclined to think that any young employee, without a father, would be someone who was defenseless. When the owner found a serving tray badly bent out of shape and inquired of Nellie as to "why," he was told that there would be more bent trays if his brother didn't learn to keep his hands at home!

That summer Nellie learned of an opening at a school in a farm area. She applied and was hired on the condition she could qualify. Since she would not be 18 until February 10, a petition was circulated among the professional and business men, requesting that Miss Smith be certified. The county superintendent stated she had passed examinations in each subject she would be teaching. At the end of the term (three months, as Iowa had split sessions), this school was to have a vacation for two weeks so her mother suggested Nellie apply at another school that was starting the following week. This she did and was hired. At the first school she lived with a school board member who was very poor. They had hot rabbit for breakfast, cold rabbit for lunch and hot rabbit again for supper. The school was a mile away and life was hectic, to say the least. At the second school, in her new home, the meals were well-balanced, her bedroom warm, and she was given milk and cookies when she came home from school. She was told, "We buy apples by the barrel so you must always pick out the best apple, that way you will always be eating the best." At both schools she was janitor as well as teacher.

In the summer of 1913, Nellie married Paul Hodgson and in 1914 their daughter, Marjorie, was born in Pella, Iowa. Some time later they moved to Des Moines, where Paul was employed by Bell Telephone Company. In 1917 they were persuaded to move to Thermopolis, Wyoming, by Nellie's uncle. Relatives were of the opinion that her health, which had been poor, would improve in the fresh, western air. In the spring of 1918 a son, Kenneth Glen, was born. He lived only 22 days.

In mid-year 1918, she accepted the position of teacher for the eighth-grade homeroom in the departmental junior high system. It was during this time that she became guardian to the Campfire Girls, who promptly went to work and planted beds of flowers around three sides of the new library. They also earned $365 and Nellie took 13 girls on a 13-day trip through Yellowstone National Park!

In 1919 she was offered and accepted a position teaching the sixth grade (her favorite). 1921-23 saw her teaching third, fourth and fifth grade the first year, fifth and sixth the following year at Gebo, Wyoming. (Explanation—In 1921 married teachers were barred by the Gebo board, but Nellie was hired to replace an unqualified teacher there.) 1924 found her working in the office of County Superintendent Myra Skelton. She also did some substitute teaching. She subsequently filed for the office at Mrs. Skelton's request. She was elected and served during 1925 and 1926, during which time she served on the state Textbook Committee, helping with the completion of the state Course of Study and the standardization of schools. At this same time Mr. and Mrs. Hodgson took it upon themselves to provide weekend board and room for three young teachers who taught in the country and came to town weekends. They also delivered them back to their respective boarding homes, one on Buffalo Creek, one in Wind River Canyon and the other 28 miles up Owl Creek, with no reimbursement from the girls, with a resultant indebtedness of $300. During 1927, 1928 and 1929 she substituted in the local school and worked in the Golden Rule store. In 1929, under her direction, the Baptist Young People earned enough money to take a busload of them to the first Baptist Camp in Wyoming, near Lander.

She taught school in 1930 at Ten Sleep, beginning at mid-year. Her family stayed in Thermopolis. In 1931 she became interested in writing insurance and opened an office on Arapahoe Street in Thermopolis and soon qualified as a member of the National Association of Real Estate Brokers. She worked at this until 1951. This same year she was chosen Wyoming chairman of the Women's Association of Real Estate Brokers. 1951 also found her selling her business in order to take her very ill husband to the Mayo Clinic in June. He passed away on July Fourth. He had been a Civil Service clerk in the post office 24 years.

In 1952 Nellie was urged by friends, the Rev. and Mrs. Edwin Bell, to visit them in Zurich, Switzerland, where he was working for a mission board. He had, at one time, served as pastor of First Baptist Church in Thermopolis. After two weeks in the Bell home, it was decided Nellie would become a member of the Bell household and share expenses for six months. During this time she went on tours of many European countries, including a visit behind the Iron Curtain to East Germany. When the ship docked in New York on her return voyage, as she was preparing to go through customs, she found her luggage was inspected by an official who simply opened and then closed the lid of each of the seven pieces, while others were having everything removed from the cases. She asked, "Why . . ." He said simply, "You have an honest face." . . . Her reply was, "Thank God," as she remembered the hours she had spent, carefully wrapping 200 very small articles. The night she returned to Thermopolis she was asked by the superintendent to substitute teach in junior high, which she did for the balance of the year. The following year she was offered the sixth grade and accepted. From then through 1967, except for one year, she taught the sixth grade. During this tenure, in 1963, she was given the Classroom Teachers' and the Wyoming Education Association's "Teacher of the Year Award" for outstanding service to the community and its youth. In 1967 she retired at age 72. From then until 1974 she did some substitute teaching, and then requested that she not be called upon to teach anymore.

Mrs. Hodgson has been a member of the First Baptist Church of Thermopolis since 1918 and has been active in some capacity or other, most of that time. She served as treasurer, a member of the building committee, was church clerk and on executive board from 1960 to 1976. She taught a Sunday school class of sixth-grade boys for 11 years. During her search for new class members, she "discovered" a bright sixth-grade boy who couldn't read. His mother assured her that he wouldn't come to

Sunday school, but he did, and Nellie worked out a plan to help him learn to read. With the cooperation of school authorities and teachers, they started with three pre-primer books and followed the course of reading through fourth grade. He went to her Sunday school room after school each day from 3:30 to 6 p.m. until the end of the school year to accomplish this. In the eighth grade he won a reading award. He later graduated from high school at Shoshoni, Wyoming.

In 1975, with the help of Beatrice Slane, she compiled a complete history of the church, its officers, committees and all activities, in identified pictures. For eight years she made two trips in the morning and two in the evening each Sunday to and from the church to the Pioneer Home to transport those wishing to attend church services. In 1948 she received a 25-year citation and gold pin from the National Red Cross for her meritorious service, and served in many capacities in the Red Cross for more than 20 years following.

At the close of World War II she received a beautiful citation from Great Britain and Northern Ireland, which reads, "On behalf of the war-distressed people and the Women's Voluntary Services, we tender thanks to you for your generous help given during the long years of battle against Nazi tyranny." It was during these war years that she was on call 24 hours a day to assist any servicemen and their families if a need arose. She was secretary-treasurer of the USO and earned her "wings" as a ground observer. She has been a continuous member of the American Legion Auxiliary since 1922, as a charter member of the Wyoming Historical Society and the local chapter. and the Pioneer Society. She is an honorary deaconess at First Baptist Church and served long on the Historical Committee. Also during all those active years, she was president of the Thermopolis Classroom Teachers, a charter member of the VFW Auxiliary and a continuous member since 1960, as well as a charter member, of the Wyoming Historical Society and the local chapter.

Although she never did "write arithmetic" on Saturdays or any other time, the contribution that Mrs. Hodgson has made to the community is remarkable in its amount and its intensity. It is remarkable also because of its "SELF-LESS-NESS." Nellie is not a wealthy woman in worldly goods, but the richness of her sincerity, the fervor of her service, the dedication and exuberance displayed, make her one of the most outstanding people that a community could claim. For more than eight decades she has been one of a rare breed, a person who invests herself in projects that may not be publicly recognized, with as much fervor as she would a project that brought personal glory and recognition. Even today, she surprises this writer with the fact that her wisdom of so many years brims with an enthusiasm that so many times is credited to the young!

— Iota Chapter

MILDRED GLADYS WENDT HOLDREN

Mildred Gladys (Wendt) Holdren was born June 12, 1912, in Kearney, Nebraska, Buffalo County. Her father was George Wendt, and Mabel Wolf Wendt was her mother. Mildred's maternal grandparents were John and Margaret Wolf and her paternal grandparents were Auguste and Millie Wendt.

Mildred attended elementary school in Pleasant Hill School in 1918 through 1925, and high school in Pleasant Hill High from 1925-1928 and then went to Kearney High from 1928-1929. She attended Kearney State Teachers' College in 1929-1930. She then went to summer school at the University of Wyoming in 1932-1955. She received her high school diploma in 1929 and her bachelor's degree in 1950 at the University of Wyoming. Mildred also has a master of arts which she received in 1955.

Mildred taught in Odessa Rural-Nebraska from 1930 to 1931. She went to Banner County Rural in 1931-1932; then she taught in LaGrange, Wyoming, in 1942-1946; Torrington, Wyoming, in 1946-1962.

The lowest salary she has ever received was $400 for eight months in 1932, and the highest salary is $6,200 which she is receiving now.

Mildred belongs to the English Lutheran Missouri Synod Church and has been a Sunday school teacher and organist for six years. She was a Scout leader in 1939-1940, 4-H leader in 1935-1938, Delta Kappa Gamma, Ruth Society, American Legion Auxiliary, Soroptimist and a Republican Junior Committee member.

— Epsilon Chapter

CAROLYN NEWELL HOWARD

When I was 17 years old in 1903 with an eighth-grade education, I started to teach in country schools in Banner County, Nebraska. I was getting $25 a month for teaching and paid $10 for board and room. All the privacy I had was back of a sheet curtain. My pay was a bond. To encourage me my father bought the bonds and paid my board. I stayed four months. When I went home for Christmas, I quit.

The balance of the winter I studied at home. In the spring I went to Esterbrook near Laramie Peak in Wyoming to visit relatives. While there I learned they wanted a teacher at a sawmill for summer school so I taught this school for $40 a month. I bought a horse and saddle and spent all my spare time riding with cowboys. It was a little log schoolhouse to which eight pupils came. I was offered a school on Wagon Hound Creek that fall with $45 a month pay and $15 for board. I moved down there from the mill.

In the fall there was a dance up at the mill which I could not miss. I had the mailman bring my horse down and Friday evening I started to ride 25 miles all alone. It would have been all right, but my horse had been starved and consequently gave out. All I could do was walk and lead him. It grew dark and I was afraid but kept on going and finally arrived. Then I danced until daylight. Someone took me home and I never saw my horse and saddle again.

When this school was out I went home to Mitchell, Nebraska. My next school was at Caldwell where Lyman is now located. I had 50 pupils from the primary to the ninth grade. I boarded at a farm about three miles from school. This was the Frank Lane School. He added to my grief by shipping cattle to Omaha late in the fall and returning with two orphans, a boy 9 and a girl 11. They started school right away. There were no seats for them and no books. The school board would not buy books. So I had to buy the books myself and crowd pupils in by putting three in some seats. This was a tough school with most of the boys 10 to 16 years old. The year before they had put the teacher out and broken up the school. I got me a good whip and I finally had them under control. I had to keep them busy. I was asked to teach another year but I didn't.

Next year I taught the Coleman School near Laramie Peak on Cottonwood Creek. It was a small log school with 10 pupils. I was there for two years and had to do my own janitor work. I boarded with Mrs. Newman, a widow, and walked a mile to school. I received $50 a month and paid $15 for board.

Next winter I was back in Nebraska teaching the lower Mitchell Valley School with 50 pupils from primary to eighth grade. The year before they had run the teacher out, three different teachers, in fact. I held them down for eight months and had to ride horseback seven miles to school. It was a terribly cold winter but I missed only one day. Next fall I didn't have a school and got a job weighing beets. Along in the winter I got restless and wanted to teach. So I headed back to Wyoming and was hired for the Adams School on Cottonwood Creek. It started February 1 and last until August 1. There were only three pupils from one family and it was real dull. We had to walk a mile and there was a lot of snow that winter. Not once did the father offer to take me and the girls. We would be wet to the waist when we reached the schoolhouse some mornings. I was glad when it was over.

In September I taught at the Waln School on Horse Shoe Creek with 10 pupils. The school was held in an old house. I had to walk three miles from where I boarded. Before the weather got bad that fall a rancher sold out and left with two of my best pupils. They moved the school up the creek to another old house and I changed my boarding place to a ranch close to school.

The last two schools I taught were near Mitchell, Nebraska, where I stayed home and rode horseback to school. The last school was the only one I taught where the school board would not do anything. They would not clear lumber out of the schoolhouse and the mice were terrible. They would not provide coal and kindling. One morning I arrived at the schoolhouse and there was only one bucket of coal. It was terribly cold. I went out and chopped off some fence posts and got a fire started. I told the children we would have no more school until coal was delivered. The school board had coal delivered the next day, but the stove smoked and they would not fix that. I dismissed school again until the stove was fixed.

Carolyn, the daughter of John and Catherine Neeley, was born in Fredonia, Iowa, May 18, 1886. Her folks homesteaded near Esterbrook, Wyoming, in 1887. When they had proved up on their homestead, they took a covered wagon and drove back to Iowa in 1900. It took them a day to drive through Omaha. They stayed a year in Iowa and then moved west by emigrant car, settling in the Mitchell, Nebraska, area. Carolyn married William Howard July 12, 1912. She belonged to the Presbyterian Church and a homemakers' extension club.

— by Mae Urbanek
— Epsilon Chapter

MYRTLE LUELLA HUNSAKER

M yrtle Luella Lewis Hunsaker was born at Burlington, Iowa, July 22, 1883. When she was 20 months old, her father, Arthur C. Lewis, met an accidental death and the family moved to Avoca, Iowa. There her mother met and married Thomas Wellington Brown and they lived on the family ranch where Myrtle grew to womanhood. She received her education in the rural schools of Pottawattamie County.

After taking state exams at the age of 16, she taught in rural schools for four years. She then attended Iowa State Teachers' College at Cedar Falls, Iowa, receiving her bachelor's degree in education in 1909. At her parents' urging she joined them in Idaho Falls, Idaho, where she taught school for five years.

Myrtle and George Maurice Hunsaker were married on July 22, 1914, and made their home in Idaho Falls until they moved to Greybull in 1919. She was the main substitute teacher in Greybull elementary schools until the death of her husband in November 1922, leaving her with three small children, the youngest being 7 months old.

After spending 16 years teaching in Greybull Junior High School, she was elected county superintendent of schools in 1938, a position she held for 16 years. Her jurisdiction covered all of Big Horn County with many rural schools, all of which she visited faithfully although roads and means of transportation in those days left much to be desired. While she was in this office she furthered her education by attending summer schools at Washington State University, where she was initiated into the national educational sorority, Kappa Delta Pi, in recognition of her high scholastic achievements.

As the president of the Wyoming Superintendents Organization, she was sent as a delegate to the National County Superintendents Association meeting in Indianapolis, Indiana, in 1947, where she served as a consultant. She was past worthy matron and a 62-year member of Fern Chapter 31, Order of the Eastern Star, as well as a member of Rebekah Lodge 10.

After her retirement in 1955 she spent her time traveling and engaging in her many hobbies. A born collector, she had extensive collections of buttons, rocks, salt and pepper shakers, potholders, sea shells and many items of interest which crossed her path. Her main interest, however, was in learning and she continued her studies as long as she was able to read. Always an individualist, she enjoyed life to the utmost and found good qualities in every acquaintance. Her last years were spent in the Pioneer Home in Thermopolis and the Basin Sanitarium where she died in June 1981.

Still living are three children, Maxine Knudson of Greybull; Robert of Henderson, Nevada; and Betty Sabec of Casper; four grandchildren' six great-grandchildren and many thousands of students who have been influenced by her teaching.

— Rho Chapter

GRETCHEN HUTCHISON

The writer Gretchen Hutchison, nee Bishop, was born April 4, 1907, at Parnell, Missouri.
After graduating from Parnell High School in 1924, college work began with the summer
session at Northwest Missouri State Teachers' College, Maryville, Missouri. Former plans of teaching
a few years to save money to attend college were abandoned when teaching afforded so much
pleasure. Consequently, some extension courses and many summer sessions (one at the University of
Colorado) were required to complete the work for a bachelor of science degree in elementary education in August 1935.

Graduate work at Ohio State University in the summer of 1939 was followed by a summer's experience as a homeroom teacher for a sixth grade at the Demonstration School, State Teachers' College, Maryville, Missouri.

Work on a master of arts degree was started at Teachers' College, Columbia University, in the
summer of 1946. Next summer the work was supplemented with valuable experiences as an assistant in
two classes. The third summer and a field course finished the work for the MA degree in curriculum
and teaching—reading diagnosis and remediation.

A few years later there came the opportunity to do more graduate work, this time at the University of Wyoming. There was time to finish requirements for a professional diploma in elementary
guidance before moving again.

Interspersed with the many years of teaching were some courses from Washington University in St.
Louis and one course from the University of Missouri.

The writer's teaching experience began in 1924 at Glendale, a rural school near Pickering, Missouri. After four years a position in the hometown school at Parnell seemed attractive. After seven
years of intermediate grade teaching there, two more followed in Burlington Junction, Missouri. The
next move was to a position in a fifth grade at Overland School in Ritenour District in St. Louis County, Missouri. Three years later remedial reading was initiated. This work occupied the next 12 years.

Teaching was resumed four years later. Thirty years were completed in Missouri before I moved
to Glenrock, Wyoming. Here in the first grade the challenges continued for 13.5 years before retirement on January 12, 1973. Good health was responsible for unusual attendance during those 43.5
years. Only two days' absence were due to illness.

During all this elementary teaching, the writer worked concurrently with adults in church, school,
civic organizations and in teaching first aid. The following include her among their memberships: the
Methodist Church, the American Association of Retired Persons, the National Education Associa-
tion, the National Retired Teachers Association, Retired Teachers Association of Missouri, the
Wyoming Retired Teachers Association, the Converse County Retired Teachers and School
Employees Association, the Glenrock Women's Club, and the Delta Kappa Society, Nu Chapter,
Converse County, Wyoming. She later transferred to Epsilon Chapter.

— Epsilon Chapter

HELEN A. IRVING

Miss Irving was born in Rawlins February 8, 1887, to Mr. and Mrs. James N. Irving, and died September 8, 1962. She attended the local schools from kindergarten through high school, attended the University of Wyoming, and worked as a printer for the old Rawlins *Republican* before launching her school career.

Her first teaching assignment was at the old Dunkard School near Encampment, Wyoming. Other assignments followed at South Spring Creek School, the Walcott School and she taught the last class ever held at old Carbon.

Her first teaching post in Rawlins was in the third grade and from that she went on to teach in the fourth and fifth grades.

While teaching the fifth grade in Rawlins she was elected to the office of county superintendent of schools in 1921. She held that office continuously until 1959, a period of 38 years.

She drove to many schools in the county by back roads that were not paved and was sometimes stranded all night. Often she had to go by horseback and snowshoe to get to school, but she always made her visits. Miss Irving is listed in WHO'S WHO IN EDUCATION and started the Carbon County spelling contest 49 years ago.

She served several terms as president of the Wyoming County Superintendents Association, was a member of the PEO, BPW (past president). She was a charter member of the Soroptimists Club and a member of the Presbyterian church. She served for 10 years as treasurer for the American Cancer Society of Carbon County, and was chairman of the Junior Red Cross. Miss Irving was asked to join the ranks of the Delta Kappa Gamma as a state founder in Wyoming in 1939 and was invited to become a state charter member in Wyoming in 1940. She was a founder and the first state president of Alpha Xi State of the Delta Kappa Gamma Society, an honorary teachers association.

Her practical experience as a teacher and her intrinsic power of initiative matured the executive ability of Helen Irving, and under her administrations a splendid work has been accomplished in coordinating the work of the public schools of Carbon County and in raising the general standards of that work.

Helen was a wonderful person, so self-effacing, so loyal. She did so much for Rawlins that, of course, could not be recorded—small things, constantly being done. Somehow we do not meet her kind any more. Probably they have been swallowed up by the aggressive type and the pattern has been destroyed. I have watched that same thing happening to plants. I know you have, too.

Good night; sleep well!

— Mu Chapter

Laura Irwin

Laura Haley Irwin, who speaks of her first week of teaching as a "nightmare," was 21 years of age and had completed 12 weeks of summer school, when an unexpected vacancy occurred in the St. Joe rural school. Laura Haley accepted. By Tuesday of the first week, she felt so incompetent and inexperienced, she decided to submit her resignation on Friday. But with hard work, her limited college training and her experiences as a pupil in a rural school, she was able to meet the challenge, and by Friday Laura Haley Irwin was on her way to a teaching career which lasted 42 years.

Laura Ruth Snyder, daughter of Mr. and Mrs. Bert E. Snyder, was born October 8, 1906, in West Chester, Iowa. After her first four years in elementary school in Longmont, Colorado, Laura moved in 1916 with her parents, her three brothers and one sister to Gould District. The family of seven lived in a one-room log cabin until her father, Mr. Snyder, completed the new two-room house in the summer of 1917. The children attended grade school in Gould District, then Laura completed three years of high school in Greybull, and graduated from Basin High School in 1924.

Laura was married to Eddie Ray Haley, and a daughter, Dorothy Lucile, was born July 26, 1926.

Laura's college training dated from 1928 to 1966, much of which was earned in summer school. In 1930-31 she attended college for 12 months and received a two-year normal diploma. She earned a bachelor of arts degree in 1951 from the College of Education, University of Wyoming, with a major in elementary education.

In 1931 she began her teaching career in Basin, teaching the third grade. At the close of the first year, she was issued a Wyoming life certificate, qualifications for which were a two-year normal diploma and three years of teaching experience.

For the succeeding two years, due to the depression, the third and fourth grades were combined, as were the fifth and sixth grades, and the enrollment in each classroom ranged from 54 to 60 pupils per grade. She was thankful to be employed, and for this tremendous task received an annual salary of $810.

In the fall of 1934 the single-grade plan was resumed and Laura Irwin taught fourth grade. During most of the summers, if there was enough money, she went to summer school; otherwise she worked at whatever job was available.

While attending summer school in 1943 she was offered a position in the Laramie schools, which she accepted. At the close of the year she was married to Verne Irwin and she returned to Basin to resume a teaching position in the Basin Elementary School.

Laura recalls, in the fall of 1944, the "hot lunch program" was started. During World War II many items were scarce, including dishes and silverware. Table service was obtained by each child's bringing his plate and silverware. It was during this time Laura was appointed building principal but continued full-time teaching.

Five years later, in 1949 when a new superintendent was hired, Laura had her first experience of being placed on a salary schedule. In 1956 when all the rooms in the elementary school, including the basement, were filled to capacity, the superintendent introduced her to the sketch of the proposed new elementary school. She recalls the thrill of that moving day in October 1957, and felt privileged to occupy a principal's office; however, she continued to teach full-time in the third grade. After the state evaluation committee recommended a full-time principal in 1958-59, Laura assumed this job, and spent half a day teaching in the classroom.

In 1969 Laura, along with other faculty members, had the opportunity to visit Meeker, Colorado, schools to study and observe their plan of departmentalization. During the summer months she worked planning and scheduling classes to develop a workable program of departmentalization for the intermediate grades. The program was launched successfully, and continues to be very satisfactory.

In the spring of 1970, Laura requested to return to the classroom to assume full-time teaching duties.

Laura Irwin, an active member of Gamma Chapter of Delta Kappa Gamma, has held chapter offices of parliamentarian, corresponding secretary, second vice president, first vice president and president. She has been active on many committees and served on Alpha Xi Necrology Committee from 1969-71. She attended many state conventions and workshops, two regional conferences, and two international conventions.

She has been an active WEA member, serving on the Structure and Organization Committee at the state level. She represented Basin at the delegate assembly of that organization. She was a member of Basin Education Association, National Education Association and Business and Professional Women's Club and PEO.

Laura Irwin is a member of the United Methodist Church of Basin. Her community activities have been many and varied. She served as a Red Cross First Aid instructor for 10 years. In 1968 she helped sponsor a "Know Your Candidate Program" for Big Horn County. Her travels have included the Dr. Goldsmith's Omnibus Tour of 22 states and Canada in 1933. She has visited most of the national parks of the West, has traveled in Mexico, spent three vacations in Canada, and traveled to both the east and west coasts in her service in Delta Kappa Gamma. Her hobbies are arts and crafts, and she is a talented painter, both in watercolors and oils.

Five of Laura Irwin's pupils taught in Basin during the 39 years she was teaching. In 1970 she taught the third generation of one family. She was presented with a plaque at awards night by the members of the three families.

In May 1971, when she retired, Basin honored her with a **Laura Irwin Night.** Approximately 200 people, five superintendents, school board members, former pupils, fellow teachers and friends presented her with a "This is Your Life" program, floral tributes, gifts, cards and telegrams.

Laura Irwin speaks of her years in the field of education: "My years of teaching have been challenging, wonderful years. The loyal support, encouragement and assistance of my family, along with the fine support and cooperation of the school board and parents, and the association with hundreds of wonderful boys and girls have enriched my life and made my teaching career a success."

In 1985 the Basin Elementary School was rededicated as the Laura Irwin Elementary School.

— Rho Chapter

VERA STEELE ISBERG

In a thriving farm valley in Kansas, our Delmar School and Methodist Church across road revealed the joy in learning and living, which I knew in early years. On the school library shelf a delightful COMIC HISTORY OF AMERICA, by Bill Nye, fascinated every pupil. Not then did I know a day would come when Laramie, Wyoming, would be my hometown and I should learn about Laramie's newspaper man and see his books assembled in the county library in his honor. Nor did I know I would do a watercolor painting someday of that old home community center.

High school days were at hand. The R.F.D. mail carried the *Daily News*—"War in Europe . . . Call for Food from America." Our Steele family moved to Yuma, Colorado, nearer town for school and church, and were able to farm more available land. Extra-curricular activities were fun in plays, projects and Glee Club. The tunes of World War I were sung by everyone in patriotic gatherings. One appreciated the active, dedicated leaders in the community. While still in high school I spent a week in a grade school room as substitute teacher and was convinced I would like a teaching career.

How enthusiastic the instructors were in that first institute for teachers! What eagerness to read returns from the first county teachers' examination! What pleasure to step through the door of my first rural school! Later, it was a privilege to have a position in the grade school in my hometown, Otis, Colorado. My first office was secretary of the county teachers' association.

After several summers and a couple of years in the College of Education in Greeley, I received my BA degree. The 10th year in Colorado I taught art in the junior high school in Fort Morgan.

I came to teach in Wyoming in 1931, serving as teaching art-supervisor in the Laramie elementary schools and as junior-senior high school art instructor. Following further study and work in the summers I received my MA degree from the Colorado College of Education. I retired in 1964. During the school year of 1966 I had the privilege to be supply instructor in art in the College of Education at the University of Wyoming.

This life member of NEA attended some of the meetings at the national convention one year in San Francisco, and was a delegate to a regional in Seattle once. The Cleveland, Ohio, location for the National Art Education Association meeting presented an opportunity to attend one game in the Cleveland Indians' stadium. WEA and LEA membership brought concerns of the profession to me and now in the present day, the local organization of the National Retired Teachers Association offers varied interests and activities.

Membership in AAUW and in Alpha Chapter 1, Eastern Star, began in 1931. In the American Legion Auxiliary one finds a place to serve and to assist in familiar educational and rehabilitation areas. The United Presbyterian Church leading me through the years, still challenges and encourages me to study, grow and serve.

By request in 1969 I submitted three articles for the centennial booklet printed for Kirwin, Kansas. Two were on the pioneer life of my grandparents. In 1972 I wrote a brief paragraph and sent photos of the grandparents to the Phillips County, Kansas, CENTENNIAL VOLUME. Then I wrote an account of the early settlers in our valley for the centennial issues of the weekly newspaper, *Phillips County Review*.

Delta Kappa Gamma Society brought inspiration, friendships and opportunities for service on chapter and state levels. The national convention in Chicago, 1952; the regional conference in Jackson, Wyoming; Green Lake, Wisconsin; Rapid City, South Dakota; Vancouver, British Columbia; and Anchorage, Alaska, all were informative and made enjoyable travel experiences possible.

For the recognition and honor Alpha Xi State has given me, I thank every member of Delta Kappa Gamma. This beautiful framed hand-printed "Certificate of Award" reminds me of the days of fellowship and work with friends in our society throughout Wyoming.

— Zeta Chapter

SYBIL JACKSON

In 1906, on July 28th, Sybil was born to Charles English Jackson and Florence Mc-Clung Jackson on their homestead in Crook County. Sybil's mother was a school teacher and taught her in her younger years at a country school near their home. The school was actually an old cellar house. There were about six students in the school, including one of her brothers. Sybil's family eventually grew to three brothers and two sisters.

When Sybil was 11 she moved to Spearfish to continue going to school, living with an aunt. Her mother continued to teach in a country school, this one close to Inyan Kara Mountain near Sundance. In 1918 a flu epidemic raged and her mother almost died. Her sister died in 1920 of what doctors called acute indigestion and in 1924 her mother died of typhoid fever. Sybil continued her education, keeping her brother and sister with her.

In 1928 she graduated from Spearfish Normal with a South Dakota teacher's certificate. Her first teaching experience was in Upton where she taught fifth and sixth grades for eight years. After teaching in Wyoming for three years, she received a life teaching certificate for Wyoming.

Sybil's next teaching job was a country school at Pleasant Valley School near Four Corners. This was for one year. Then in 1937 she came to Newcastle and taught seventh grade for about two and a half years. In December of 1939 Sybil was appointed as Weston County Superintendent and served in that capacity for 22 years. She lived in Newcastle and traveled around the county. One of her duties was to visit every classroom once a year. Weston County at that time included 29 country schools as well as Upton, Newcastle and Osage town schools. During the last four years as county superintendent, much was happening with redistricting and many of the country schools were being closed down. In the late 1950s Sybil began a petition campaign to eliminate the county superintendent position. Because of her efforts, Weston County was the first county in the state to vote out the county superintendent position.

At this time the University of Wyoming was inquiring about someone to be a student teacher supervisor. She said she would like to do this and the county commissioners gave her permission even though she was still county superintendent. She covered the whole area including Gillette, Upton, Sundance, Osage and Newcastle. She served in this capacity as student teacher supervisor for 12 years. Sybil had no advanced degree at this time, but had taken numerous graduate courses. The university felt her experience was more important than having an advanced degree. Also, during this time she worked for school District 1 part-time. Her position with school District 1 included helping beginning teachers and doing anything that she felt needed to be done around the school. One of the places you could find Sybil was in the lunchroom during the noon hour supervising the students.

After having a car accident near Hulett, Sybil finished out the school year and officially retired in the spring of 1973. Since retiring, Sybil finds herself more jobs to do than before, but says, "What's nice is, I don't have to do them all!"

Over the years Sybil belonged to NEA and WEA. She has been a member of Delta Kappa Gamma since 1960—her first two years were with Theta Chapter in Gillette; then she became a charter member of Lambda in Newcastle in 1962. She also belongs to the Pythian Sisters, Flowering Fingers' Garden Club, Retired Teachers Association, AARP and Weston County Senior Citizens. Sybil has been a member of the Reorganized Church of the Latter-day Saints since she was 18 years old.

Another accomplishment that Sybil achieved to benefit school District 1 is that about 1941, she got the teachers to organize and develop a local teachers' association as well as the classroom teachers' association.

A highlight in Sybil's life came in 1979 when she was honored by Lambda Chapter of Beta Sigma Phi as "Woman of the Year." Sybil was honored for her contributions to education as well as her community services. Newcastle and Weston County have been very lucky to have this dedicated lady working for them.

— Lambda Chapter

VERDA JAMES

V erda James, Beta Chapter, has served both as a local president of Delta Kappa Gamma and as state president of Xi, the state affiliate. She has been elected to eight terms in the Wyoming Legislature as a representative from Natrona County, and her last term was elected as Speaker of the House, the first Wyoming woman to be elected to that position, and the second in the United States. As a legislator, she was chairman of the Education Committee of the House, five of her eight terms.

Born in Stratford, Ontario, Canada, she received her early education in Michigan, South Dakota, Minnesota and Iowa; and her BA degree from the University of Iowa, and her MA degree from the University of Denver. Her teaching experience has been at the elementary level, high school and at Casper College. She served as assistant state superintendent of schools in the Wyoming State Department of Education, and as assistant superintendent in the Casper schools.

Presently, she is representing Casper College as a member of the Wyoming Community College Commission through a four-year appointment by Governor Hathaway. Twice she has been appointed to the governor's statewide Committee on Education.

Verda is a longtime member and a past president of the Casper Business and Professional Women's Club. A few of her activities past and present include the Central Wyoming Counseling Center Board; a United Fund worker; state president of the Wyoming Education Association; life member of NEA; state parliamentarian of the Federated Republican Women's Club; AAUW; Friends of the Library; a board member of Meals-on-Wheels; Synergae of St. Mark's Episcopal Church; PEO; OES; and legislative chairman of the local NRTA organization.

She has served as chairman of the Wyoming Commission on the Status of Women, and is currently on its advisory board.

Honors received through the years include the Carol Lane Certificate for her work in safety education; the local American Legion Award for outstanding teaching; the Wyoming Education Association award for distinguished service to education; and the state Delta Kappa Gamma award which goes to an outstanding member. She holds an honorary life membership in PTA.

Verda is listed in WHO'S WHO IN AMERICA, WHO'S WHO IN THE WEST and WHO'S WHO IN AMERICAN WOMEN.

In 1979 Verda had the distinct honor of having a new elementary school in Casper named for her—the Verda James Elementary School. This multi-million-dollar school opened in September 1979.

— Beta Chapter

MARY LOUISA JOHNSON

Mary Louisa Johnson was born in Albia, Iowa, July 1, 1908. She received her early education in Powell and graduated from high school there in 1926. She then took fifth-year normal training in 1927 after which she attended the University of Wyoming, receiving her BA degree in 1957 with a major in education and a minor in English and foreign language. Since then she has attended Western State College in Gunnison, Colorado, the University of Washington in Seattle and Eastern Montana College of Education in Billings.

She also attended the Broadway Vocational School and the Induction School, both in Seattle and the Pacific University in Forest Grove, Oregon, where she studied radio production and planning for individual learning.

Mary taught in rural schools in Emblem, No Wood and Big Trails, grades one through four, and one through eight at Wapiti and grades one and two at Deaver. She came to Powell to teach grade one in 1939 but left during the war years to work in Seattle as a clerk at the Naval Supply Depot and the Puget Sound Bridge and Dredging Shipyard, as an accountant for the Frederick & Nelson Department Store and the Greyhound Bus Terminal, and as a junior visitor and case worker for the Washington State Welfare Department.

She returned to teach grade two in Powell in 1947 and remained in that position until her retirement in 1974. Since that time she has often substituted in Powell elementary grades.

Mary participated in the beginning of the "Initial Teaching Alphabet" reading program in the Powell schools. This was a program which originated in England and was very successful in Powell schools for about 14 years.

Because of the lack of publisher's editions of the reading texts, the program has been discontinued in the Powell schools.

Mary holds memberships in the National Education Association, the Wyoming Education Association, National Retired Teachers Association, American Association of Retired Persons, American Association of University Women, and was a delegate to the delegate assembly from the Northwest District in 1953.

She is a charter member of Gamma Chapter, Delta Kappa Gamma, International Honorary Society of Women Educators, having been secretary, vice president and president of that chapter from 1954-1958. She has been state delegate to Laramie, state membership chairman and state expansion chairman for Alpha Xi State.

She also belongs to the book club of the Republican Women's Organization and a fine arts club in Powell. She is a member of the Women's Association of the Presbyterian Church in Powell, Deacon Presbyterian Church, and has been chairman of several "circles" in the Presbyterian Women's Organization.

She served as vice president of the Classroom Teachers' Association in Powell, as its delegate to the regional convention in Seattle in 1953 and as its secretary in 1954. She was named "Teacher of the Year" by the Powell chapter of Future Teachers Organization in 1962.

Mary is interested in oil painting and doll making and has shared her experience and knowledge in several speaking appearances before groups of high school students and at PTA meetings.

Mary is also fond of travel, having taken two trips to the East Coast with visits in Washington,

D.C., New York, Pennsylvania, New England and eastern Canada; a trip to the World's Fair in Seattle and on to Hawaii; a visit to Alaska, a fall foliage tour from Billings, Montana, to the East Coast, Quebec and Pennsylvania; a Caribbean cruise and; after her retirement, a trip to the Canadian Rockies.

— Gamma Chapter

LETHA B. JOHNSTON

I was born Letha B. Frederick in Bethany, Illinois, on April 17, 1905. My mother's maiden name was Emma Clark and my father was E.M. Frederick. There were four children—all daughters—probably not the entire answer to a hard-working farmer's prayers. I lived on a farm near Humeston, Iowa, from the age of 10 and before that on a farm in Illinois.

Vernon Johnston and I were married in Jackson Hole, Wyoming, in 1947. We made our home in Rawlins where "Jiggs" (no one called him "Vernon") was a heating engineer for Northern Gas Company. We adopted two children, Bill and LeAnn. Bill has three girls and LeAnn has one. Even from adopted children, girls seem to be a family tradition. Jiggs and I had a very happy marriage and, although he was younger than I, he survived a first heart attack by only five years and died at the age of 45 in 1960.

All of my elementary education was in country schools, and I am grateful for that experience. I graduated from Humeston High as salutatorian in 1923 at the age of 17. All that was needed at that time to teach a country school in Iowa was 12 weeks of college, so I spent the summer at Cedar Falls Teachers College. As I was not yet 18 (a teaching requirement), I took a "refresher course" in husking corn for my dad, harvesting 1,500 bushels. It is difficult to separate my education from my teaching experience as, with so many teachers of that era, I gathered my education as I went along. I finally got my BA from the University of Wyoming in 1955 after many summers and untold extension courses. By 1959 I had everything for my MA except that I never quite managed to finish a thesis along with teaching and raising a family by myself. Maybe some day?

At the age of 18 I was hired to teach in a one-room school in High Prairie, Iowa, and followed a year there with three years in another one-roomer in Sprote, Iowa, which enabled me to live at home and walk the four-mile round trip. Having earned the magnificent sum of $80 a month and with board and room costing me only $3.50 a week, I was able to save enough to go to college the next full year, which then qualified me to teach in a city school. So I moved to Cedar Falls where I taught fifth grade at the Lincoln Elementary School for 17 years. My $80 a month went to $120 (until the Depression knocked it back down to $95), where I had had 25 pupils I then had 42, but it seemed easier with only one preparation to make each day, for one grade instead of eight.

The principal, an ex-military man and wonderful administrator, told me that 10 of my original 52 children would be sent to another room. I chose the 10 and was told later that I had chosen the 10 most troublesome ones. I will always remember how he used to stand at the head of the stairs each morning with his big gold watch in his hand and mildly remind any teacher coming in late that she surely should expect as much of herself as of her children. We were seldom late, I assure you!

I had traveled in the South and the West and now, feeling the need for a change of scene, I accepted an offer from Mr. Lee in Rawlins. He, being an Iowan, liked to hire from that region and I was soon on my way to new adventures. I taught one year, then married Jiggs and was forced to give up my job as married women were not permitted to teach in Rawlins at that time. I taught in Cheyenne one year and returned to Rawlins when Mr. Lunney called me back. After two years with a sixth grade at Mountain View, I was made elementary supervisor in 1959, a position I held for five years, finally giving it up because of too many unpleasant late night phone calls and because of family responsibilities. My next job was as teacher of the fifth grade and as principal at Mountain View from 1964 until I retired in 1970. Since then I have been teaching home-bound children, and it seems I shall never really

85

let go unless they haul me away in a straight-jacket. Teaching has always been a great fulfillment to me.

With the exception of the New England states, I have traveled all over the United States whenever I had a free summer. One summer I spent in Panama after having visited Cuba and several Central American countries. I was hired to teach in Panama in 1941, but as soon as I was there to do so, the authorities put me on a ship for home. Many ships were sunk by U-boats in the Gulf that year and some people I had known were lost, so it wasn't a very pleasant sea voyage. I also traveled to Hawaii in 1975 with Iowa friends, the Anderson family, and again in 1979 with a tour sponsored by the University of Wyoming.

I guess I should know about everything now, having read over 2,000 books since my retirement. At least I am learning how little I do know about my world, and each book is another window on that often lovely place. I seem to be a "doctor" of African violets as many friends send their sick "pets" to me; perhaps my good mother passed some skill on to me as I usually manage to save them. As an avid collector of demitasse cups to the present sum of 80 and of cookie cutters totaling 147—some over 100 years old—I am rich in one small area. Ceramics has also been my joy for years. Backyard gardening is for me mostly flowers, but if prices continue to rise, I may convert to beans and squash. In golfing I have won only one small cup—for my purported putting skills. The Good Lord had better be generous with the years if I am to win another. I have long worked with the Blood Bank and this year am helping with the Meals for Seniors program. Constant activity hopefully fools Father Time, and I have therefore recently joined the Women's Club. And, of course, I am a proud member of Delta Kappa Gamma.

Reminiscing, I can see again my first automobile, a new 1933 V-8 Ford which costs $550. It was surely a love, almost as great as my first teaching assignment—or perhaps even a new husband. My mother said I was a better driver than my two sisters, although they had learned earlier—at least until I ended up in a ditch one icy winter day. Part of the bargain when I bought the car was that the mechanic would teach me to drive—poor fellow.

I see again that first year of teaching and a tough boy coming at me with a knife that seemed a foot long. With all my 120 pounds I wrestled the knife from him and struck with the nearest weapon of my own, a geography book applied vigorously to his backside . . . the cyclone at Sprote and the children clinging to me as we rushed to the basement and huddled against a wall as the wind blew all the books and papers out the open window upstairs . . . and I see 42 children and myself on a train ride from Cedar Falls to Waterloo where we visited the engine roundhouse then took a streetcar back home. The only problem was one new coat left on the train but dropped off by the train crew the next day, though not before I had heard from a very irate mother. Forty-two children and a teacher not much more than a child—a most pleasant and successful outing. Could we do it today?

I have found that there are shy children, frightened children or just those with problems of which no one is aware, and if a teacher will go that additional step (exhausted though she may be) to find the key, she may save a child from lifelong despair and failure. What a wonderful reward that can be!

I was born a premature infant weighing 3 pounds, 3 ounces, and I slept in a shoe box on the oven door of the old Majestic kitchen range. But Mother took care of all the runts and cast-offs of our farm community, so that kind of devotion probably saved my life. The doctor told her to be good to me as I would never live—BUT HERE I AM!

— Mu Chapter

Marjorie Haines Keeler

I was born in Newcastle, Wyoming, in 1908 and spent most of my life in Newcastle and the surrounding area. I attended both elementary and high school there. Twelve of us who began first grade together finished in the same class, all graduating May 27, 1926.

Most of our class was eagerly looking forward to graduation as we either had jobs or were going on to school. Times were rough and money was not plentiful. At last, the long awaited evening arrived—graduation from NHS! There were 38 students in my class and 12 would be going out to teach in rural schools, an almost unheard of proportion today! I had been a member of the normal training class offered during our senior year. In this class we received some of the best teacher's training that was ever to be offered in Wyoming. Our instructor, Miss Velva Lewis, was a very positive person, dedicated to her work. I feel she contributed greatly to the development of my understanding and ability to present subject matter with patience, especially to the slow learner, or to the so-called "kid who missed the boat."

My first job was that of teaching the LAK School which was located on the LAK Ranch, about six miles from Newcastle. I was able to stay at home and commute back and forth most of the time on horseback. My salary was $95 a month, which was one of the highest paid wages throughout the state at that time.

These first two years I taught grades one through six in a very small building. All of our programs had to be held in a ranch house, the home of three of my students. This family contributed much to a most successful and happy year for all of us.

In 1928 a new building was constructed, and we moved into it after the Christmas holidays. My class had grown to eight by this time and was composed of the children whose parents worked on the ranch. During the next four years we had many good times here, the school being the center for any community fund-raising event, programs, dances, box socials, taffy pulls and card parties. It was centrally located and situated next to what was then considered a good gravel road. I taught here for four years. Each year brought a few more students, as the district decided to bus to our school the South Dakota students whose families lived just across the Wyoming line.

This new building, along with two others in the county, was given honorable mention by the Wyoming Education Department for being the only "Standard School" in the county. To be considered standard, schools had to meet specifications that the state department had drawn up regarding proper lighting, location of windows, amount of floor space, blackboards, cloakrooms, cupboards, heating and many other things that seemed very important at that time.

I was teacher, playground supervisor, nurse, janitor and "speech therapist," as there was always a student who needed help along these lines. I was not trained to do this last job, but after much research and help from every source available, I believe that I may have helped a few. If nothing else, maybe I helped to give them some confidence to try to overcome this shortcoming. Our county superintendent oversaw all of the country schools. She usually visited us about four times a year and was much help to us.

Altogether I spent six years in this district. In 1932, due to a cut in the budget and several ranch families moving, it was decided to transport the students left on the ranch, along with the South Dakota students, to the Sweet School farther on up Beaver Creek. I was hired as a teacher for this school and would have had probably 21 students, all grades. I resigned to take a job at Luzon, South Dakota, as I was to be married and Wyoming District 2 was not hiring married women.

The relationship that I enjoyed in my first six years of teaching cannot be and was not equaled at any place I've ever taught. Children were eager to learn and uncomplainingly did with whatever they had, although our district was tops about ordering supplies. This school board was composed of "self-made" ranchers, who were a very cooperative and appreciative group of men.

John Keeler and I were married on September 16, 1932. We ran a few head of cattle on a place we had leased near Luzon, South Dakota. I continued to teach at Luzon for the next two years, where I had 18 pupils, grades one through eight, mostly big boys. It seemed all the neighborhood troubles were brought to this school, so there were many discipline problems. My previous experience as a teacher helped make these two years somewhat easier. My first year's salary was $65 per month, payable in warrants; sometimes they were payable at the end of the month, but other times two months would go by without my being able to cash a warrant. (I did not know that this method of payment to teachers was being used when I signed my contract.) My second year at Luzon was a bit better; my wages were raised to $80 per month, payable once a month, which did make some difference.

We remained in the Luzon area for about two more years. During this time, our son, Wendell Lee, was born in Custer on May 7, 1935. I had the Luzon Post Office until it was discontinued in May of 1936. My father had passed away in April, so we moved back to my folks' home place in Wyoming. We remained there until 1944, when my husband took steady employment with the Wyoming State Highway and it became necessary for us to live in town. By now we had another son, Jerry Eugene, born May 14, 1940.

Jerry was about 6 years old when I went back to the schoolroom as a substitute. This I did for about two years, but due to my mother's last illness, I was forced to alter my plans and care for her until she passed away. I returned to the classroom full-time in 1951 as a fourth-grade teacher. This was an eventful year, as the room I stepped into had 46 pupils and it was lots of work. After 16 years out of the classroom, lesson plans were no pushover! The next year I became the teacher of one of three sections of fifth-graders. I remained with the fifth grade for the next 15 years, each year bringing new challenges. Although I enjoyed all the others, I believe this particular age of children was my favorite.

For several summers after returning to teaching, I attended BHSC at Spearfish, South Dakota. I took a leave of absence during the spring term of 1961, and in August of that same year I received my BS degree in education.

Due to my husband's poor health, we moved to California in 1967. I taught in a unified district while out there and was very happy. We came back to Wyoming in June 1968 and I became a fourth-grade teacher in Cowley that fall. I remained there for two years, then for the next three years I taught in Lovell, retiring in June 1973.

Since my retirement my husband and I have lived on a small acreage in Cowley. I am still a member of WEA. I was a charter member of Lambda Chapter, Delta Kappa Gamma, when we organized March 17, 1962, and held the office of recording secretary for two terms. I am still a member of Eastern Star in Newcastle.

In reflecting back, it seems that the relationship between school and society has been almost lost. Today, teachers have to take part in so many extra-curricular activities that they have sacrificed the efficiency and effectiveness of their teaching. Before all of this professionalism, we did much more "person-to-person" teaching, thus gaining more respect from the children in the classroom.

Among my former students are a few engineers, teachers, ranchers, pharmacists, insurance salesmen, homemakers, lawyers, a Rhodes Scholar, and an associate professor at the college in Madrid, Spain, as well as medical and dental technicians and doctors. The rest of my former students can best remember my giving them much encouragement in whatever line of work that they chose to follow.

I chose teaching, first of all because I knew that I had to make my living. During my junior year in high school, both banks in Newcastle failed and my parents' life savings were suddenly gone. I had no choice but to go to work and help pay back a part of what my mother had sacrificed for my education. I've never been sorry that I did choose as my profession that of teaching.

With all of the help I had had from school boards, county superintendents, patrons and pupils, I was able to carry on for 28 years as a teacher in the schools of Wyoming, two years in South Dakota and one year in California. I can see that there are many things that help to reveal some of the true reasons why teachers teach.

— Lambda Chapter

PHILLIS ANDERSON LANNING

This autobiography was written by my mother, Phillis Anderson Lanning, when she was honored as a pioneer teacher by Theta Chapter of Delta Kappa Gamma March 1974 in Gillette. No changes of the original writing have been made. She was 87 years old when she wrote her autobiography. She passed away August 1977 at the age of 90.

I was born near Anna, Illinois, Phillis Mary Anderson, to David and Ida Anderson. My father farmed with my grandfather, and we lived with my grandparents while my dad was building a house on his farm which was part of the land owned by Grandpa. In the meantime, my mother died, so we lived with them as my father married again. I went to country schools until eighth grade, then to Union Academy, an accredited school supported by the Presbyterian Church. I received a scholarship to this school as other high schools charged tuition and that seemed the best plan for my education. My aunt had been a primary teacher for years and I think they thought I should follow in her footsteps.

So I graduated from Union Academy with honors in 1907. The following year, after applying and interviewing school boards in our county, I thought I would have to give up. But at the last minute they needed a teacher in the second grade in the school where my aunt had taught for 20 years. I was an assistant to a third-grade teacher, taking my classes out for recitation. I received only $35 a month, but this gave me a start. I had no normal training as at this time it was not considered necessary. Experience was what counted. Most of my salary went for room and board. I shared a room with the primary teacher and went home weekends, so I managed to save a little. We had only seven months of school where I taught and some of the girls were writing for summer terms of three months in Wyoming. Four of the girls had schools spoken for when my friend, Maude Appell, and I decided to go, too. So we made plans to leave the last of April. We were all excited with the prospect of an experience I shall never forget.

We had not been far from home except for St. Louis once or twice in short train trips to work, so the big terminal there, where many trains back into the gates for the arriving and leaving of passengers, was quite a sight. We had a few hours to wait before taking the train to Omaha. We had to arrange for a berth on the Pullman so kept the clerks at the information desk busy with questions. Had to change trains again in Omaha. Not as nice accommodations as the Burlington but was very exciting to the two Illinois teachers who were going out West! And to be chosen to tell about our experiences 60 years ago, I'm very thrilled to be one of the group.

When we arrived in Aladdin, or rather when we got on that little train carrying freight and passengers to that little coal-mining town 10 miles down a beautiful valley, it seemed as though we were going to the end of the world after riding in a Pullman from St. Louis. The coach, discarded from Northwestern, was used, with torn upholstery, no uniforms—only overalls—mostly rough-looking men. It made us wish we were back in God's country. We talked as we rode, and the country down that little valley was very pretty. We were surprised when we got off the train to find Mr. Fred Aikman, one of the school board members, to meet us. He loaded our suitcases into his spring wagon and we were off to his home about eight miles away.

We found his wife and family made us feel welcome to spend the night. One of our friends, Serna Davie Sims, was boarding with them and teaching the Aikman School. Serena now lives in Hulett. Connie Grear, a cousin of Serena, as well as two other Jonesboro girls, had found schools in the district, which was large at that time. We did not get together until the teachers' institute in Sundance some time during the three-month term of school. They were trying to follow a course of study, but not many schools were well enough organized to get much accomplished in the three months. There was no state aid to help pay the teachers. In fact, when I taught the Farrall School, Mr. Ellsbury cashed my warrants so I could have money to pay for my board and my fare home. He held my warrants until they came due later. I mentioned before how the district was all in one and Maude Sims, county superintendent, rode horseback to visit the schools. I dare say she did more visiting than the superintendents of later years.

I taught Upper Oak Creek in the summer of 1909. My pupils were Ruth and Esther Anderson, Sam and Lottie Barlean, Theo Derickson and Tommy and Helen Robinson. I boarded at Carlsons, rode horseback—a gentle horse—with Helen in the saddle and Tommy, at back, was my gate opener. We rode three or four miles with six or eight wire gates to open.

The Fourth of July came during the time I was there. First there was a barn dance in Aikman's new barn. There we planned a trip to the Devil's Tower so the six Illinois teachers could meet. We drove, Hilma Carlson and I, in a light wagon over the Bear Lodge in a road full of boulders, through their place to Alva where we met the Aikmans, Ed Simm and Oscar Carlson. The rodeo, the first I had ever attended, was held in the streets and was very thrilling to those who like such things. I enjoyed the trip to the tower which we made the next day. We had a tent and camped beside the river. Mrs. Carlson had prepared a turkey, a ham, pies and baked homemade bread for our trip of three days. We had nice weather the first part of the time, but it rained going home so we were like drowned rats when we finally got back.

This is a resume of an article I gave at a Delta Kappa Gamma meeting in Gillette several years ago. Here I am again, March of 1974, recovering from a broken hip—still interested in the history I had penned in this article. My daughter, Phillis Habeck, is teaching in Moorcroft and wants to use it for publication in their book, LET YOUR LIGHT SHINE.

My husband and I live in Spearfish, South Dakota, Evans Lane, where we have a little home by Spearfish Creek. Ned was 90 years old in February and I am nearing 87. Our activities are limited, but we still enjoy having friends call on us. We celebrated our 60th wedding anniversary last year. We spent 22 years in Montana, Belle Fourche, South Dakota, Wyoming and now Spearfish, South Dakota.

Our family of seven children are all living and have homes of their own. All were here for our 60th wedding anniversary.

Again, I feel honored to have my name among the One-Room School Teachers of Wyoming.

— Theta Chapter

LILLIAN ARTHUR LEITHEAD

Lillian Arthur Leithead was born in Ansley, Colorado on March 2, 1907, to Lyle Cole and Gladys Miller Arthur. My parents were separated and divorced shortly after I was born, and I was given into the custody of my grandparents, Samuel and Idella Arthur, who were pioneers and longtime residents of Boone County, Nebraska (in the Primrose area).

I graduated from the normal training course in Ansley High School in 1925 and started my teaching career with eight grades in Primrose, Nebraska, with the next year at Comstock, Nebraska. Being somewhat dissatisfied with teaching, I left to take a position as a receptionist in a doctor's office in Hot Springs, South Dakota. When I arrived there, I found the job no longer existed and I worked as a waitress until I found work in a rural live-in school known as the Finger Butte School northwest of Albion, Montana.

I left there at the half year since I discovered I did not have enough college credits in education. After attending Black Hills Teachers College in Spearfish, South Dakota, I taught in a one-room school near Teckla, Wyoming.

My next position was in a one-room school near Oelrichs, South Dakota. The Depression was keenly felt. Warrants were issued which had to be held until the teacher was notified that there was enough money to cash them. I felt very fortunate with my $60 a month as so many were out of work. I failed a first-grade girl, so my contract was not renewed.

Feeling unsuccessful as a teacher, I went into nursing at the Lutheran Hospital in Hot Springs, where I stayed for two years. I had a chance to return to teaching if I would kick back part of my salary to individual members of the board of education, but I refused.

I returned to Nebraska to fill out a teacher's term in a sod building with plenty of ventilation around the windows and hordes of little sand lizards in the spring. My certificate expired that year so another girl and I hitchhiked to Basin to work for the Woodruff Seed Company to get enough money to return to school.

With an arrangement with the county superintendent, the school board at Hyattville, Wyoming, hired me even without my certificate. The school was up in the mountains and had four boys for students—in fifth, third and 10th grades. The boys had "ganged up" on their previous teacher and caused him to resign. The teacher's home was comfortable but without modern conveniences. The school week was six days and the salary was $40 a month. I attended summer school at Laramie that year.

I next taught eight elementary grades in the Looman School in Hyattville for $75 per month. Room and board was $20 a month. I walked two miles a way each day in spite of snow and temperatures that sometimes reached 40 degrees below zero. My contract was not renewed because I had used more coal that year than any other teacher before me.

I sealed my doom as a teacher when I married Milo Mills Leithead on June 9, 1937, in the Salt Lake Temple in Salt Lake City, Utah. I had met him in Hyattville the year before.

In 1942 I became an assistant for two teachers in the Lovell, Wyoming, school for the first term, leaving there to return to the university at Laramie where I received a two-year diploma.

After working for the UP Railroad and the United Airlines in Cheyenne, I returned to teaching, this time two girls of one family at the JHD Ranch, near Cheyenne. This was a lonely time since my husband was working elsewhere.

This problem was solved when I was given a contract to teach third and fourth grades in Ten Sleep, only 12 miles away from the ranch where my husband worked. Here I stayed for three happy years.

After a year at Grass Creek, Wyoming, while my husband drove the school bus into Thermopolis, I accepted a fourth-grade position in the Hill School in Thermopolis where I started a symphonette band and accompanied them on my accordion.

Besides their regular routine, the symphonette band played at several community gatherings. While there I also helped a boy discover his artistic talent in painting.

In 1952 my husband and I moved to Worland where he went into partnership with another barber. I taught one of the fifth grades in the South Side School. I later transfered to the fourth grade at the East Side School and still later to the new West Side School. When the special ed pupils came to the West Side School, I found a new and interesting challenge. While working with these pupils, I found my experience with the accordion to be a big asset. I also bought a double keyboard organ and accompanied my student musicians. I enjoyed teaching in Worland until my retirement in 1972.

After my retirement I became a home-bound teacher for a handicapped boy with a keen interest in music. This continued until October 1, 1974, when my husband and I moved to a 160-acre farm in Bluffton, Alberta, Canada.

When I'm not busy with the animals and my garden, I'm doing some needlework, practicing my piano lesson, reading, walking, writing poetry, or just plain napping and counting my blessings for good companionships, good health, active church and for the wonderful neighbors and friends I have known.

I received a BA degree from Wyoming in 1956 and also attended Northwest Community College in Powell and Eastern Montana College in Billings.

I became a member of Delta Kappa Gamma in Worland on May 12, 1956. I joined the American Association of University Women and the International Reading Association, the WEA and the NEA. The International Reading Association printed in booklet form many of my poems and presented me with a copy.

Precious memories still linger as I recall school days. Some of these were bitter; some very joyful; all were precious. I am still writing poems for special occasions, taking music lessons and trying to get the most out of life, giving some small part in return.

GREETINGS FROM WYOMING

A big "Howdy" from Worland, Wyoming
And my "Thanks" for warm friendships and fun.
Hospitality knows Arizona
Can hardly be matched or outdone.
But if you would come to Wyoming,
We'd just love to give it a try
In the shade of our cool lofty mountains
That seem to shake hands with the sky.
We love our great open spaces
"Where the deer and the antelope roam."
We have generous smiles on our faces
In our pride for the place we call home.
"Women's Lib" is "old hat" in Wyoming
Where equality and suffrage began.

Where our nation's first National Monument
And Yellowstone Park are so grand.
"Girl Scouts' Center West" in our mountains
And the "Tyrolean Band" in our town
Inspire and give hope to the critics
Much good in our youth can be found.
Our sugar beets sweeten your beverage
And our lamb chops and pork chops are fine.
There are dairies and beef to your liking
And steaks that are superbly prime.
Now before you deem this a commercial
And are tempted to just tune me out—
This message: "Come visit Wyoming
And you'll see what I'm talking about."

— *Lillian Leithead*, Sigma Chapter
Worland, Wyoming

ELIZABETH PLAPP LESLIE

In the town of Prairie du Chene, Wisconsin, on January 4, 1881, a daughter, Elizabeth Tresa, was born to Agnes Beowar Plapp and Jacob Plapp whose destiny was planned to help educate many a child.

She attended grade school at a Catholic convent at Milbank, South Dakota, and graduated from high school at Barron, Wisconsin, in the year 1901 and was granted a teaching certificate.

Her first teaching experience was at Paskin Lake, Wisconsin, for which she received $20 a month and did all janitor work including building the fire and keeping the building warm all day.

She also taught at Barron, Wisconsin, and Grano, North Dakota. In 1908 she taught at Glasgow, Montana, and homesteaded a tract of land.

On August 9, 1909, she was united in marriage to Fred J. Leslie and to this union were born four children, Elizabeth, Agnes, Annabell and Richard.

During this time she resided with her family at different locations in Montana, as her husband also taught school.

The summer of 1920 found her back in normal school at Dillon, Montana, to receive her normal certificate for teaching in Montana.

She then taught at Landusky, Montana, near the Canadian border, and at that time a rather primitive country. She had several Indian children in school and had many experiences she loved to relate to her children. She also taught at Stricker, Montana, and each weekend she rode on a locomotive to be home with her family in Eureka, Montana. Being in mountainous country, this locomotive was used to help other trains up the mountains and as Stricker was at the top she had easy access for trips back and forth. Her father, being an engineer, had given her rides on his locomotive and so she enjoyed the trips as it brought back fond memories of her childhood and home life.

In 1928 she and her family moved to Otto, Wyoming, but she continued to teach in Montana until 1934 when she accepted a teaching position in Otto.

In 1937 she attended Eastern Montana Normal School at Billings, Montana, and renewed her normal certificate. She then taught school in Otto, Wyoming, and Burlington, Wyoming, until 1950 when she retired under the Wyoming Teacher Retirement Plan and moved with her husband to Port Orchard, Washington.

For two years she did private tutoring for welfare department children at Port Orchard. In 1970 she and her husband retired at Bridger, Montana, near one of her daughters and they reside there at this time.

Although she was crippled for life after having had rickets as a child, this in no way kept her from leading a normal life. Teaching children was her whole life, from her own to all others she came in contact with. I'm sure many a child was richer in life after being taught by my mother. I know I was.

— by Agnes Aagard
— Rho Chapter

JOSEPHINE IRBY LESTER

When I was a little girl on an isolated Wyoming cattle ranch, reading everything I could get my hands on, I was once intrigued by the story of a princess who spoke seven languages. I realized that I was no princess, but I could learn other languages. Thus began my motivation to become a linguist, and I worked at it ever after.

On November 4, 1902, I was born in Arlington, Oregon, a little Columbia River town. My parents were Joseph Kendrick Irby III, a transplanted North Carolinian, and Oregonian Mary Hurlburt Irby. My mother's story is told in the 1965 edition of LET YOUR LIGHT SHINE (page 127, Mary Hurlburt Scott). My mother and I came to Wyoming in June 1906, arriving just as an unseasonable snowstorm blanketed the lilacs. Then my mother alternately taught school and attended university classes. I began my education in the basement of the University of Wyoming's towered "Old Main" where Miss Adsit's teachers' training department had its beginning.

During the summer of 1911, Mother and I went up into the Green River Valley where she taught a summer term. In this valley we were destined to remain when Mother married David Harvey Scott, a pioneer cattle rancher. My education continued in a little one-room log schoolhouse which my pony and I reached every morning after fording Green River. In the winter I traveled on skis.

Rumor has it that I was the terror of the very young, inexperienced teachers who came to the Bronx School because of my penchant for asking questions. I passed the county eighth-grade examinations when I was 12 years old. With no high school near I was shuffled off to Hermiston, Oregon; Pinedale, Wyoming; Westminster Collegiate Institute in Salt Lake City; and finally was graduated in 1920 from Washington High School in Portland, Oregon. After that I could and did return to Wyoming, to the university at Laramie. In June 1924 I received my BA with a major in French and minors in Spanish and English.

My first school was near the home ranch. Later, I was instructor and principal at Baggs High School. It was during this time that I met and on March 24, 1928, married Henry B. Jones. When the school term ended in 1928, we loaded our Lares and Penates into our Model T and set forth for the Green River Valley. My husband became manager for my step-father's ranches. There our four daughters were born: Mary Josephine, 1930; Kathryn Lucille, 1933; Patricia Anne, 1934; and Lois Eileen, 1936. During these ranch years I helped organize a group of writers and painters into the Sublette County Artists' Guild, which has subsequently published four volumes of prose and poetry.

In November 1940 a fatal car wreck took both my husband and my step-father. This catastrophe catapulted me back into the educational field. I returned to the University of Wyoming for a master's degree which was granted in August 1941.

Then my daughters and I returned to the Green River Valley, and I taught in Pinedale High School for the next four years. Subsequently I taught two years in Montello, Nevada, during which time my eldest daughter graduated from high school, and I attended the University of California at Berkeley on a family life education scholarship from the Rosenberg Foundation.

Autumn 1948 brought our return to Wyoming, this time to Riverton, where I taught languages in the high school for the next eight years. In 1950 I was married to Willard Lester. During the academic year 1953-54 my four girls, my mother and my step-son, Jack Lester, were all in attendance at the university in Laramie. Other universities that I attended for summer terms included the University of Montana (together with my youngest daughter), the University of Colorado where for six weeks I lived in the Foreign Language House and spoke no English, also Willamette University, Salem, Oregon, for a foreign language workshop.

In 1956 my husband and I went to Coos Bay, Oregon, where I taught for four years at Marshfield Senior High School. Here I was instrumental in the installation of an excellent 30-position foreign language laboratory. Unmechanical as I am, I learned to operate it and found it a valuable aid.

Always I endeavored to make my classes as fascinating to others as language study and use were for me. In Latin we learned "amo, amas, amat" and saw Julius Ceasar through the Gallic Wars, but we also became conversant with mythology. Each year we held a Roman banquet and a Roman wedding. French classes sang chansons and held a Mardi Gras. The main feature for Spanish classes was a pinata party. We always started modern language classes with a conversational warm-up. We tried to make our classes delightful as well as practical.

During my teaching career in Riverton I was initiated into Delta Kappa Gamma at the installation of Eta Chapter on March 21, 1953. Other organizations to which I still belong include Riverton Chautauqua Club, Order of the Eastern Star (worthy matron in 1945 at Pinedale), DAR, DAC, NRTA and the American Association of Retired Persons, which I served as state director from 1965-1970 and organized chapters in Laramie, Rock Springs, Casper and Sheridan. I am a member of the AARP National Membership Recruitment Committee and am membership coordinator for Wyoming, Montana, Idaho, Utah and Colorado. In 1967 I was chosen as an "Outstanding Civic Leader" by the Outstanding Americans Foundation. My church affiliation is Christian Science.

Publications include: articles in Nevada and Wyoming educational publications, Delta Kappa Gamma's LET YOUR LIGHT SHINE, Ralph McWhinnie's THOSE GOOD YEARS AT WYOMING U, poems in the BULLETIN OF DELTA KAPPA GAMMA, WYOMING PAINTBRUSH, OREGONIAN VERSE and the CHRISTIAN SCIENCE SENTINEL. During my final year of teaching, my book, FOOTPRINTS IN THE SNOW, copyright 1963, was published privately.

My husband, Willard Lester, passed on November 26, 1968. I continued to make my home in Riverton. I have always loved my work, my family and my associates of all ages. My career gave me opportunity to share my love and lore of languages. My retirement from teaching gives me leisure for writing and study, and I enjoy my work with retired people. Giving others a realization of dignity and purpose in later years is also rewarding.

— Eta Chapter

FLORENCE LARSON LIVINGSTON

I, Florence Larson Livingston, was born July 2, 1910, about 10 miles west of Billings near the cemetery. For many years what is now Central Avenue was known as Cemetery Road. The doctor came out in horse and buggy to deliver me, but he forgot to record my birth. When it came time for me to sign up for Social Security I had no birth certificate. Fortunately the church in which I was baptized still had its records.

During World War I my folks moved to Tacoma, Washington, so that my father could work in the shipyards. It was while in the fourth grade there that I knew I wanted to be a teacher. I dearly loved my teacher and the many things we did in the classroom.

We returned to Billings after the war. My eighth grade was spent in Milwaukee, Wisconsin. There my teacher had a large class and often asked me to help her.

My high school years were spent in Billings. I took all the normal training courses which were offered. Eastern Montana Normal School, now Eastern Montana College, had started the year I finished high school so I was able to stay at home, help my father in a small cafe, and attend the college. I graduated with a two-year diploma in June 1930. Times were hard and teachers were a dime a dozen. Also, I was a Catholic, which I didn't hesitate to put on my application. The placement officer suggested that I just write "Christian."

Finally, I was offered a school 20 miles north of Wibaux, Montana. A friend of mine got one 20 miles south of Wibaux. Great! We'd get to see each other. We saw each other only once during the nine months of school.

My school was two miles from where I was to room and board. I say "school." It was an old deserted ranch house. The battered desks were pushed into a corner, the books in a pile on the floor. With the help of my landlady we got the desks and books in order. The first time I went to town I bought sandpaper, paint, varnish and material for curtains for the windows.

I had to ride horseback to school until the weather got very cold. Then the horse was hitched to a buggy. I had never ridden a horse so by the time I arrived at school the first day, I was sick to my stomach, probably mostly from fright.

One day I looked out the window and said, "Someone's dog is in the yard." A student replied, "That's a coyote."

Some packrats had their home in the attic. We could hear them scampering back and forth and see them go down the side of the building.

I paid $25 a month for room and board and had to sleep with my seventh-grade student. It wasn't too bad because she was warm and I was very cold-blooded. In the winter the water in the pitcher would freeze.

I returned to this area for a second year, but this time I had a tiny schoolhouse. Before the year was over a couple of families moved away and I was left with only two pupils, children of the family with whom I was staying. They then had me teach in the bunkhouse.

After another year I got a third- and fourth-grade position in Wibaux itself. The best part of that was that I didn't have to do my own janitor work and the plumbing was indoors.

Due to drought the ranchers in Wibaux were having financial problems. As a result, the district didn't have enough money to pay teachers. My salary was $95 a month. The bank cashed our warrants at a discount so I really received only $65.

The next fall I took a rural school north of Billings. Back to janitor work and outdoor plumbing, but I enjoyed working with the rural children. They were always so appreciative of everything that was done for them.

In the fall of 1936 I took the position of teaching the first four grades at the Allendale School west of Billings on the Laurel Highway. The teacher of the upper grades was Glenn Livingston. He was also the principal. I married my "boss" December 28, 1936, but not before I had the permission of the school board to let me finish the year. At that time our contract said if a woman teacher married, she would be dismissed. I finished that year and also taught the next.

In the fall of 1938 we went to Missoula, Montana, so that Glenn could get his BA. Our son was born that fall. Glenn worked part-time at a grocery store and I cooked one big meal a day for three college students to help with the expenses.

We came to Cody in the fall of 1942. Our son, Don, was 4 and Barbara 3. By then teachers were at a premium but I had no intention of going back as long as the children were small. I took some extension classes and correspondence work. Then we both started going to summer school in Laramie. I received my BA degree the summer of 1950 and Glenn received his master's.

I went back to teaching the fall of 1948, teaching second grade and then moving to third at the Eastside School in Cody where I continued until I retired in the spring of 1972.

While teaching I held various offices in Classroom Teachers and worked on many curriculum committees.

When in Laramie I joined Kappa Delta Pi, an educational honorary. I am one of the charter members of Gamma Chapter of Delta Kappa Gamma. I have served as recording secretary, vice president and president of the latter.

In 1970 I received the "Award of Appreciation" plaque from school District 6. In 1977 Glenn and I received a plaque for services rendered to the community.

After retirement I volunteered for community work such as delivering rolling meals, helping at the nursing home, visiting shut-ins, and teaching religious classes at church. Because of health problems, I had to stop after a couple of years. I still take part in some church activities.

I belong to AAUW and a PEO chapter. I like to read and play some bridge. I have knitted 14 afghans and make both punch hook and latch hook rugs and wall hangings.

In the summer we enjoy having friends and relatives at our cabin on the Clark's Fork River, in the Sunlight Basin area 62 miles from Cody.

We have eight grandchildren and, so far, one great-grandson.

I feel that I have lived a full and satisfying life because of my many years of teaching.

— Pi Chapter

Edith Longwith

I t was March 6, 1977. A crowd had gathered in the auditorium of the new John Early Building to share in the dedication of this new facility on the Sheridan High School campus. Among participants on the platform were the superintendent of Sheridan schools and the president of the Board of Education of school District 2. But the dignitary on whom many focused their attention, and was the real reason they were there, was a lady who had given herself to the needs of young people in the community for whom the school system, up to her coming, had had no real place.

Later in the ceremony this modest, unassuming woman seated there on the stage, was to be lauded for her many accomplishments in the field of education. She was to be honored by having the part of the new building used for the handicapped dedicated to her. In recognition of this she was to be given a miniature replica of the plaque which had been placed at the entrance to the special education wing. There, for all to see, is this well-earned tribute:

"This educational facility is respectfully dedicated to Edith Longwith who set the pace and direction for special education in our schools. With great compassion, she directed the best efforts of her students, her faculty, and herself."

These words speak for all those who knew or worked with her at any time during the 29 years she taught in the Sheridan schools.

Though she shied away from publicity or recognition, she was a recipient of the two highest awards given to teachers in the state of Wyoming—the School Bell Award and the Gold Key Award.

Edith was born in Fort Collins, Colorado. At a very early age the family moved to Eaton, Colorado, which became the scene of a very interesting childhood. She remembers how her parents went out of their way to see that their children had many varied experiences. She comments, "They took us on field trips—now, too many parents depend on the schools for that!"

Most of her growing up years, however, were spent in Wheatland, Wyoming, where her father continued as mortician. Hard work seems to have been a habit with her, and she showed a remarkable degree of responsibility while still very young. At 10 years of age she was employed by a family that had a new baby. For the many household duties she performed daily, she was given $10 a month.

When Edith was in the seventh grade she attended school full-time and worked a regular shift in the restaurant owned by her parents. At the end of that year she took an eighth-grade test and passed it. This earned for her the privilege of going right into high school. When a junior, she transferred to Nebraska Wesleyan Academy at University Place in Nebraska. All the time she was a student there she worked for her room and board. During these last two years of high school she earned 25 quarter hours of college credit. In this way she qualified herself to be a teacher.

She was too young to have a certificate when she started teaching, but she soon proved her worth as she accepted and attained success in a position at Baggs, Wyoming. At that time the little village was so isolated that when you went in, you were "in" for the year. Living in an old hip-roofed hotel was a scary experience, but the pool hall operator assured the boarders that "school teachers are just as safe here as cattle rustlers are where they operate." In this school she taught the third and fourth grades with pupils coming from both Baggs and Savery. In November she rode in an open stage from Baggs to Wamsutter for a teachers' meeting. Instead of being given commendation for this evidence of her professionalism, she met criticism—"That young teacher was 'out' of her classroom!"

The following year she taught the third and fourth grades in Chugwater and the next year moved on to the coal mining town of Gebo. As always, she took a keen personal interest in her students. It was here she became aware that one of her students needed her eyes tested. Edith got permission from the parents to take her to Thermopolis where glasses were prescribed. One of the first comments the young lady made after being fitted with the glasses was, "Does everyone see across the street?" Edith was also instrumental in getting help for a young Finnish boy who had been crippled from a bad fall. Years later a former student who had grown up there in a very poor home with a large family told a friend of Edith's how, when she was his teacher, she had bought him a pair of new shoes. Those who know her will confirm that this was not unusual.

In 1936 she made her last move before coming to Sheridan. She taught until 1941 in Winton—north of Rock Springs. Here there were about the same nationality groups as there were in Gebo. Her pupils were the second- and third-graders.

In addition to her school duties, she worked tirelessly to establish a library in this community. It would be a branch of the county library at Green River. When receiving praise for her efforts, she responded with, "Who wants the credit if we can get a library?"

Her first assignment when she came to Sheridan five years later was the "Opportunity Room" at Central. Nineteen boys, all bigger than Edith, were her first charges. They were all ages with different kinds of handicaps and most were severe discipline problems. She was at Central until 1950 when she moved up to Hill School, where she taught until she retired in 1970.

She began in this old building with her "Opportunity Room" on the second floor. Since the restrooms were in the basement, many difficulties presented themselves in working with physically handicapped students.

You could go into Hill School almost any day and find some students busy working on math, English or typing; others would be sanding furniture or weaving; and still others would be sewing something to wear or perfecting their culinary skills. An annual project was to serve a complete Thanksgiving dinner to the board of education, the administrators and the students. This was usually done on the Tuesday before Thanksgiving.

Junior and senior high students who came and went those years she was teaching will long remember the teas, the Christmas sales, the programs, the style shows, the parties in the old gym, and the many field trips. A memorable one was an airplane trip to Casper followed by tours through Old Fort Caspar, the observatory, and other places of interest before boarding a bus for the ride home.

The expenses for these special trips were paid for out of money earned from the sale of items made by the students themselves for the annual Christmas sales. Those "in the know" are aware that Edith helped out now and then along the way, too. The young people privileged to be part of these unusual adventures will probably never completely realize how much the foresight and dedication of a caring teacher enriched and broadened their too often commonplace, humdrum lives.

Though she started alone, her staff grew to include six certified teachers besides herself, and several aides. Her year's work often included summer sessions, too. As the program grew, she was both the principal and a classroom teacher.

Her BA degree was from the University of Wyoming, but all the undergraduate work after she started teaching was gotten in summer school and through extension and correspondence courses. Her MA was earned at San Francisco State in the year 1960-61. In order that she might pursue her studies there, she was given the first federal scholarship ever offered by the state Department of Education for Special Education. She graduated with honors. She also took advanced work at other universities and participated in many workshops, conferences and local, state, regional and national planning sessions.

Realizing the scope of her teaching activities, one would think that was the extent of her service to the community, but a closer look reveals that she was very active in many other ways. Many of these "extra curricular" activities involved the welfare of youth.

She was always active in the work of the local teachers' association—serving as treasurer for a term and accepting many other responsibilities too numerous to mention. She was an active member of the Classroom Teachers Association, attended a regional meeting in Spokane, and then was president of the local organization for two years. She was secretary-treasurer of Wyoming Education Association's Northwest District for 14 years.

The Wyoming State Board of Education chose her to be the state's delegate at a meeting in Portland on vocational training for the handicapped. They also sent her to a similar conference in Las Vegas. Later, she represented the state two more times at meetings of the Northern Plains Regional Conferences on Rehabilitation at Minneapolis and Saskatoon, Saskatchewan. In 1948 she was Wyoming's delegate to the International Conference of the Council for Exceptional Children in New York. She attended this international conference again when it was held in St. Louis in 1965.

Edith was a charter member of the state and local Association for Retarded Children for many years and was state president in the late '50s. She did all of this while being a cornerstone of the local group. It was through the sponsorship of this organization that Edith Longwith helped in the birth and growth of a sheltered workshop for handicapped persons in Sheridan. She had attended the convention of the National Association for Retarded Children in Philadelphia in 1950.

Sheridan's Kappa Chapter of Delta Kappa Gamma claims Edith Longwith as a charter member. She had been a member of the Gillette chapter just prior to the formation of Kappa. She was vice president and president locally—each for two years. Then she went on to be state recording secretary, second vice president, first vice president, and then state president in 1967-69. She also was on the national committee for personal growth and services. Under her leadership, while research chairman of Alpha Xi State, the first edition of LET YOUR LIGHT SHINE was published. In 1974, on a trip to Russia, she served as a member of the International Seminar in Education of Soviet Republic Schools. In recognition of her outstanding leadership she was named to receive the 1973 Delta Kappa Gamma "Achievement Award" at the Alpha Xi State convention that year.

Edith was a member of Business and Professional Women from the mid-'20s until her retirement. While teaching in Gebo she was president of the Thermopolis club and was state president for two years.

It was in the '40s that she joined the American Association of Women. She dropped out for a few years while she was organist at the Methodist Church, but rejoined when she had more time. During the years she served in various capacities on the board. She was program chairman for one term and more recently was the treasurer.

It was in 1970 that Miss Longwith received the Wyoming School Board Association's Golden Bell Award for outstanding educational contributions. Her nomination letter stated that she was credited statewide with the development of the special education program in Sheridan as well as being a moving and influential force behind the growth and development of special education in the entire state.

A certificate of appreciation presented in July 1971 by the Governor's Committee for the Handicapped states, "Edith Longwith deserves special recognition for a significant contribution to the welfare of this state for her inventive ideas, resourcefulness, and dedicated interest to the many handicapped in Wyoming."

Then on April 3, 1977, she was named a recipient of the Wyoming Education Association's Gold Key Award at their delegate assembly in Sheridan. In nominating her for the Gold Key, the Sheridan Central Education Association declared, "Miss Longwith devoted much personal time and attention to 'her children,' not only taking them into her home, but also spending many weekends at her cabin in Story with small groups of handicapped children." The WEA recognized that "the lives of boys and girls have been enriched and that the educational program has been improved because of these years of service."

Those close to Edith know that the reason she bought a cabin in Story was so that she could give "her children" a chance to get out in the open away from their homes and where they could exercise a greater degree of independence. She wanted them to have the experiences of camping and living for a few days with their peers. Friends also tell how she would take out-of-town children into her home when they didn't have a place to stay, so they could take advantage of the summer special education programs.

Maybe a secret of excellence in all her undertakings is revealed in this little interchange: Confronted with, "You don't have to meet any standards," her immediate response was, "Oh, yes I do—I have to meet my own!"

Retirement was not the end of her service to others. Even while teaching she was a Red Cross volunteer at the girls' school where she taught arts and crafts. She continued serving as a Red Cross volunteer at the Veterans' Administration hospital for several more years after her teaching days were over. In fact, she was chairman of that volunteer program for some time.

Her interest in libraries was still keen as she was on the board for the Friends of the Library for several years and was president for two years. One of the librarians, years later, talked about all the delicious breads and other treats Edith would make and bring to the library for special occasions and for the staff to enjoy.

Her last administrator said of her, "She is the most outstanding teacher I have ever known. You hear the words 'concern' and 'dedication' a lot, but they're superior when they apply to her. Her attitude toward kids with handicaps was something else. It was not wallowing in sympathy. She tried to help them. She expected their best and she got it. And she got their respect, too."

Evidence of the high esteem in which she was held by her students and co-workers was displayed in the gala "party-tea-talent production" presented in her honor shortly before her retirement. Every person enrolled in the special education program—from the smallest pupil in the primary room to the most sophisticated senior—had some part in the tribute. Their deep, sincere love and respect for her and all she stood for couldn't be put into words but their thoughts were briefly epitomized in the inscription engraved on the silver tray they present to her: "Presented to EDITH LONGWITH, in appreciation of her exceptional dedication to all the students whom she served. May 25, 1970."

This is the Edith Longwith who came to be known throughout the state for her pioneering work in the area of special education. Her successful leadership in a field too long neglected earned for her the title "Miss Special Education" of Wyoming.

It would be impossible to guess what thoughts were in Edith's mind that day in March 1977 as she stepped toward the podium to receive her citation. Surely there must have been some flashbacks of treasured incidents from her teaching days. And certainly, it's very possible that, as she expressed her appreciation for the honor, she could have felt her real reward was the joy of knowing she had "opened doors" for countless boys and girls she had touched along the way.

— Kappa Chapter

HELEN OSTBY LOTTES

What a wonderful experience my first year in school was for me! Not only did I learn to read, but I also learned songs, poetry, and an appreciation of art, and a love of school. New doors were opened which influenced me in the years to come. To my first teacher, Helen Ostby Lottes, I owe a debt of gratitude.

Helen Lottes, nee Helen Ostby, was born on January 31, 1900, in a Scandinavian community 12 miles north of Fargo, North Dakota, the seventh child of Kari and Gelinus Ostby. She attended the Sheyenne School in this community and later came back to teach there for five years. She graduated from Fargo High School, attended NDAC, now the North Dakota University at Fargo, and the Moorhead State College at Moorhead, Minnesota. After teaching rural schools for many years, she took a business course, but decided teaching was her career so went back to teaching and attended summer school working toward her degree.

Helen thoroughly enjoyed her teaching experiences in the rural schools. Her students won many honors in state fair competition and Cass County, North Dakota, declamatory and music contests held every year. The music trophy was won by the Maple River School.

In her rural teaching experience, the church and school were the centers of interest. Many and varied programs were held. The teacher worked hard for excellence of performance and the pupils tried hard to succeed.

There were basket socials to raise money for library books. The big programs were attended by the entire families, and lucky were those who found sitting room.

With a talent for organizing, Helen was instrumental in beginning PTAs in some of her schools, where she served as secretary and president. These were social as well as educational meetings and there was always music and singing.

In 1936 Helen was married to John J. Lottes at Billings, Montana, and it was then that she came to live in Cody, Wyoming. During World War II she went back to teaching and taught at Eastside School in Cody from 1944 to 1960. During this period she had a year's leave of absence when she received her bachelor of science degree in education at Moorhead State College in Moorhead, Minnesota, in August of 1954.

She considered it a great honor to be asked to join the new Gamma Chapter of Delta Kappa Gamma which was organized in May 1949. At that time she began serving as second vice president, followed by first vice president and then president from 1954 to 1956.

Now, retirement days have come when the time goes by too fast. Five winters spent in Arizona and Texas were most enjoyable, so she feels no regrets for an early retirement. She enjoys a little tutoring now and then and occasionally there comes a nostalgic feeling of wishing to be back in the schoolroom. However, the mail brings cards and letters from friends, relatives and former pupils all over the United States, and not infrequently a former pupil stops by to have a visit with the teacher, who smiles a welcome at the door to each and every one.

MY FIRST-GRADE TEACHER
She rose up early every day,
To be prepared for those who came,
To smile a welcome at the door
And greet each one by name.

She taught 3 R's and taught them well,
But always time was there
To teach each child a little more
Of what was right and fair,

Of what was beautiful and true,
Of what was just and good;
And all the while, she taught each child
To do the **best** he could!

— by Cordelia "Dee" Holst
Teacher and Delta Kappa Gamma Member

—Pi Chapter

CHRISTINE D. LYNCH

I was the third child of a family of five. I was born to Nettie Coin Davis and Pearl W. Davis in Jewell County, Kansas, on August 17, 1901. All but one of us became teachers. My mother was also a teacher.

I graduated from high school in Superior, Nebraska, in 1919. We were required to complete a normal training course which permitted one to teach.

My teaching and work experience is as follows: one year, the intermediate grades, Mount Clare, Nebraska, (1920-22); two years, eighth grade, Loup City, Nebraska (1920-22); five years, junior high school in Red Cloud, Nebraska (1922-1927); 15 years, co-owner in a cleaning establishment in Red Cloud, Nebraska (1926-1941); one and a half years, librarian in junior high school, Red Cloud (1941-1943).

June to September 1943, served in Women's Auxiliary Army Corps, re-enlisted in Women's Army Corps in September 1943 and received honorable discharge in August 1945. Basic training at Fort Devins, Massachusetts, and assigned to Personnel Department, Fort George G. Meade, Massachusetts.

Worked at Fort Francis E. Warren Exchange for four months, August to November 1945; worked for Office of Price Administration from November 19, 1945, to December 13, 1947.

Three and a half years, sixth-grade social studies, Torrington, Wyoming (1947-1950); one year, fourth grade, Alta Vista School, Cheyenne, Wyoming (1950-1951); two years, fourth grade, Clark School, Cheyenne, Wyoming (1951-1953); 14 years, social studies in McCormick Junior High School, Cheyenne, Wyoming (1953-1967).

In the summer of 1953 I received a BA degree from Colorado State College in Greeley, Colorado. I also attended the state teachers' college in Peru, Nebraska; the University of Nebraska in Lincoln, Nebraska; the University of Wyoming in Laramie, Wyoming; and the University of Wisconsin at Madison, Wisconsin.

When I started my first year of teaching I remember the school board member who gave me my contract saying, "You should be paying us to practice teach the first year," because in those days one only had to complete high school and pass the state examinations, which were required before being issued a certificate. I guess that to him I looked a little "green" and a little young. Normal training in high school was required if one planned to become a teacher. Incidentally, I was fortunate to have an excellent normal training instructor.

My second year of teaching was in a Polish settlement. This school year started out as a very rough one and ended beautifully. My room assignment was an eighth-grade class. They had "run out" two previous men teachers. On that first day when the school bell rang and I had gone into the classroom, I was greeted with a hurricane of chalk, erasers and large old history books. It took me a little less than two weeks to settle these boys and girls and let them know that I intended to remain as their teacher. Not too much teaching transpired except to get them to stay in their seats, quit throwing things, etc. At that time in Nebraska, it was against the law to touch a child with anything except a rubber hose. The school director there ran a hardware store and he gave me a piece of hose from a spray pump, similar to a bicycle pump. He said, "Now carry one piece with you and use it." Needless to say, I did. Many of the boys were older and much taller than I. I well remember one red-headed and freckled-faced boy, who drank perfume or hair tonic for the alcohol that was in it. Well, I won the battle that day, too. From that day on I had no more trouble and we all became the best of friends, both students and parents, and we had a good school. The last month of school before leaving I never paid for a meal. The parents had me in their homes to eat, yes, and even breakfast—and were they ever good cooks! The food was excellent and I was treated royally.

It was a year or two later, and in another town where I was teaching, that I was in charge of a large group of students in a study hall in a large high school. Some of the boys' "pastimes" seemed to be that of spitting "BeeBees" through their teeth, which often sounded as if it were sleeting inside. To locate the guilty one was almost impossible. One particular boy became most trying at times. He was not mean but full of the "old Nick." I well remember one morning opening my desk drawer to get a slip of paper and there was a big old gray rat that was dead. I slowly closed the drawer, went about my business, and avoided the culprit entirely. That evening after school he came in to me and said, "Why didn't you scream or something? I didn't have any fun at all, after all that work to get it in your desk." Not too long ago I was in the bus depot and who should I see but this young man. He was in uniform and was a highway patrolman from Colorado. He was a very nice, courteous young man and he had to remind me once again as to how disappointed he was about the rat episode.

The most rewarding experience is to have the boys and girls come back from college and say, "I don't know how you ever put up with me. You were strict, but I learned from you."

As I look back I've had a small part in helping to mold a few lawyers, senators, teachers, nurses, technicians, engineers, architects, etc. To read about them and their work today makes teaching far outweigh all of the "hardships" endured. Doctors seem to be my greatest contribution to society.

Some of the offices held in organizations were: vice president, Cheyenne Classroom Teachers' Association, 1956-1957; in Delta Kappa Gamma, charter member of Epsilon Chapter, April 25, 1950; Alpha Xi State offices, editor, *Alpha Xi Roundup,* 1957-1959, parliamentarian, 1960-1962, and corresponding secretary, 1969-1971. Local offices held in Alpha Chapter were: vice president, 1958-1960, parliamentarian, 1966-1967 and 1968-1970.

Memberships in other organizations included: National Education Association, life member; Laramie County Retired Teachers' Association, charter member and second president; National Retired Teachers' Association; Wyoming Retired Teachers' Association, life member; American Legion, Francis E. Self Post 6, 1950-1981; and Women's Army Corps Veterans, Wyoming, member at large, 1965-1970.

Honors received include being elected, in 1980, by the Laramie County Teachers' Association as a candidate to the 1981 White House Conference on Aging.

— Alpha Chapter

Ollie E. McCleskey

I was born at the turn of the century on Christmas Day, December 25, 1903, in De-Ridder, Louisiana, in Calcisieu Parish; down in the Cajun Country. I was given the name Ollie Elizabeth—Ollie after my mother's brother; Elizabeth from my father's mother.

My parents were John Burton Wyrick from Tennessee; and Carolyn Luttrell from Missouri. My mother's Uncle Edward came over to America on an old barge called "The Glory" from England. My paternal grandparents were A.G. Wyrick and Lottie Collins, a part Cherokee woman.

I have two brothers, Leonard E. Wyrick, born in Texas, and T.J. Wyrick, born in Oklahoma.

We left Louisiana and moved to Idabel, Oklahoma. Ida and Bell were two of the first white girls born here; and "okla" means red; "homa" means home—so Oklahoma means home of the "red people" (Indians). Idabel is the county seat of McCurtain County. We moved here in 1909, two years after statehood. I attended elementary and completed high school in May 1923.

The first morning after our arrival in Idabel, it came a big snow. As I had never seen snow, I thought it was a big "Jack Frost."

In 1925 I started my teaching career, a vocation I had long admired and wanted. My first experience was really something else. My father and I decided to go see Mr. Mark Willis, who was president of Willis Springs School Board. At that time (1925) few women had cut their hair, "bobbed hair" it was called.

Mr. Willis approved of my credentials and finally said, "Miss Wyrick, do you have bobbed hair?" As I had on a close-fitted metallic cloth turban, I guess he couldn't decide for himself. Before Daddy and I left, Mr. Willis asked me to please remove my hat to let him see that my hair was long. As I had a lot of long thick hair, he seemed so surprised when I removed my hat, and I might say, quite pleased. The job was mine. Here for the next four years I was teacher, janitor, nurse, supervisor and "general flunky" for school District 49. The first year I received $90 per month, the following three $105.

I taught next in Eagletown, Oklahoma (one of the oldest towns in Oklahoma)—elementary four years, high school seven years.

I left Eagletown for Tom, Oklahoma; here I taught for five years—three elementary and two years high school English and art.

The years 1945-1956, 11 in all, in Broken Bow, Oklahoma, I taught art, science, biology and chemistry. Several of my art pupils won places in the state art shows. I had an art pupil who won a year's scholarship to Europe.

A sad event in my life was the death of my dear father February 1954. This left me so alone, but in 1955 I married Frank D. McCleskey, an employee of Exxon Oil Company, the best and dearest man in my life to me.

My husband was transferred to Frannie, Wyoming, where we moved to Deaver, Wyoming, on Teachers' Row, house No. 3. I taught English and art, and was high school librarian. I was there seven years.

Later we moved from Deaver to Powell, Wyoming. During the years, of course, I earned several degrees from Southeastern State, Durant, Oklahoma; an MA from Oklahoma University; and hours of graduate work from the University of Wyoming.

Mrs. Wiese, an art instructor from NWCC, Powell, is a person with deep concern for her pupils, and has a dynamic personality. I wouldn't have missed her classes and knowing her for the world. I love her!

I was initiated into Delta Kappa Gamma, Alpha Epsilon 1950, Idabel, Oklahoma, and was transferred to Gamma Chapter in 1956 in Wyoming.

My husband and I have enjoyed our travels in Mexico, Canada and Alaska. I also paint, fish and collect antiques, especially plates, cups and saucers.

My favorite Bible scripture is the 23rd Psalm; my song, "Whispering Hope"; my color, shades of blue.

My years of teaching and association with young people taught me regardless of age, sex or creed—there is no profession as satisfying and fulfilling as the age-old profession of "pedagoging." I am thankful and happy that I taught when . . . I could love and respect my pupils and they could love and respect me.

My 38 years taught me three things—leave a man's religion, politics and dog alone—those are his personally.

Some of my pupils are now doctors, lawyers, homemakers, teachers, business people, one priest, also one first-class "hippie." The wonderful art pupil, whom everyone loved and admired, and who won a scholarship to Europe, is now a "hippie" in Dallas, Texas.

There are days I would like to receive a wee note from each pupil, telling me his goals and places in life, for I love them all.

I realized on my last birthday I have never seen so many years in such a short time. I have lived through three generations of nieces in one family, hot wars, cold wars, depressions, recessions, tight money, no money and a terrible tornado.

I have taught everything from tight-rope walking to toe dancing but have never been able to "cry pretty" or "fall gracefully."

My husband told me today, "If the snow melts before noon in Wyoming, it is summertime."

One day a child said to me, "Miss Wyrick, next to my mother I love you best." I can still see that sweet child's face and hear those words. I consider that my dearest compliment.

I still say, *"There is nothing like youth!"*

If I had but one wish in this world, it would be for **everyone** to be able to see.

My constant hurt is to know children go to bed hungry.

— Gamma Chapter

Berenice K. McIntosh

Born in Oakdale, Nebraska, Berenice Koetter, daughter of Dr. and Mrs. Max Koetter, came to Wyoming with her parents when she was 9 months old. They settled in Burlington where her father set up a medical practice for the town and the surrounding area. Three years later her father died. Dr. Koetter owned the only drugstore in town and Mrs. Koetter managed it after his death. Several years later she married the druggist, A.E. Schlaf.

Since there was no high school in Burlington at that time, Berenice was sent to Denver to live with her mother's older sister to go to school for the eighth grade and high school. She attended Manual Training High School there for two years, then the aunt moved to Long Beach, California, and Berenice was sent there to finish her high school at Long Beach Polytechnic High School. She went to Colorado University at Boulder her freshman year. Since she was interested in becoming a doctor and also much interested in art, she took some pre-med subjects and also one art course, along with the required English, etc.

Returning home to Burlington for the summer she found that the family finances were a bit short so she decided to teach at the St. Joe School the next term. By taking a methods course by correspondence to add to part of her credits from Boulder she could get a "C" class certificate, which qualified her to teach one year. This was the 1923-24 school year. There were 20 students in all grades but the third. The building was very small, and the room was barely large enough for the teacher's desk, pupils' desks, the organ and the old-fashioned "pot-bellied" heating stove. When the weather permitted, Miss Koetter took the children outside for calisthenics and physical education activities. This really stirred up some of the community as nothing so revolutionary had ever been done before, but Mrs. Bertha K. Van Devender, who was then county superintendent of schools, heartily agreed with Miss Koetter and approved the outdoor activities.

During the coldest part of the winter, Miss Koetter had to room and board at a ranch home, but when the weather permitted, she rode to and from her home in Burlington, a distance of five miles, on horseback or in her little open Ford "Bug."

It was during her first year of teaching at St. Joe that Miss Koetter performed a service above and beyond the call of duty. The children brought hair clippers and scissors to school so that Miss Koetter could trim their hair during the noon hour.

In 1924 Miss Koetter attended summer school at the University of Wyoming and, after passing examinations in six required subjects in addition to the summer school credits, she was granted a class "A" certificate which entitled her to teach for three years. That year she taught the fifth and sixth grades in the Burlington School.

In the spring of 1925 she was married to A.F. McIntosh and they moved to Midwest, north of Casper. She did some substituting in Edgerton, near Midwest. Their older son, Herbert, was born there. In 1927 they moved back to Burlington, where Mr. McIntosh worked for her step-father for several years. That fall before school was to start, the fifth- and sixth-grade teacher resigned and Mrs. McIntosh was asked to take the position. She taught that year and the following one, but did not return the third year as they moved out on a ranch that spring.

In 1931 she taught the Odessa Rural School on Shell Creek east of Greybull. It is often referred to as the Stone School. In 1933-1934 she taught the third and fourth grades at Burlington in the same building that she had gone to school in her first three years. It is now the lunchroom and kitchen. In 1934 her husband got the contract to carry the mail on the Burlington-Basin Star Route. At times when he had other duties with the livestock, etc., she carried the mail.

In 1936 their second son was born. In the meantime she enrolled in correspondence and extension courses to keep her certificate valid. In November 1938 Mrs. McIntosh was asked to complete a term for a teacher who had resigned. She finished that term and the next one teaching fifth and sixth grades. The following year she was given the third and fourth grades and made elementary principal. In 1941 she attended summer school at Eastern in Billings, Montana. In 1943 she resigned because of ill health.

After a year of rest, she taught seventh and eighth grades and served as elementary principal in Burlington again for two years, from 1944-1946.

In 1946 she and her husband bought a ranch so she discontinued her teaching for the time being. In 1948 she worked for the Big Horn Rural Electric Company at Basin for seven months and served a year on the Burlington School Board.

In August 1950 the Otto School Board called on her to teach the first, second and third grades as their teacher had resigned and moved to California. She was a bit hesitant about getting back into harness, but a few days later, when a severe hailstorm cleaned out their bean crop, she told them that she would take the job. This meant a 10-mile drive each morning and evening, but she enjoyed the little youngsters so much that she stayed there for seven years. In 1957 she returned to Burlington and taught the sixth grade for four years and the fourth grade for one year. In 1962 Mrs. McIntosh taught at the Antelope Point School near Reedpoint, Montana. Since her husband's health was failing and her step-father had died she came back to teach at Burlington again to be at home and nearer her mother. This time she was placed in the junior high teaching English, reading, social studies, girls' physical education, science and art. In 1968 she was appointed head teacher and coordinator in the junior high. In 1970 she taught sixth-grade math, seventh-grade English, reading, literature and social studies and junior high and high school art.

She enjoys painting and craft work. She is especially talented in music, drama and dance and has helped to produce many excellent operettas and programs which have been well received and appreciated by the local school patrons.

Many of her summers were spent in Laramie, where she continued her studies at the University of Wyoming. In August 1964, 40 years from the time she first enrolled at the University of Wyoming, she received her bachelor of arts degree in education. It had been a long struggle but she was especially pleased to have her diploma presented to her by her former superintendent, Dr. Ivan R. Willey, who was then dean of the College of Education. He and his wife, Evalyn, had become very good friends of the family while at Burlington. In 1965 Mrs. McIntosh was voted "Pioneer Teacher of the Year" in the Gamma Chapter area by the Delta Kappa Gamma Society. In 1966 she joined the Delta Kappa Gamma and continued as an active member.

In addition to her teaching duties, Mrs. McIntosh has been a wonderful mother to her two sons. Her 15 grandchildren and 10 great-grandchildren, ranging in age from 3 months to 27 years, are her pride and joy. Because of the death of her older son's wife, she reared in her home three teenage grandchildren while they finished their junior high and high school education, as well as carrying a heavy school load.

Even though she chose a pre-med major in her first year at college, Mrs. McIntosh was happy in the teaching profession and was a dedicated teacher. She loved children and has always been loved and respected by all those who have been fortunate in having her for a teacher and co-worker. She gives a lot of credit for her success to some of her former administrators including Delia B. Foley, Frank Kraus, Ivan Willey, Robert Yorgason, Phillip Whaley and Rogers C. Ririe, who held her in high esteem, not only as a teacher, but as a friend. Several years ago at an award assembly, one of her eighth-grade pupils, Clifford Alexander, paid a fine tribute to Mrs. McIntosh. It is a typical example of the love and respect her pupils have shown for her.

In 1971, during the summer, Mr. McIntosh's eyesight was rapidly failing and the lady who was caring for her mother became ill and could no longer stay with her, so they sold the ranch and moved to Cody to care for her mother. She resigned her position with the school at Burlington. At a community gathering she was presented a beautiful flower arrangement by the faculty, and a watch, engraved on the back, "From the parents and students in appreciation of 33 years service." She had taught 35 years in all plus some substitution at Burlington and Edgerton.

Mrs. McIntosh was a 4-H leader for six years, spent many hours helping in her step-father's general store and, with Fred Maller, banjoist, Ray Nicholson and Bill Maller, violinists, and Mrs. McIntosh on the piano they formed a dance band and played for many dances.

Mrs. McIntosh's mother passed away in 1973, and six months later her husband was terribly ill and has been a semi-invalid since, partly because his eyesight was about gone. They have a wonderful collection of records for their stereo and enjoy them very much. They also enjoy their family and many friends and trips around the surrounding country.

Her husband and son Herbert died in 1980 and Berenice in 1983.

— Pi Chapter

MILDRED MCKELVY

Mildred McKelvy was born in Corydon, Iowa, in 1908, a daughter of John and Martha McKelvy, who were farmfolk of Scotch Irish ancestry. She was the youngest of six children and remembers a home of security and love, but with no financial frills.

As a very young child she informed her parents that she wished to be a music teacher and clung to this decision through the years. A chronic ear infection and respiratory problems sometimes threatened the desire, but determination resulted in college training which enabled her to teach for 44 years in her chosen profession. Her college education included a year of normal training, four years at Simpson College in Indianola, Iowa, earning a bachelor of music degree; graduate work at the University of Washington in Seattle, the University of Wyoming at Laramie, the University of Toronto in Toronto, Canada, and Brigham Young University in Provo, Utah.

Quoting the next four paragraphs directly from Miss McKelvy:

"My first experience in teaching was in a rural school of Park County where I made the fire, swept the floor, baked potatoes in the ashes for the children's lunches and felt a freedom that was wonderful even though I had all grades except the seventh.

"We not only worked hard in class, but took our lunches down to the creek, picked watercress to put in our sandwiches (we didn't worry about ticks) and celebrated a birthday by playing 'hare and hound' over the surrounding hills. We made up problems in math using candy recipes from the fudge we brought to the Halloween party, measured the length of the flagpole by its shadow and did all sorts of things that are now considered innovative ideas.

"At the age of 17 (I was to be 18 in two months) I started teaching at Lower Sage Creek in Park County. It was an experience I still like to remember. It was a happy time with 23 pupils. I always felt that the second grade probably suffered the most from lack of teaching time. The first-graders had to be taught how to read and there was always so much to do in the upper grades. Thankfully, my second-graders were pretty sharp and learned in spite of neglect, if there was any. I vividly remember one second-grade boy who always asked to study the encyclopedia after he had finished his assignment. Perhaps he just liked to look at the pictures, but it seemed to be his favorite book. The children were easily disciplined, noisy and full of fun, but always respectful.

"In my third year of teaching I accepted a job in an Ohio oil field. There I taught the upper grades and had my first case of difficult discipline. The boy was a handsome but pampered child who wanted attention. He was a challenge which I enjoyed and the results were satisfactory."

Mildred taught three years in the rural schools with a normal training teacher's certificate and was anxious to go to college for more training.

After three years, a diploma in public school music allowed her to accept a job in the Powell Junior High in 1932 teaching music, geography and English. After three years of teaching this assignment, she entered college again to get her bachelor's degree.

Then followed seven more years teaching in Powell. This time the assignment was music in the high school and junior English.

In 1943 she accepted a job as supervisor of music in the Sheridan schools. Although she liked the town and people in Sheridan very much, Mildred discovered that her interest was in actually teaching rather than in supervising other teachers. After two years she resigned to take a year of assessment of the situation. However, the need for teachers during the war years made her give in to the local super-

111

intendent's plea to teach and she accepted a job as English and geography teacher in the junior high at Powell. Then followed a couple of years of trying other areas—in Missoula, Montana, as a seventh-grade homeroom teacher; Yakima, Washington, as a music teacher in the junior high; and finally as a sixth-grade teacher in Cody, Wyoming. A year later the elementary music teacher in Cody moved out of town and Mildred was enticed into that field, which she found very interesting. She stayed in elementary music in Cody until 1956 when she returned to Powell to teach elementary music 13 more years until her retirement in 1969.

Mildred had time to work in Classroom Teacher groups, was president of that organization in both Powell and Cody. She worked in Delta Kappa Gamma, International Honorary Women Educators group, as charter member of Gamma Chapter, holding many local offices, including that of president, and finally became state president of Alpha Xi State from 1973-1975.

She loves to travel and would have done more if finances had allowed it. Trips to both coasts, to the Banff (Canada) area, Quebec and Montreal, Hawaii, Alaska, the New England states, national parks of the Western states, the Smoky Mountain area, and the Caribbean, were some of the trips she especially enjoyed.

Her hobbies included gardening, reading and collecting bells.

Miss McKelvy was a member of the Presbyterian Church where she was organist for many years. She was a member of the PEO Sisterhood and Mu Phi Epsilon, an honorary music society.

Mildred died January 31, 1984.

— Gamma Chapter

112

ROSE MARY MALONE

I was born in a Minnesota farmhouse six miles from our county seat of Stillwater, in the same house in which my father was born. Incidentally, the house is still standing; at least part of it must be more than 120 years old. The farm was a government grant to my grandfather for his service in the Army during the Mexican War.

My mother was reared on a farm two miles from my father's home; the two families were among the oldest settlers in Washington County. My first two years of school were in the one-room country school my parents had attended, one mile from our farm. Because my sister, three years older than I, would have had to walk to school alone, I was allowed to enter when I was 5. At my third-grade level, a two-room school was built at the little village of Lake Elmo, two miles from us. There I finished my elementary education. We walked to school except on stormy days, the length of our farm and then along the lake through the village.

Life in our farm home was very pleasant. Long winter evenings we sat before the coal stove reading aloud to each other and eating russet apples from the barrels laid by in our cellar. Perhaps it was to be significant in my life that our two-classroom school also boasted as an addition a very attractive little library. I can still remember vividly the oak bookcases with glass doors, the bay window, the table and chairs for those whose lessons were prepared and who had the privilege of withdrawing to read. A love of reading was mine by inheritance and by environment. When I was 11 we moved from one end of the farm to the other, to a new house built in six acres of oak woods, close to the bank of the lake, and among other homes that lined the road up through the village. Then we entered village life.

In those days no provision was made for rural children to attend high school, no transportation to the nearest high school at Stillwater. Therefore, my sister and I were sent to boarding school in St. Paul, Derham Hall, a preparatory school for the College of St. Catherine. It was near our home, and we frequently were with our own family and our uncle's in Minneapolis. I had a nearly disastrous attack of scarlet fever my freshman year and was out of school because of illness when I should have been a sophomore, but I managed enough credits to graduate with my class at the end of two more years. Then I was offered the chance to complete college in three years at the College of St. Catherine if I could keep up my grades. Emerging triumphantly with my BA, I was "ready" to teach at the age of 19. Then came three years in small Minnesota high schools, a variety of subjects, with emphasis on English and history. Since I had minors in science and mathematics, I taught those, too.

Graduates of private Catholic schools were then at some disadvantage in the public schools of Scandinavian-dominated Minnesota, hence I took a year to get an MA in education at the University of Minnesota. Meanwhile, I worked part-time at the West Publishing Company in St. Paul to help finance my further education. That firm offered to put me through law school and employ me in their lawbook publishing business. I worked for them a year while considering such a career. But I could not afford to abandon the expensive training I already had and could not face years of low income while I was being trained in another field. Besides, I liked to teach.

The next year I went to Montana to teach in the little town of Geyser near Great Falls. That was a fun year, a very happy memory. Friends I made then have been close to me ever since. I had been attracted to Montana by my father's sister, who was a pioneer physician in the Judith Basin. Upon her death I went to Asheville, North Carolina, to teach two years in a private college. During that time I bought my first car, and toured the South and the coast up to Atlantic City.

I liked the West better than the East and wanted to return. Even though the Depression had made a change of job difficult, fall of 1929 found me in Douglas, Wyoming, where I taught for 15 years, and the last three as high school principal. I loved Douglas, and still enjoy going there. I met Mr. Walsh when he was on a North Central evaluation team for Douglas, and he suggested I apply at Casper. This I did and moved to NCHS in Casper in 1944. After two years in the classroom I combined teaching with some hours in the library. In 1948 I became assistant to Edith Hegwer in the NCHS library. Having attended summer school in 1947, 1948 and 1949 at Denver University I received my MA in librarianship in 1949. When Mrs. Hegwer moved with Casper College to its new campus, I became head librarian at NCHS, which position I held until I retired in 1967. But school work was not over for me even though I had been employed in it for 44 years. Casper College invited me to become western history librarian on a part-time basis. This has been one of my happiest assignments.

Minnesota was my first home, and I have strong ties there. My sister moved to California in 1938, and I spent many vacations with her in San Diego and San Francisco. We bought a home in San Diego. When she died in 1955 I sold the San Diego house and now consider Wyoming my real home.

What are my hobbies? Reading and studying western history, and travel almost anywhere about the state, over the nation, and abroad when I have time and money.

Teaching and librarianship have been a rewarding lifetime work for me. I am a life member of NEA, of ALA, and of the Wyoming Historical Association, and a member of many other organizations. I am proud to have held offices in several of these organizations, including Delta Kappa Gamma.

— Beta Chapter

Pearl Wilson Alcott Marsh

On August 8, 1904, the E.B. Wilson family arrived at the tiny community of Camp Worland on the west side of the Big Horn River. At that time the family consisted of Edward B. Wilson, his wife, Viola Templin Wilson, and their six children—five sons and one daughter, Pearl. Pearl was born on October 29, 1892, in Central City, Nebraska. The Wilsons moved to Nez Perce, Idaho, in 1897.

They had been on the road 40 days, leaving Nez Perce on June 30. They were a motley looking caravan. Their vehicle was a covered wagon drawn by four horses. On the back of the wagon was a huge cupboard, with the baby's highchair on one side and a rocking chair on the other. Tied behind was a single buggy, and behind it trailed the family milk cow.

Their route of 800 miles had taken them through Yellowstone Park at the height of the tourist season. The road was a one-track trail and, in many narrow places along the mountain, the older children had to hurry ahead a half mile or so to warn people coming from the other direction to seek a turn-out in the road so the vehicles could pass each other.

Upon their arrival in Camp Worland, they ferried across the river on Eddie Conant's ferry as Mr. Wilson had been out previously and had purchased 160 acres from the Hanover Land Company on the east side of the river. Mr. Wilson had never farmed before but felt a farm was the place to raise five young boys.

The family lived in a tent for several weeks while the father and sons worked hard to clear away the sagebrush and to build a home of rough lumber, which had two walls filled with dirt for protection from the winter cold.

That first winter, in order for the children to go to school, the older brother drove the buggy to Neiber, which was about seven miles away. Pearl remembers that the next year school was available in Camp Worland. One-half of the Rupp Store building was an empty warehouse that the men working for the Hanover Canal used as a dormitory. During the day, the bed rolls were piled against the wall and the room was used for school. The children sat on nail kegs and grocery boxes, and the recitation bench was a plank. There was a 2-by-2-foot blackboard that the teacher and pupils used. Miss Carrie Ley taught the three-month fall term and Mrs. Alice Rhodes taught the spring term.

The next year, school was conducted in the little Halstead house on the east side of the river. Much of the town was relocated on this side of the river by this time because the Burlington Railroad had surveyed on the east side of the river. The teacher was Miss Helen Coburn, who had just passed the state exam for teachers. The only heat was furnished by a pot-bellied stove. Pearl recalls with glee that when Miss Coburn's fiance came to call at recess, the big boys stuffed the stove pipe with gunny sacks, causing the stove to smoke. Everyone thoroughly enjoyed the unexpected holiday.

For the next couple of years, school was held in the basements of the two new churches and the opera house stage where Pearl's freshman year was spent.

In order for the Wilson young people to complete their high school education, it was necessary for them to go to Basin and live there three years. Harry and Pearl bached their sophomore year; the next year, she lived with the local dentist, a Dr. Dodge, and helped his wife with the housework. Pearl remembered staying with Mrs. Percy Metz when Judge Metz was away conducting court in the other counties of the district. When Pearl was a senior, the family moved to Basin where they sold milk.

Upon graduation from Basin High School in May of 1912, her parents sent her to summer school at the Wyoming university. She well remembers that trip. Her family took her to Thermopolis where she boarded the stage and went over Bird's Eye Pass to catch the train at Bonneville. The stage trip took an entire day.

That fall she taught the school at Basin Gardens and taught all eight grades for two years. She had about 16 pupils. Pearl lived across the road from the schoolhouse with the Bollman family in a stone house, which still stands there.

The next year, she was promoted to the Basin public school. The building was not large enough for each grade to have its own room, so each teacher taught one grade and half of another. Pearl's assignment was second grade and half of third.

In 1915 she enrolled at Nebraska Wesleyan University in Lincoln, Nebraska, and received her BA degree in 1919, with a major in education and dramatics.

Pearl then taught sixth-, seventh- and eighth-grade English and grammar, with the sixth grade for her homeroom, in Worland in the old Emmett Building.

From this job she went to Alexandria, South Dakota, where she was high school English teacher for two years before she moved on to Lead, South Dakota, where she taught English, drmatics and public speaking.

In 1925 Pearl returned to Worland where she taught English in the high school. During these years she trained three young people who took state honors at a declamatory contest. She recalls this with pride, remembering that Ernest Clark placed first in oratory, Vivian Hayes Laird first in dramatics and a third in public speaking, whose name she cannot recall.

One of the hilarious incidents she remembers with the Worland faculty was that it was the custom of the Hatfields (Mrs. Hatfield was county superintendent of schools) to invite the teachers to their ranch (presently Circle J) for a weekend in the spring. This particular year it was the last weekend of school and baccalaureate services were scheduled for Sunday night. Ford Company had furnished the cars and all of the faculty except the principal, Mr. Emmett, had gone up on Saturday and stayed all night. They had a lovely time, but on Sunday it began to rain. The group started back to town, slipping and sliding on the muddy road. One car turned back but the car Miss Wilson was in struggled on although it grew late and dark. Finally, the gas tank ran dry so there was nothing to be done except for the driver to walk seven miles to the Morgan Ranch to telephone for more gasoline while the ladies sat in the car listening to the coyotes howl all about them. It was six o'clock on Monday morning before the party arrived back in town, muddy, bedraggled and tired, and went to bed. The second car came home the next day. No school that day!

Mr. Emmett had carried off baccalaureate by himself. Even the music teacher was with the others.

Miss Wilson left the teaching profession that spring to marry Arthur Alcott, a local farmer, and they lived north of Worland for many years. They raised two children, Kathryn, now Mrs. Dean Kempf, and Robert. Mr. Alcott died in 1956 of a heart attack.

In 1963 Mrs. Alcott married Earl Marsh, a retired farmer from Iowa. They now live in Worland.

— Sigma Chapter

WILHELMINA MILLER

On February 17, 1888, Frank and Lena Miller became the parents of Wilhelmina Miller in the territorial town of Cheyenne. The event went unrecorded as no birth records were kept (but certainly to the happy parents, their third child was a blessing).

Frank Miller and Lena Rieper had emigrated from neighboring districts in Germany in territory adjoining Denmark. Frank came to America at the age of 20. On his way across the country he lived on a farm near Boone, Iowa, for two years and then came to Cheyenne to work on the railroad in 1873. He worked as a fireman on the run between Cheyenne and Sidney, Nebraska.

Lena came about a year later after living with a sister on a farm in eastern Nebraska. She told stories of the herds of buffalo that roamed the prairies and the Indians who peered in the windows and frightened them. All they wanted was food!

Frank and Lena met in Cheyenne and were married in 1882 by Rev. Saunders, one of the first ministers of the Congregational Church.

The family spoke German but quickly acquired fluency in English. Dorothea, four years Wilhelmina's senior, went to Corlett School and brought English home to her little sister who could handle the language easily before she started school.

She anxiously awaited the day when she, too, would be a pupil in Miss Leonard's first-grade class; but when September came, she had to wait, since her birthday was in February. By the time school was ready for her, she had no desire to go. But go she did, four years to Corlett School, four years to Central School, and four years to Cheyenne High School, graduating in 1906 with a class of 23, three of whom were boys.

She learned to love the out-of-doors in early childhood from her mother who was an ardent gardener. Her flower beds surrounded the house and yard with their bright colors.

Her childhood included happy days skating, playing along Crow Creek, playing basketball in the gym and cycling with the family. The family had three bicycles; she shared a bicycle with Dorothea. She had to take turns staying home when the family took Sunday outings to visit friends at a ranch six miles north of town.

The girls and their friends were ingenious at entertaining themselves, a fact she chided her students with in later years. Once they cleared a vacant lot, next to Central School, installed the nets and enjoyed their own tennis court. Unfortunately, the owner decided to sell the lot soon after the games were underway!

Wilhelmina's father was then working in the Arp and Hammond Hardware Store. His transportation was on his bicycle. He worked from 6 in the morning 'til 8 in the evening. Some of the wares were displayed on the sidewalks in front of the store to attract business.

He must have been proud as both his daughters graduated from Colorado College in Colorado Springs. Wilhelmina, having majored in German and biology, began to seek a job as a school teacher. Most girls had chosen the same career, and jobs were hard to come by.

Finally, on the first day of January 1911, as the thermometer dipped to a minus 20 degrees in the daytime, she stood in three feet of snow at the depot in Monument, Colorado, and waited as a school official helped gather her luggage and settle her into a room behind a small cafe where she was to take her meals and live during the next five months. This proved to be her first real experience teaching fifth, sixth, seventh and eighth grades.

The next fall she accepted a position in a one-room rural school 11 miles northeast of Cheyenne. On Sunday her family walked with her to the edge of town where she got on her bicycle and rode the prairie trails to the ranch where she boarded. Then on Friday she rode back to town to spend the weekend with her family.

Her students ranged from first to eighth grades, with one or two pupils in each grade. One morning as she sat at her desk, she looked up to see a porcupine in the entryway, apparently trying to avail himself of some learning. Quickly she closed the door of the classroom and shoved the offender out the front door with a broom. As it ambled down the path, she was relieved that Phil's dog, who often accompanied him to school, would not suffer from a nose full of quills which would surely have been the case if the porcupine had arrived a few minutes later.

At Christmas time she accepted a position in Thermopolis, teaching German and social studies in the high school. The position was perfect for the training she had received at Colorado College. Getting to Thermopolis was no easy task since no trains ran north of Thermopolis, and there were no highways through the canyon. The three-day train trip would take her to Sidney, Nebraska; to Billings, Montana; and finally south to Thermopolis.

The teachers in Thermopolis knew how to have fun. They enjoyed swimming in the hot springs, horseback riding and socializing. The teachers chaperoned the basketball team to Shoshoni, on the other side of the mountains. Fur coats and hot bricks helped to make the trip possible for travel by stagecoach.

Her family longed to have her home with them in Cheyenne, but because of a ruling that two members of the same family could not teach in the school system, she could not return to her hometown as long as Dorothea was on the Cheyenne staff.

After four years in Thermopolis, she took a position in Albuquerque, New Mexico. Those four years spent in Albuquerque were most interesting. Here was an opportunity to visit and study the customs and culture of the Pueblo Indians and the Spanish Americans. Many trips were made to the various villages around Albuquerque, Santa Fe and Taos, to see their dances and watch them at their hand work.

In 1919, when her sister began to work on her master's degree in the state of Washington, Wilhelmina came to Cheyenne to live with her mother and continue her teaching career in Cheyenne High School. Her father died in 1918.

At Cheyenne High School she taught community civics. A textbook for social studies had to be revised from year to year to meet the conditions of a growing community. It provided Wilhelmina with an enjoyable challenge along with the opportunity to take the classes to see and study the various industries.

By 1923 the junior high school classes had been separated from the senior high school and Wilhelmina taught social studies, world history and American history in the new Central High School.

Extra-curricular activities took much of her time. Camera Club work and Campfire groups were organized, which involved two-week trips to campgrounds in the mountains during summer vacations.

Students in the Camera Club used to pile into cars, including the Miller family's Case car, and visit points of interest 20 to 25 miles from town, such as Granite Springs and Sherman Hill. They took a lot of pictures and enjoyed themselves.

That Case car, complete with side curtains and running boards, covered many miles from Cheyenne to Denver, Fort Collins and Greeley. One day Dorothea announced on the way back from the reservoir west of town that she was going to get the car up to 25 miles per hour. The noise the motor made as it approached that speed was so loud that the girls decided they had better slow down!

Love of the out-of-doors and study of "how the rest of the world lives" led her to travel as often as possible. Those travels included an omnibus college tour in 1931, which went through the Southern states, East Coast to Maine, and back along the St. Lawrence River to Chicago.

She made two trips to Alaska, the first in 1926 and the second in 1953. The last trip to Alaska took her to Kodiak Island, Fairbanks and north to Kotzebue where she saw the Eskimos as they lived north of the Arctic Circle.

She also traveled around South America by ship and plane in 1951. Her first plane ride had been in Detroit while on the omnibus tour.

Closer to home, she enjoyed hiking along mountain trails which led to climbing three mountain peaks: Pike's Peak in Colorado Springs, Long's Peak from Estes Park, Arapahoe Peak from the University of Colorado at Boulder. Wilhelmina climbed the Grand Teton as far as the first glacier.

One summer, 1933, was spent following the Oregon Trail across Wyoming by car wherever possible. She went to summer school sessions in colleges around the country always trying to mix business with pleasure.

In 1955 she retired and was then able to spend more time pursuing her hobbies of travel and outdoor life, gardening and relaxing in her cabin in Estes Park. She was an active member of Women's Club, the Green Thumbers, Pioneer Club and various church organizations. She taught Sunday school for 25 years at the First Congregational Church where she was a member from 1907.

In 1960 she was asked to write an autobiography for her 50-year class reunion at Colorado College. In that autobiography she assessed her teaching career this way:

"Most of these past 50 years have been spent in teaching. I attempted to teach American history and citizenship. How successful have I been? Well, that is a good question. As I meet the doctors, the lawyers and the Sunday school teachers, the housewives, the salesmen, etc., etc., I often wonder."

Certainly her students never wondered. On December 8, 1965, they paid her the high tribute of naming the city's newest school the Wilhelmina Miller School. At Miller School she was a familiar figure as she met with the school's principal to arrange for new books for the library which she donated. The school and the city speak of her as a classroom teacher in secondary education, a friend to Cheyenne and a real pioneer.

Wilhelmina Miller died on August 26, 1980, in Cheyenne, Wyoming.

— Alpha Chapter

ALFHILD MINNIS

Alfhild Johnson, daughter of G.A. and Anna Almen Johnson, was born in Grafton, North Dakota, May 21, 1897. She received her education in the grade and high schools there after which she attended the University of North Dakota in Grand Forks and State Teachers' College in Valley City in that state, receiving her special teaching certificate in 1928.

She taught several years in her home state—grades three, four and five in Adams, three years; all grades in Concrete, one year; first grade in Marmarth, four years; and in Devil's Lake, one year before coming to Greybull in 1929.

She taught second grade there for three years and shared teaching grades four and five during World War II before finding her special niche in grade one in 1946 in which position she remained until her retirement in 1968.

She married John R. Minnis in Billings June 1, 1932, and they had one daughter, Mrs. Charles S. Wood of Colorado Springs, Colorado.

She is a member of Session, the UPW and the Priscilla Circle of the Presbyterian Church where she taught Sunday school for 30 years. She was worthy matron and treasurer of Fern Chapter, OES. She also belongs to the PEO and is a past president of the Greybull Unit of the American Legion Auxiliary in which organization she is still very active. During her teaching career she belonged to the CTA, PTA, WEA and NEA.

She is interested in a variety of areas including bird study. She has traveled extensively and spent two winters in Puerto Rico and three summers in Pensacola, Florida, where she attended Pensacola College.

Members of Gamma Chapter of Delta Kappa Gamma, which she joined in 1954, honored her at the time of her retirement with the following tribute:

TRIBUTE TO ALFHILD MINNIS
by Laura R. Irwin, Feb. 1, 1969

I'm pleased to have the privilege of paying tribute to a very dedicated teacher who has devoted many years to the education of little children.

Today, I'd like to take you with us on a little journey. Put on your cloaks of imagination and step upon the magic carpet with me. As we ascend, I'll quickly turn back the pages of time, to the year 1915. We go sailing over the Big Horns in a northeasterly direction and find ourselves floating down to land on the plains of North Dakota. Boys and girls of all sizes are playing in front of a tiny one-room school building.

The door opens and out steps a charming young lady. Can this slip of a girl, barely out of high school, be the school mistress? Ah, yes, it is none other than our own Miss Alfhild ringing that bell to start her career as a teacher. It all began that fall, following her spring graduation from high school and summer school at the University of North Dakota. It was a very brave, but very frightened, little "schoolma'am" that rang the bell that first morning.

She worked diligently as school teacher, janitor, school nurse and yard man and earned her salary of $55 a month. After two years she accepted another position at the fabulous salary of $70 per month. Several times Alfhild tried other vocations, but she was destined to be a teacher and after each new venture found herself back in the classroom.

She continued her college training and earned a life certificate in North Dakota. After 12 years of teaching there, she accepted a position in the Greybull schools, where she taught three years before her marriage. She gave up teaching for a few years, but before long, she was back in the classroom again. It wasn't until 1946 that she started teaching first grade, which she found so challenging that she continued with it until 1968 when she retired from teaching.

She started her career in an era when the equipment, supplies and school environment were very simple and meager as compared to present times. It took much courage, skill and true love of children to meet the challenge Through her many years of dedicated teaching, Mrs. Minnis has given hundreds of children that very important "good start" in school life along with the development of self-confidence, pride and the satisfaction of accomplishment.

She has won the affection, admiration and respect of her pupils, co-workers and many friends.

This is the message her superintendent sends to her:

"To Mrs. Minnis:

"I have enjoyed working with you these many years and have appreciated very much our association as friend, neighbor and teacher. I know that in this I hold the thoughts of all who have known and worked with you. Also, I know that we have relied on your sincere, stable influence and have been held to the proper pathway by your guidance and counsel.

"I know that you have, and no one has more right to have, an honest pride in having helped to direct the lives of the many, many children who have been fortunate enough to have had Mrs. Minnis as a teacher. Numerous students have made remarks to me such as: 'I got off to a good start because I had Mrs. Minnis as a teacher,' and, 'I am glad I had Mrs. Minnis for a beginning teacher.' In these and many similar remarks I sincerely concur.

"On this day you are being honored, I wish to extend my sincere congratulations and to say once again that many, many children, adolescents and adults are better people for the encouragement, advice and help you have given them—me included." Signed Hillman W. Snell, superintendent of schools.

Her principal says: "Mrs. Alfhild 'Allie' Minnis devoted many years of her life to the education of hundreds of pupils. Today we are able to express to her, in a small measure, our gratitude for her dedication to the children of Greybull. Her patience, her tolerance, her cheerfulness and her optimism are traits appreciated by her contemporaries. Posterity will remember her many achievements.

"May this tribute be a reward for a job well done!" Signed Frank R. Gruden, principal.

One of her first-grade pupils, now a high school senior, said: "Mrs. Minnis, many students have had the rewarding experience of being in Mrs. Minnis' class. First grade is a frightening time, but Mrs. Minnis seemed to make it bearable. An animal cracker would help us over the hump of counting to 100, which in the first grade was a feat worthy of a Nobel Prize. If we weren't perfect angels, which was sometimes true, we were sent to the little corner kingdom. The pictures she chose for us to color were the heroes of our time, like Peter Pan and Humpty Dumpty. We were no DaVincis but for Mrs. Minnis we tried our best. Really, I'm rather sad Mrs. Minnis retired from teaching the first grade. I wanted my first-grade picture put on the bulletin board in the school lunchroom when our class graduates.

"Now you know why I feel so honored to have the privilege of paying this tribute to Mrs. Minnis."

— Rho Chapter

MARIE SALISBURY MONIGHAN

Marie Salisbury was born in Mitchell, South Dakota, August 29, 1903, daughter of Joseph B. and Anna (McGoran) Salisbury.

She attended grade and high school in her hometown before spending two years at Southern State Teachers' College in Springfield, South Dakota, and Northern State Teachers' College at Aberdeen in the same state. She also attended summer schools at both those colleges as well as at Boulder, Colorado, and the University of Wyoming at Laramie. She received a BA degree from the University of Wyoming in 1954.

She met George Monighan of Oil City, Pennsylvania, when he was visiting his brother, the Right Rev. F.P. Monighan in Isabel, South Dakota. They were married June 1, 1937, and moved to a permanent home in Cody, Wyoming. The Monighans have one son, F. Patrick Monighan, who, with his wife and three children, lives in Buffalo, New York.

Marie taught school in Selby, McIntosh and Isabel, South Dakota, for 13 years, being grade school principal in Isabel. She taught third grade in Cody for 27 years until her retirement in May 1969.

She was a member of NEA, WEA and the Cody Classroom Teachers' Association and belongs to the National Association of Retired Teachers, the American Association of Retired Persons, AAUW and Gourmet Group.

In 1949 she became a charter member of Gamma Chapter, Delta Kappa Gamma, and served that organization as second vice president and on the recruitment, scrapbook, membership and personal growth and services committees.

She was also a member of St. Anthony's Catholic Church, St. Anthony's Altar Society, Royal Neighbors, St. Rose's Bridge Club and the Cody Country Club.

She was primarily interested in sports and reading and died in 1983.

— Pi Chapter

HELEN RICHARDS MORGAN

On a beautiful fall day in October 1973, this interviewer had a most interesting visit with one of Worland's early teachers. Helen Richards Morgan was visiting with me in her home where she has resided since 1931. The rooms were lined with her loved books and other mementos of a happy and busy life.

This 81-year-old lady was most gracious, with an alert mind and so willing to share her memories with others.

She was born July 14, 1892, at her mother's parental home in Pleasant Hill, Illinois, which was the custom in those days. When her mother could travel, she was taken to the Richards' home in Annada which was named for her aunts. She attended the local schools until she had completed the eighth grade. Her mother and father were both interested in education, and wanted their girls to receive a fine education so they were sent to Lindenwood Girls' School in St. Charles, Missouri. Helen graduated from this school in 1910 and went on to Washington University in St. Louis where she got her BA degree in 1913.

She did not recall that she really had any special teacher training, rather she had taken many foreign languages, history and English. She took what was considered a fine education for a lady of those times.

In the summer of 1914, she decided that teaching was the occupation she was best fitted for and her first position was at Center, Texas, but she did not like Texas.

She seemed like a vital person who loved adventure. She said in looking over the positions that were open she found the young community of Worland needed a teacher. She applied and arrived at this community of about 450 to teach German, Latin and English and sometimes history in the old Emmett Building in the fall of 1915. When asked how her parents felt about this, she said, "I suppose they felt rejected and hurt that I would choose to go so far away, but I was young and it was what I wanted to do." Like many a young school teacher, here she met and fell in love with a young aspiring lawyer—Noel Morgan. They were planning to be married but about that time his country needed Noel's abilities in the Army in World War I. So, Helen remained in Worland teaching and they were married in January 1920. She did substitute teaching until the birth of her first child in this same year. She recalled that students liked to pull pranks and that discipline was a problem, which sounds so familiar to the ears of any teacher.

She had hoped that one of her children would follow their father's footsteps but their professions show great parental influence. Leon Richards is a journalist; Phoebe Trimmer (who was named after Noel's mother) teaches in elementary school; Harriet Hixenbaugh (named after Helen's mother) is a journalist and news editor; Alfred works for the government in the Civil Aeronautics Administration; and Oyer (named after Noel's father) is a minister of the Methodist Church. Helen has been a member of this church since she was 8 years old. All of her children graduated from the Worland High School.

While her family was growing up she was kept very busy helping a young lawyer become established and with her organizations. She is a charter member of the American Legion Auxiliary, and PEO. When her children were in school she was active in PTA and has been very active in Women's Club and, of course, the Methodist Church.

Her husband died November 6, 1961, but she has continued to be active in her organizations and keeps abreast of the times with an avid interest in reading.

— Sigma Chapter

ESTHER MYRDAL

E sther Myrdal was born in Edinburg, North Dakota, and attended grade school there. She graduated from high school in Park City, North Dakota, and received a bachelor of science degree with honors from Valley City State College in Valley City, North Dakota. She also attended the University of Washington at Seattle, the University of Southern California at Los Angeles, Colorado State College at Greeley, the University of the Pacific at Stockton, California, and Sacramento State College at Sacramento, California.

She taught four years in elementary schools in North Dakota and Montana. She went to Powell, Wyoming, in 1935 and taught the fifth grade until 1949 when she became fourth-grade teacher and building principal in Parkside School in Powell, serving in that capacity until 1968 when she moved to Escalon, California. She taught fourth grade there until her retirement in 1972 when she moved to Arcadia, California.

Esther was honored by the Powell Chamber of Commerce in 1965, for 29 years of public school service.

She is a charter member of Gamma Chapter, Delta Kappa Gamma, and served as its corresponding secretary from 1949-1952. She was state corresponding secretary in Alpha Xi State from 1952-1954.

She was a member of the Powell Classroom Teachers Association and once served as its vice president. She was also a member of WEA and NEA, having been a delegate to the NEA convention held in San Francisco. She belongs to the Lutheran Church.

Miss Myrdal is especially interested in doing oil painting and watercolors. She participates in community activities, attending special showings of painting and sculpture in the museums in the Los Angeles area.

Since her retirement she has visited many of the United States, including Hawaii and Alaska. She has traveled to Mexico, the Scandinavian countries, Central Europe, Great Britain, Ireland, Italy and Egypt. She also took a Caribbean cruise through the Panama Canal with stops in South America.

—Gamma Chapter

124

Nellie Avis "Jayhawker" Pate

" **A** former teacher and Girl Scout executive will serve as marshal of the 1970 Central Wyoming Fair and Rodeo Parade, sponsored by the Casper Lions Club."

Nellie Avis Pate will lead the parade which begins at 10 a.m. Wednesday.

At 82, Miss Pate looks back on a full life of teaching and counseling young people, Girl Scout activities, church work and some adventures in the outdoors.

Born in Holton, Kansas, at 8 years of age an attack of scarlet fever left her with a severe hearing loss. Nevertheless, at 18 she began her first teaching assignment in a one-room country school in Kansas with 65 youngsters in grades one through nine.

She remembers the salary was $37.50 a month. What seems like a small sum nowadays went fairly far in those days. Board and room was $8 a month; a pair of hose cost 10 cents; and a long pair of kid gloves cost 75 cents, she recalls.

After teaching in village and city schools, she became county superintendent in Jackson County, Kansas.

On May 31, 1931, Miss Pate stepped off the Burlington train in Casper and unknowingly entered a new life. She came to spend the summer with her friend, Mary Nichols, and ended up staying.

During her first few years in Casper, Nell Pate worked with the Girl Scouts as a troop leader, activity director, treasurer and member of the Girl Scout Council and finally acting director upon the resignation of Christine Reynolds. The highlight of her years working in Girl Scouts was the building of the "Little House," she recalled.

In 1937 she became a boys' counselor at Natrona County High School and later became dean of girls in 1946. While in this job she sponsored the Girls' League and Big Sisters and the May Hamilton Future Teachers Club was reactivated. The Future Nurses Association and the Pep Club were organized and she instituted the orientation teas for incoming freshmen.

"I considered the counseling of students the most important service I performed," said Miss Pate.

In her younger years Miss Pate was an avid collector of Indian artifacts. She and Mary Nichols went out into the country looking for the artifacts and managed to survive two spring blizzards, sand traps, gumbo slicks, high centers and rattlesnakes.

"One time we were on a narrow trail winding up a steep incline. We couldn't turn around and finally were stopped by a washout. We had no alternative but to back down that twisting road for almost a mile," remembered Miss Pate.

"Because of my impaired hearing, Mary kept a close watch on my wanderings in snake territory. One time she ran back toward me and yelled, 'Stop!' A large rattler was coiled in the shade of a small sagebrush beside my path.

"But my closest call came when we had a Victory Garden during World War II out at what is now Dempsey Acres. It was a chilly fall day and as frost was forecast, we thought we had best get what we could from the garden. I reached over to pull a pea vine towards me and found myself face to face with a coiled rattler. Because of the cold it did not strike and got away before we could get the shovel from the car. We finished picking the peas but never went back."

A member of the First Christian Church, Miss Pate served as a deaconess, treasurer of the church and its building and memorial funds, and was a member of its building committee. She is a charter member of Beta Chapter of Delta Kappa Gamma, an honorary teachers' sorority, and has received an American Legion award given for outstanding contribution to community and nation.

— Beta Chapter

HELEN HAYES PATTERSON

I was born February 4, 1909, in Harlan, Iowa, and Harlan is my home today.

In 1926 I was graduated from high school here and spent the next two years in Des Moines attending Drake University. My degree in education came a good many years later after numerous summer school sessions at Drake and the University of Wyoming where I also did graduate work.

In 1957 I married Dr. G.R. Patterson, an old family friend, and moved to Minden, Iowa, where he was a practicing veterinarian. It was close to Harlan where his family also lived so I renewed many old acquaintances. His granddaughter married and lives in Billings so I am now a step-great-grandmother to her three children. After my husband's death I eventually moved back to Harlan.

My first teaching experience was at Persia, Iowa, where I had seventh and eighth grades for two years and on to Harlan where I taught junior high school social studies for 10 years. In 1941 I went to Powell to teach sixth grade and junior high English for two years and until 1957 I was elementary principal and supervisor.

In college I was a member of Delta Gamma, a social sorority, and Kappa Delta Pi, an honorary education society.

When Delta Kappa Gamma's Gamma Chapter was organized, I was a charter member and the first vice president. I then served two years as president. After I moved to Iowa, I helped organize Beta Iota Chapter here in Harlan, and I have enjoyed this association with teachers in this area.

I belong to several organizations here in Harlan—AAUW, NRTA, Eastern Star and two study clubs. I am an active member of the Congregational Church to which I have belonged all my life.

I enjoy playing bridge, reading and doing a piece of needlework occasionally. However, my favorite pastime is planning trips and I have done some traveling. I have gone to Hawaii twice, have had a Caribbean cruise with Mary Johnson, and have been to Mexico as well as to several places in this country. Last spring I flew to the Netherlands for an extended visit with my brother and his wife, who live in The Hague. We enjoyed seeing much of this country, Belgium, and the Moselle and Rhine River areas in West Germany. I plan another trip there this fall.

I have been a Delta Kappa Gamma member almost 30 years now and have enjoyed the organization and my many friends who are also members.

— Gamma Chapter

LINA PERINO

ina was born to Ruffel and Mecia Hathaway in 1910 at her Grandfather Beard's farm near Champion, Nebraska. She is the oldest of three children—one sister and one brother.

She started to school in a one-room rural schoolhouse only two miles away from her birthplace. Her father filed on land south of Rozet, Wyoming, that year moving the family there in early spring. So, Lina finished the school year in a school south of the homestead.

Liking to practice what she had learned each day in school, Lina would go home and teach her little sister. She was so successful that when her sister entered school in the fall, she stayed in the first grade only one month and was then advanced to the second grade. She and her sister went all the way through elementary and high school in the same class, even graduating from high school together.

When schools in the Rozet area were consolidated, children were transported in a horse-drawn covered wagon, seats along the side, and a wood- or coal-burning stove in the middle.

Times were hard for the homesteader, so to help finance the necessary farm building and fencing, Mr. Hathaway went to Nebraska each fall for the corn husking. Since the whole family went with him, they would spend from late October until early March with Lina's grandparents and attend school there.

Then in early spring, they would return to Rozet where they would finish the school year. Later on, Mr. Hathaway worked on the railroad during the winter months so the children could remain in one school. In 1924 Lina's father gave up farming and moved the family to Rozet where he worked full-time on the railroad. Two years later he transferred to Newcastle where Lina completed the last two years of high school, graduating in 1928, proud of the normal training certificate she had earned.

That fall Lina began teaching at the Howard Well School. She taught at the Oil Creek and Plum Creek schools and was married January 1, 1936, to Joe Perino. Married women were not allowed to teach at that time, so Joe and Lina kept their marriage a secret until she could finish her term of teaching.

Being a ranch wife was very enjoyable to Lina, but in 1943 she was asked to teach the Horton School. After consulting with Joe, she finally accepted. After riding horseback six miles, opening a dozen gates to go home on the weekends, and then spending the weekend cleaning, washing clothes and baking, it is no wonder she felt she was needed at home the next year.

However, Lina returned to teaching again when the teacher at Beaver Creek School quit at mid-term. After discussing recertification with the county superintendent, she started to work the following week.

When the parents at Horton School heard Lina was teaching again they asked her to return to Horton in the fall. It was much closer to the ranch, so she accepted and remained there until the spring of 1950.

In 1948 the Perinos, in partnership with Joe's sister and husband, had bought a ranch north of Belle Fourche, South Dakota. They moved their trailer house to Belle Fourche at the close of the term but returned in the fall. Lina taught and Joe drove the Newcastle bus.

The next fall, Lina taught at Horton while Joe worked at the new ranch and again she was a weekend wife. This time she had to drive a hundred miles to get home.

By the spring of 1950 the cattle herd was built up so Lina once more became a ranch wife. And over the next four years she and Joe would move their trailer house to the summer pasture near Colony, Wyoming, look after cattle, and put up hay; then they moved the cattle back to the home ranch in the fall.

Joe became very ill in 1953 and he was forced to give up ranching, so Lina applied for a teaching job and taught at the Grieves Rural School for the next three terms. In 1957 she moved to the Gertrude Burns Elementary School in Newcastle where she taught first grade, kindergarten, and Title I remedial reading until her retirement in 1972.

Lina attended the University of Wyoming, Black Hills Teachers College at Spearfish, South Dakota, and Chadron Teachers College, Chadron, Nebraska. She earned a bachelor of arts degree in elementary education, minoring in art, at Black Hills Teachers College in 1961. All of her college education was earned through summer sessions, correspondence, extension classes and workshops during her teaching years. It was scattered over a long period of time, but she enjoyed it all.

Remarking on the many changes in Weston County's schools during her 32 years of teaching, Lina recalls her first school when water had to be carried each day from home and the room was heated by a wood and coal stove. When she returned after an absence of several years she found the school had installed a Warm Morning stove which would hold a fire all night so any leftover water was not frozen by morning. When she returned in 1953, there had been installed an oil-burning heating stove and Skelgas lights. An apartment was built at this time, at one end of the schoolroom, and was equipped with gas for cooking and lighting and a cistern pump—but she had to carry out the waste water! The last rural school she taught in had modern plumbing and electricity in the school building and a modern trailer house for the teacher.

It has been said that "time changes all things," and this is certainly true of teachers' salaries. When Lina began teaching she received $520 for eight months' work. There were 30 rural schools in the eight districts in Weston County—there are now two districts and no rural schools.

Lina is a member of the Altar and Rosary Society and has worked with religion classes. She has also worked with 4-H groups, belonged to NEA, WEA, IRA, PTA, Newcastle Education Association, Newcastle CTA and Northeastern Wyoming Reading Association. She was initiated in Delta Kappa Gamma, Lambda Chapter, in 1963, serving as corresponding secretary, recording secretary and historian, not to mention the many committees, breakfasts, banquets and initiations she helped to do. She is active now in the Retired Teachers Association, local, state and national, and the Senior Citizens Center. In 1975 Lina decided to lose some unwanted weight, so she joined TOPS, lost 53 pounds and became queen of 1976, and a very lovely and svelte queen she was and is.

"Light Up Your Life" is a good title for this lady's biography, for Lina has certainly given the light of knowledge to many, particularly in the all-important area of reading. The reflected light from the rainbow of life falls gently upon her as she now enjoys all the things for which she never had time. A multitude of friends and relatives, gathered over the years, fill the pot at the end of the rainbow to overflowing.

— Lambda Chapter

HELEN AND MARTHA PETERSDORF

They were known, respected and admired in Riverton, in Fremont County, and across Wyoming, and now they are gone, everyone remembers these kind, dedicated, philanthropic Petersdorf sisters; Helen a professional teacher, Martha a registered nurse.

Both were born in Indiana, Helen on January 7, 1880, and Martha on November 25, 1883. Their father, Frank, was a prisoner at Andersonville during the Civil War. Because of ill health, their mother, Henrietta, a registered nurse, came west in 1908 and homesteaded near Riverton; later she built a hospital in Riverton. Since her mother was here, Helen came out to visit in 1908; Martha first came in 1911. Eventually, both came to stay and to begin their many years of continued and exceptional service to education and to health at both the local and county levels.

Over the years people, in speaking of them together, said, "Helen and Martha" or "Martha and Helen." It didn't matter nor does it matter now. Nature, fate, chance, or was it God that made a team of these sisters? Working together, they made outstanding contributions to their state, their county, their local community, and to their fellow men. Countless lives have been enriched in some way by casual contact, by professional association, by philanthropic benefits, or by close personal friendship with Helen and Martha.

Educationally, each went her own way, Helen to Purdue and Indiana University and then on to Vineland, New Jersey, to secure special training for work with retarded and handicapped children. Before coming to Wyoming to stay, Helen had taught for three years at the Iowa State Training School at Glenwood, Iowa. In Wyoming, Helen was at the opening of the Wyoming State Training School in Lander, helping to admit the first patients. Martha was graduated from Bellevue Hospital School of Nursing in New York City, and for a year she was night supervisor of nurses there. For a time she was superintendent of what is now Natrona County Hospital in Casper. In 1918 she enlisted from Riverton and served in the Army Nurse Corps during World War I. After her discharge in 1919, she entered Columbia University, specializing in obstetrics and communicable diseases.

In Riverton's early days Helen taught for many years, most of them at the junior high school.

After Martha's return to Riverton, she opened the Wind River Hospital for Indians, assisted in the dispensary at St. Michael's Mission, and did duty at Bishop Randall Hospital in Lander. One year she taught a third grade in Riverton. She was one of the first public-health nurses under the Shepherd-Towner Maternal and Infant-Hygiene Program. She volunteered her services at St. Stephens Mission and at the state training school when they had epidemics and there was no setup to care for such emergencies. By 1928 Martha was the librarian at the Riverton Community Center which was supplied with donated books and furnished with reading and card tables, chairs, a piano and a sewing machine. The center was used extensively by clubs, church groups, Red Cross members who met there to sew, and by the two local doctors when they gave smallpox vaccinations. The material was furnished by the state Board of Health, and from this type of circumstance, the school communicable disease or health program evolved.

Martha acted as social educational assistant (school nurse) to the schools. An occasional epidemic of scarlet fever, measles or diphtheria indicated the need for annual checkups for the students. Teachers were required to give preliminary checkups during the first six weeks of the school year. Students needing further attention were screened, and then a team from the state Board of Health brought eye charts, an audiometer and other equipment and conducted the clinic. During these years Martha also served as volunteer welfare worker.

In 1930 Helen left classroom teaching when she was elected county superintendent of schools, and Martha found time to drive her around the county to visit her country schools. In 1944 Martha became the county health nurse. For years the sisters had worked together; now they were an organized team of working professionals. Both were filled with understanding and tolerance of human beings. Helen's great concern for children transferred to her teachers, particularly her rural teachers, during the more than 25 years she was Fremont County Superintendent of Schools. Always, she was eager that her rural teachers continue their education, and often she would suggest means that might be available for completion of necessary courses. To the job of county health nurse Martha brought her ceaseless crusade for health, better health for everyone. And so this team of sisters went about their tasks together since Helen did not drive a car. Martha was the chauffeur, the teammate, the confidant, the counselor, the fellow planner as they covered the schools of Fremont County, Martha checking health needs while Helen helped teachers meet and solve their problems and initiate new programs. Helen championed school consolidation and during her years in office saw the number of districts in the county reduced from 52 to 12 or 13.

Helen was county superintendent from 1930-1958, and Martha was the county health nurse, 1944-1953. Of these years of teamwork at the county level, Martha wrote: "Between us we advised and secured many improvements in the rural school system. These included the annual checkup for students, immunization projects, attention to physical condition of students, improved sanitation, and better salary status for rural teachers. Plus many other possible benefits available upon request from local associations."

Because of her interest in children and youth, Helen provided much material assistance for many capable and ambitious young people. At the time of her death she was financing a boy at the University of Wyoming. And Martha, in her involvement with health, was a leader in promoting hospital bond issues and in giving generous gifts to Memorial Hospital in Riverton.

Also, as a team, Helen and Martha helped to organize the Girl Scouts in Riverton. They had a very dedicated interest in the local branch of the county library and in St. James' Episcopal Church.

Both of the Petersdorfs were consistently cooperative and active participants in the promotion of community welfare. Their involvement was physical, material and spiritual. Their humanitarian services were innumerable. They never glamorized either themselves or their activities; nor did they ever say or do anything to make their good works appear spectacular, but their daily deeds in service to others rounded out two gloriously successful lives.

Both Helen and Martha set up substantial trusts to ensure continued financial benefits to others after they were gone. Helen provided a fund for needy Fremont County high school seniors who wish to continue their education. Martha's trust fund was given to Fremont County Memorial Hospital in Riverton, Wyoming, to be used for needs of the hospital.

Their love of travel led Helen and Martha off on many happy wanderings: to South America, to Europe, to Hawaii, Japan, Australia, Hong Kong and on around the world.

Education was Helen's life, and Martha said, "Promotion of health has been my life's work." Helen lived until December 18, 1965, Martha until September 28, 1970.

Prepared by Madge McGrew Jewett
August 2, 1971, Eta Chapter

— Eta Chapter

ESTHER ANN PICARD

Esther Ann Picard was born November 18, 1905, in Ruso, North Dakota, to Fred and Augusta Wilmovsky. She grew to young womanhood in this area where she attended both elementary and high school from 1911 to 1924. During her high school years she lived in town and worked for her board and room in order to get her education.

At the beginning of the winter quarter in 1925 Esther entered college at Minot State Teachers College, Minot, North Dakota. She again worked for her board and room and attended winter, spring and summer quarters in order to earn a standard teacher's certificate in elementary education. That fall she taught for the first time in a rural school 10 miles from her home. She was quite uneasy with this job as the school was famous for "running off the teacher." Esther took a volleyball to school the first day and interested the big 12- to 17-year-old boys in the game of volleyball. They became so interested that she had no trouble with them and taught the entire year.

The school day for Esther started before 8 o'clock, as she had to get the fire started in the heating stove, the water in and materials ready for the day, before classes began at 9 o'clock. She ended classes at 4 o'clock, but then had the janitorial work to do before gathering together materials to take home for further attention. Her day at school ended around 5 or 5:30. Her compensation for her work was $80 a month for months taught. If she wanted to duplicate materials for a class, she had to make a hectograph. This was done by pouring a thick gelatin mixture into a large cookie sheet. When it set up, she wrote with a special ink on a sheet of paper. The paper was pressed firmly upon the gelatin until the ink was transferred to the gelatin. The paper was then removed and clean sheets of paper were pressed, one by one, on the ink-imprinted gelatin. About 20 clear copies could be made.

During her first year of teaching she was bothered a great deal by traveling salesmen. The school was at a crossroads of two main roads. She often bought something so they would leave as they interrupted her classes.

Esther's second and third years were spent in a rural school near Garrison, North Dakota, and her fourth year near Williston, North Dakota. Each summer she attended the full session at Minot State Teachers College.

In the fall of 1929 she was offered a job to teach in Shoshoni, Wyoming, at the fabulous wages of $125 a month with paid vacations. She had a close friend there, so took the train to Bonneville and from there the taxi to Shoshoni. When she started to get out of the taxi she looked around and said, "Oh, no! Not here!" The taxi driver urged her to stay overnight before making up her mind. She stayed, taught there two years. It was there she met her husband. She was married to Armand Picard August 24, 1931, and moved to Worland, Wyoming, where she has lived since that time.

The summer of 1930 she spent seven weeks traveling with Southwestern University Tours of Wichita. They started through the Southern and Eastern states and a part of Canada. They started and ended the tour in Iowa. The second year she went with the same tour group, but this time they traveled the middle and Southwestern states and northern Mexico. Esther made the route plans for this tour. These tours began her interest in traveling which became worldwide in later years.

There were restrictions on married women teaching so she did not begin teaching when arriving in Worland.

The years of 1932 and 1933 she taught private kindergarten at the Baptist Church. She started the third year there, but was asked to teach at the Durkee School in grades one and two. Durkee School was about six miles north of Worland. After two years there she retired from teaching.

In 1938 Esther was asked to open the school on South Flat and stay until someone permanent could be hired. She stayed on and finished the year.

A daughter, Ardis Ann, was born to the Picards July 5, 1940. Esther enjoyed being home with her daughter for about two years, but again in 1942 she was asked to teach fifth and sixth grades at Durkee. She taught there from 1942 to 1944, at which time Durkee was consolidated with Worland, and she was asked to join the staff in the Worland school system where she remained until her retirement in the spring of 1971.

Her first year in the Worland schools was spent in the Emmett building where she taught seventh-grade geography and was asked to start a junior high library. She was given a large table and about 200 books. This was a very discouraging start, but she was equal to the task. She worked hard to collect the various books the teachers wanted for their students, and compiled one of the best Wyoming history reference collections in Washakie County. She also collected much needed materials in all areas. She studied the needs and worked hard to gain them. She had to move the library four times before it came to rest in the present building. When she retired she left a library of 10,000 books, all indexed and catalogued.

It was while teaching at the Emmett Building that Esther recalls a rather unusual experience. A rather busy boy tried to fit his head inside his desk (one of the kind that had no movable parts). He got his head wedged in but was unable to get it out. They tried everything including oil, but to no avail; finally, they called the superintendent, Frank Watson. He came immediately and tried everything he could think of. Finally, in desperation, he got a saw and cut the desk apart. It was a happy boy and teacher when he was finally extricated.

In order to complete work for a degree Esther attended summer school from 1948 through 1951, at which time she received her degree in English and social studies. In succeeding years she gained more credits in library work. She also attended a special workshop for the organization of a migrant school in Worland.

For many years she encouraged the eighth-grade classes to sell candy. The proceeds bought much needed materials for the school. The 1949 class purchased the first stage curtains for the junior high. They were proud of them as they were of heavy royal blue velvet and so badly needed. The 1950 class was the first to use them.

Besides her many duties at home and at school, Esther found time to travel. In 1963 she traveled the Western states and Hawaii. She spent several weeks in Hawaii. She went over by luxury liner and flew back.

In 1969 she spent five and a half weeks traveling in the Orient. She visited Wake Island, the Philippines, Cambodia, Thailand, Taiwan, Japan and Hong Kong.

The spring of 1974 she spent in the Holy Land, traveling through Israel, Lebanon, Judah, Jordan and Judea. She also spent some time in Rome, Italy.

In 1976 she traveled in England, Holland, Germany, Belgium, Liechtenstein, Austria, Switzerland, Italy, Monaco and France. In all of her travels she kept detailed diaries. These diaries read like a fairy tale.

Esther was active in many school organizations including the Wyoming Education Association, Washakie County Education Association, National Education Association, Wyoming Librarians and the American Library Association. She served as president of the Wyoming Library Association for six years.

— Sigma Chapter

CHARLOTTE RANNEY

The state of Michigan provided the locality on August 6, 1904, for the birth of Charlotte Mac-Kellar. This same state also made possible an excellent and easily accessible education for me. Eastern Michigan University and Columbia Teachers College of New York City endowed me with sufficient speech training to enable me to acquire a teaching speech position called "auditorium" in the Lincoln School of Flint, Michigan. Here enthusiastic students wrote plays, constructed scenery and presented these productions to equally delighted parental audiences.

The deaths of my mother, my father and two brothers caused me to take a leave of absence from the Flint public schools and come to Wyoming to seek comfort and visit friends. On the train on my trip to Lander an attractive insurance collector pointed out desolate ranch homes to me and said, "Many ranch wives try to live here, but because of the intense isolation, they lose their minds."

Later my marriage to Edward Aldon Ranney, and moving to a ranch home, just couldn't have had anything to do with my application to the local district school board for a teaching position! The unsuspecting neighbors who knew only my husband's oustanding ability and integrity petitioned the board to hire me, which they did, and built a tiny schoolhouse about the size of a piano box right in the middle of an alfalfa field. The door could scarcely be closed when the 17 pupils in all eight grades and the teacher from the "East" went inside. This teacher had never even visited a rural school in her life!

No water was supplied and "teacher" never ceased to marvel at the dexterity of the riding processions. They tied bottles filled with water on one wrist, swung a lunch pail in the other hand, and rode a galloping horse to the school door, arriving eagerly in a cloud of dust! "Teacher's" arrival at school at 7:30 a.m. for the preparation of material for about 40 classes was defeated by the joining of the walking procession who started from home the minute they saw me walking on the road and by running were easily able to catch up with me.

My probation included teaching beginners to read, teaching myself eighth-grade arithmetic along with playing running games during recess and noon. Added to the frustration of building reluctant fires to warm the building and thaw the ink, was the carrying out of the warm, live ashes. These duties were nothing compared with the dust raised on those stormy days when I swept the floor covered with dried mud, tracked in from the clay road and the alfalfa field.

By Christmas time the beginners were learning to read in spite of me, and what I had learned about upper grade arithmetic was colossal! The Christmas program presented a huge problem. Since the schoolhouse hardly accommodated the pupils, there first was no way to manage having a dressing room, a stage, a tree and, most of all, room for the doting parents and the excited younger brothers and sisters. This difficulty was solved by having the program in our home. Our Kohler light plant gave us lights for the tree and the play, while my piano helped the monotones with the singing of the carols. The appreciation of the audience was shown by a parent board member who said as he was leaving, "Mrs. Ranney, there will be no school tomorrow. You have all worked overtime this evening." His wife added, "It's a good thing you have a vacuum cleaner."

My husband and I always lived in the same home on the Shoshone Indian reservation. We studied and learned much about their culture. I found my 23 years of teaching them exciting and rewarding as I watched the educational, economic and social changes among them. From their lack of interest in education to their present desire for higher learning, from living in tents, drying their meat on racks to shopping now in the supermarket and driving new cars, from laundering clothes in the creeks to using the laundromats, I have secretly hoped that I have some small part in this trend.

Many years later a pupil of those days wrote this article in our local paper: "I would like to nominate a person to be displayed in print as one who has made a large contribution to Fremont County. The person I would like to nominate is Charlotte Ranney. Mrs. Ranney first taught at the Booth School in 1932. She came from Michigan. My folks were so taken with her that they circulated a petition to hire her. I went to her school for several years and feel that she made a large contribution to what is good about me. While I went to her school, she always had several pupils place high in state examinations. I can't remember all of her pupils, but I doubt that there were any that didn't profit from her teaching. In this day and age there are many who call themselves teachers, but in reality are only there to put in their time and collect their pay. Mrs. Ranney was not one of these. Most sincerely, Clyde L. Carpenter.''

My gratitude to you, Clyde. You have lightened my widowhood and gladdened my retirement, and my heartfelt thanks to the many young people who taught me so much.

— Eta Chapter

Selma Raudsep

S elma Raudsep was born in Baltika, Estonia (in Europe), on October 25, 1902. Her parents were Ann Kotkas Raudsep and Hans Raudsep, both Estonians. When Selma was 4 years old, they moved to America. Selma's early schooling did not begin until she was 8 years old because of the distances to travel to country schools. All of her grade school education was in country schools and it was not uncommon to have to walk four to six miles to school. Because of this, school often consisted of only five months out of a year. Also, because of not speaking English, she found school very difficult.

Graduating from Moorcroft High School in 1924, Selma had taken the "normal training" during her last year, which qualified her to teach. Her teaching experiences were all in country schools beginning in 1924-27 in Crook County, then from 1927-1929 in Campbell County. She taught all eight grades. In the meantime, she was taking summer school classes and extension courses from the University of Wyoming and Black Hills State College to keep up her certificate. In 1955 the Wyoming State Department required that teachers have a four-year degree, so she set about acquiring that. Selma received her BA degree in elementary education from the University of Wyoming in August of 1960. All this time, from 1948-1963, she was teaching in another country school in Campbell County, then from 1963-1965 in Crook County, still teaching all eight grades. From 1965-1970, teaching six grades, Selma taught at the Black Thunder School in Weston County. She retired from teaching in 1970 and still lives in Newcastle.

Selma has belonged to many organizations including being an NEA life member, WRTA life member, NRTA, AARP, Rebekah Lodge and Weston County RSP. Her Delta Kappa Gamma experience began on April 29, 1955, as she became a charter member of Theta Chapter in Gillette. Then in 1966 she transferred her membership to Lambda in Newcastle. Selma held the office of president of Theta from 1959 to 1960 and state recording secretary from 1966 to 1968. She is a member of the Lutheran Church.

Selma is very interested in outdoor life and reading is her main hobby. One unusually interesting place Selma worked was at the Wyoming Girls' School in Sheridan from 1945 to 1948. Selma says of her education, "I got my formal education the hard way, so I appreciate the value of it." We all owe a lot of respect and gratitude to our dedicated country school teachers of years gone by.

— Lambda Chapter

ALICE I. REID

Alpha Chapter, Cheyenne, honors Alice I. Reid who was an outstanding musician, educator and civic leader. She is now retired and lives in Loveland, Colorado. Alice is a state founder of Alpha Xi. She was the first president of Alpha Chapter, three-year president and executive secretary of Alpha Xi State and Northwest regional director of Delta Kappa Gamma.

This coverage seems inadequate when contrasted to the variety and scope of her contributions. The quoted material is Alice's unless otherwise cited.

Alice I. Reid was born in Bedford, Iowa, May 17, 1892. Her parents were George and Sarah Elizabeth Gardner Reid. In 1917 Alice was graduated from the music department of Simpson College, Indianola, Iowa. She was a member of Mu Phi Epsilon, national honorary music sorority.

She began her teaching career in West Side, Iowa, where she introduced a music program into the school system. After three years, she moved to Harlan, Iowa, and was supervisor of music for five years. She then moved to Ottumwa, Iowa, to supervise music in the elementary and junior high schools.

In 1926 she accepted a position as elementary and junior high music supervisor in the Cheyenne, Wyoming, schools. She served in the department of music of the Cheyenne public schools until her retirement in 1957.

During the 40 years of her active career in education (and since her retirement, too), Alice Reid was continuously devoted to improvement and growth both professionally and personally. Her summers were spent in the further study of music and in traveling.

Her music studies included two summers at the University of Wisconsin, two summers at Northwestern University, one summer at the University of California-Berkeley, one summer at the University of Northern Colorado in Greeley, "many summers" in study at Lamont School of Music in Denver, Alice wrote, "My work there consisted of opera and vocal training." She studied one summer at the Austro-American Conservatory of Music in Mondsee, Austria.

Alice was dedicated not only to furthering her music education but also to promoting programs of the professional organizations to which she belonged. While in Cheyenne Alice was a member of the Classroom Teachers Association. She served as legislative chairman and was vice president of the organization. She was a member of the Wyoming Education Association and served as president of the Southeast District 1954-1955. At all times she was a member of the National Education Association.

Alice was instrumental in organizing Delta Kappa Gamma in Wyoming. She was pleased to be a state founder. She had this to say concerning that honor:

"During the months of April and May 1940 invitations were extended to many qualified teachers of Wyoming to become members of an organization known as the Delta Kappa Gamma Society. The teachers contacted felt it would be an honor to be a member of such a group. Thirty-six women responded to the invitations and met in Cheyenne June 1, 1940, to form the nucleus of Alpha Xi State Delta Kappa Gamma.

"Various members of the group were designated by Dr. Blanton, the national founder, as charter members and others as state founders. I was designated as a 'founder.'

"On Saturday morning, June 1, Miss Blanton called me to meet her at the Plains

Hotel as soon as possible to assist her in preparing for the initiation ceremony. As I hurried on my way, I felt a bit of concern at being able to comply with her wishes. However, I found her to be not only very efficient but also very nice to work for. She assigned me such jobs as listing names, ordering flowers, and completing any duty necessary at the moment.

"The Wyoming women were thrilled with the beautiful ceremony at which Dr. Blanton, with the assistance of several honored guests from Colorado, presided."

Alpha Xi existed as the sole Wyoming chapter for almost a year. April 26, 1941, Alpha Chapter was organized and the officers were installed at the Colorado state convention in Greeley. "I was installed as the first president of Alpha Chapter and served for four years." For 10 years Alice had a perfect attendance record. She scheduled an emergency appendectomy to be performed between meetings!

The president's scrapbook covering Alice's term of office contains many interesting articles, clippings and pictures. One clipping, dated November 1944, is especially unusual:

WYOMING CHAPTER
Alpha Chapter—Albany, Goshen, Laramie and Platte Counties

Members of Alpha Chapter have been very busy with war activities as well as the usual routine of educational work. We have participated as blood donors, canteen workers, nurses' aides, knitters for the Red Cross, motor corps drivers, and hostesses at the United Services Organizations. We have made the following financial contributions: five dollars each to the Red Cross Hospital Fund, and the War Fund. We have purchased a Wyoming Tuberculosis Bond and a fifty dollar war bond. . . ."

Alice did not lose her enthusiastic involvement with Delta Kappa Gamma. Her loyalties to the society continued through her years in education as well as in her retirement. Her participation includes the following:

1948—Elected to state presidency. She served three years as president and executive secretary. During this time she organized five chapters: Gamma, Delta, Zeta, Epsilon and Theta.

1949—Delegate to Northwest Regional Conference, Glacier Park, Montana. She was music chairman for the meeting.

1950—National Convention, Dallas. Music chairman and soloist.

1951—Northwest Regional Conference. Again music chairman.

1952—National Convention, Chicago. Member of national chorus. Another Alpha member, Frances Lake, and Alice sang duets for regional programs.

1953—Regional Conference, Green Lake, Wisconsin.

1954—National Conference, Boston. She worked on the Public Relations Committee. Later, she wrote an article on public relations that was published in the *Delta Kappa Gamma Bulletin* in the fall of 1954.

1955—Northwest Regional Conference, Gearhart, Oregon.

1956—National Convention, New Orleans. Alice sang in the national chorus and was elected Northwest regional director. Delta Kappa Gamma became an international organization at this convention.

1957—Alice planned and directed the program for the regional conference in Jackson, Wyoming.

1958—International Convention, Minneapolis. She arranged the regional program and sang in the International Chorus. "It was my privilege to introduce Dr. Edith Greene as the banquet speaker."

Reviewing this chronology, one realizes that Alice did not miss one year of energetic participation in society activities. Her work inspired Wyoming chapters to present Alice with a life membership at a state convention in Gillette. "I was so pleased and thrilled! I appreciate so much the thoughtfulness and kindness of all . . . My work with Delta Kappa Gamma has been a pleasure to me."

Alice's influence in the Cheyenne community is immeasurable! She was one of the founders of the Cheyenne Community Concert Association. She was a loyal member of the Presbyterian Church and choir. Her friends and colleagues remember her multiple creative talents. She enjoyed art work and since her retirement has sold many of her paintings. She wrote skits. She enjoyed directing and acting.

Alice and Frances Brodie, another Alpha member now deceased, built a house at 310 N. 13th, Loveland, Colorado, and moved to that home when both had retired. Alice wrote that she has "59 rose bushes and a small garden with raspberries and strawberries." She transferred her membership to

Alpha Mu Chapter in Loveland. She has been corresponding secretary and music chairman of that group.

Perhaps the following lines written by Frances Brodie in 1946 for an Alpha Chapter program on "Riding Hobbies" is a fitting close to this tribute to a really outstanding woman educator, devoted civic leader and talented artist, Alice I. Reid:

Friends of mine have hobbies galore . . .
I'll name some of them, and you name more.
There's Alice Reid, of her I'll tell
She has many hobbies and rides them well.
She can bake a cake and mix a stew;
There's scarcely anything she can't do;
She'll paint a picture, oh so fine . . .
Crochet and embroider any time!
She drives a car in an expert way
And sings most pleasingly any day.
She plants gardens, collects creamers, too,
Cups and saucers, peppers and salts, not a few.

— by Treva L. Davis, Alpha Chapter

— Alpha Chapter

Flora Shufelt Rivola

F lora Rivola was a valiant, warm-hearted, forward-looking woman, who achieved her bachelor of arts degree "the hard way," when she had already become a grandmother. This was from Yankton College in Yankton, South Dakota.

She was born Flora Belle Shufelt to Alice (Hanford) and John Wentworth Shufelt December 1, 1881, in Antwerp, Ohio. The family moved to Dakota Territory in 1884, mostly by train, partly by wagon. A woman on the train said to Alice, "Your girls all have fine heads of hair, but it will all get blowed off when they get to Dakotey!" (It didn't.) Flora attended rural schools, sometimes with her father as the teacher. The family moved to nearby Yankton, so Flora could go to high school and to Yankton Academy. By this time Dakota Territory had become the states of North Dakota and South Dakota.

She began her teaching career in rural schools near Yankton when she was 17. With her first salary of $25 per month she began paying for a parlor organ, and music lessons for her younger sisters.

After teaching four years, she married Charles E. Rivola in 1903. When he had bicycled out to see her at her school, she had introduced him as the superintendent. The next time this happened, one of the older pupils said, "Yeah, we know! Superintendent of you!" They lived in Yankton and had two daughters, Glennys and Helen, and a son, Robert. Besides caring for her family, she did much church and community work. She also took a few courses at Yankton College. She and her husband bought a big three-story house near the college and rented rooms to college students. At first there were stoves in every room, which added a great deal to her work in caring for the rooms. After three years they had a furnace and bathroom installed.

In 1917, with her emotions stirred up by the world war, she began writing poems. For the next 30 years or more her poems were published in such magazines as *The Atlantic Monthly, Century, Scribner's Poetry* (of Chicago), *The New Republic,* and quoted in *The Literary Digest.* She gave poetry programs, which she called lecture-recitals, to women's clubs, teachers' institutes and other groups all over South Dakota. The state president of Women's Clubs, Mrs. C.P. Shaw, wrote of her, "Mrs. Rivola possesses a personality that wins her audience at once. She touches the heart strings of all." She helped Dr. J.C. Lindberg of Aberdeen, South Dakota, organize the South Dakota Poetry Society, and to begin publishing the South Dakota poetry magazine, *Pasque Petals,* named for the state flower. Both have flourished for over 50 years.

Mrs. Rivola's poems have been published in many issues of *Pasque Petals,* and in these anthologies: LITERATURE OF SOUTH DAKOTA (1918), DAKOTA LITERATURE (1928), ANTHOLOGY OF SOUTH DAKOTA POETRY (1938), PRAIRIE POETS (1949), PRAIRIE POETS II (1958) and posthumously in PRAIRIE POETS III (1966).

Being widowed in 1926, she began again teaching in rural schools. She was county superintendent of schools in Yankton County for two terms and deputy in the same office for two terms.

For years she called herself the "perennial student" at Yankton College, taking courses whenever she could manage it. She taught and studied on a fellowship at Northern State Teachers College in Aberdeen, South Dakota. After receiving her degree at Yankton College in 1936, she taught in a private school, Pratt Institute of Individual Instruction, in Omaha, Nebraska, for two years.

Her teaching continued in elementary schools in Nebraska, western South Dakota, and northeastern Wyoming (in Arvada, Rozet and Osage). She enjoyed arranging school programs, and often wrote plays for them. She was an inspiring and much-loved teacher.

When she retired in 1952, she lived with her son in California, and later with her daughter, Helen, in Gillette, Wyoming. Her death in 1964 ended a life of joyful service.

(This story was prepared in 1977 by Helen R. Fawcett, a daughter of Flora Rivola.)

— Theta Chapter

FLO ROGERS

THE "BOOKWORM LADY"

After 44 years with primary school children, Miss Florinda Eleanor Rogers retired to a life filled with service to others as well as pleasure to herself, enjoying her many friends, her good health and her satisfaction of "a lifetime of service to the children of Casper."

She was born on a farm at the edge of a country town, Readstown, Wisconsin, July 9, 1895. It was a hot summer day when her father, Francis H., gathered together the other four children and took them to the wheat field to help him with the harvest, whilst mother, Edwina Hale, and the mid-wife stayed at home to greet the new baby. Father was a farmer in summer and operated his grist mill in the winter.

When "Flo" was nearly 5, the family moved in a bob-sled to a bigger country town, Viroqua, which was 12 miles distant. Here their home was maintained until the death of the parents. She was graduated from Viroqua High School in 1914, from LaCrosse, Wisconsin, State Normal in 1916, and received her BA degree from the University of Wyoming in 1946. She taught in Wisconsin for seven years before coming to Wyoming in 1923 where she finished an uninterrupted teaching career of 44 years with primary school children. Most of the time in Casper was spent in the Jefferson School second grade, under the able principalship of Miss Dell Stinson. During the last five years of her service as primary coordinator, she organized the "Bookworm Club" for second- and third-graders of the city in an effort to stimulate their reading both at home and at school.

She will be ever remembered by generations of Casper school children as the "Bookworm Lady," the smiling, friendly soul who opened up to them the world of books and a lifetime of reading.

— Beta Chapter

MUSA AND MARIE ROSS

The "Ross Girls" taught in Casper, Wyoming, the greater part of their teaching careers—Marie from 1914 and Musa from 1918 —when they both retired at the ages of 73 and 71, respectively. Records of their previous teaching experiences are not readily available, but they came here as very successful teachers with considerable experience. In those early years Casper was growing from a small cow-town into a booming oil community with its fast-growing schools. The Rosses pioneered through this period of growth and confusion with serene and orderly classrooms, and their pupils learned the three "R's" without fuss or frills.

Claudius and Permilia (Rodes) Ross, parents of Musa and Marie, moved from Clymer, New York (where they were both born and married), to Trempealeau County, Wisconsin. Here Marie and Musa were born and lived during their early childhood. While they were yet small children, the family made another move to the rich farmlands of Iowa, where they received their education and began teaching. It was here that their school teacher-farmer father died.

After a time the spirit of adventure called them to leave the security of their rural community. They and their only brother, Merton, also unmarried, each settled on homesteads in South Dakota. That exciting experience completed, their next frontier adventure was to the state of Wyoming where they finished their teaching careers in Casper. "The Girls" enjoyed people and Musa was noted for her quick wit. They loved to travel and made several trips to both the East and West coasts. They were artists of exquisite needlework and china painting

They were members of the First Presbyterian Church of Casper and charter members of Westminster Guild which was organized in the early 1920s. Their homesteads, inheritances from parents and brother, together with their own successful investments, left them in very comfortable circumstances. Musa's death, March 1959, left Marie the last survivor of the family. She passed away in January 1960.

First Presbyterian Church of Casper was the beneficiary of the Ross estate. One half of it was used to set up a permanent scholarship for divinity students at the San Francisco Theological Seminary at San Anselmo. The Ross Chapel, which was built with the remainder of the legacy, was dedicated March 3, 1963, a lasting tribute to the lives of these two pioneer teachers who had adopted Wyoming as their home nearly 50 years before.

— Beta Chapter

MAUDE C. RUNSER

On a cold winter January day in 1901, a little red-headed cherub made her appearance as the eighth child of a family of 10 in Lynnville, Iowa. Maude was the daughter of Marcus Alvin and Ruth Copeland James. She received her schooling in the Lynnville public schools for the first 11 years and in 1917 took her last year of high school in Douglas, Wyoming, where her widowed mother and two younger brothers had taken up a homestead 18 miles north of Douglas. An older brother and family had already become established near there.

During her last year in high school she took normal training under the able direction of Clara Belle Bowman. She furthered her education preparatory to teaching with two years at the University of Wyoming and later graduated with a BA degree.

Maude started teaching at Keeline, Wyoming, and taught there two years in a rural school and then taught the primary grades in Keeline for four years. In 1920 she married Harry L. Runser, who was associated with his father in ranching in the Manville area. Later, Maude and Harry bought a ranch adjoining the parental holdings. In 1923 they disposed of their land and cattle and moved to Guernsey and later to Sunrise, where Maude taught for two years in the primary grades. In 1927 James, a son, was born to the Runsers. However, in 1958 tragedy came to the family with James' sudden death. Then for many years she left the profession due to ill health.

In 1943 she returned to her chosen profession as primary teacher and grade principal in Fort Laramie. The last 22 years of teaching were spent in the Guernsey schools. All but three years of this time she was a teacher of the first grade. She set up the first remedial reading program in Guernsey during three years and then returned to first-grade teaching.

Maude has authored articles relating to the 6-year-old in university publications and the *WEA Journal*. She was one of the first two teachers in the state to receive the Professional Standards Certificate of Wyoming. She was instrumental in organizing the first Guernsey Education Association. She was a member of NEA, WEA and GEA. She also served on various committees of the WEA.

She has been a very active member of the United Presbyterian Church, having served as deacon and church organist for 36 years.

She is a past matron of Alvada Chapter 43, OES, and past president of the Epsilon Chapter of Delta Kappa Gamma and a member of Kappa Delta Pi. She is a biographer in the first edition of WHO'S WHO OF AMERICAN WOMEN, also of WHO'S WHO OF AMERICAN WOMEN OF THE WEST. A keen participant in the work of the Republican Party, she has served as precinct committeewoman, county vice chairman, state committeewoman, and was a delegate to the National Republican Convention in San Francisco in 1956.

In 1966 she retired from teaching after which she and her husband, who was also retired, traveled to Alaska and Mexico and many parts of the continental United States. In 1970 the Runsers celebrated their 50th wedding anniversary with a reception and many of the men and women whom she had taught as 6-year-olds were present to enjoy the festive occasion. After spending five delightful years of retirement, tragedy again befell Mrs. Runser when her husband died, but she still maintains her home in Guernsey.

Wyoming's schools and their interest have made up a large part of her life. There is no question that Mrs. Runser served with distinction the schools of Wyoming.

— Epsilon Chapter

ELIZABETH DUFFIELD RUSSELL

A very special baby girl was born April 2, 1888, in Bladen, Nebraska, to Clarence and Eudora Duffield. She was given the historically beautiful name of Elizabeth. Brown-haired, gray-eyed, Elizabeth grew to tall, slender young womanhood in that prairie state. She attended local schools there and graduated from Nebraska Wesleyan University. Later on, she took graduate work at the University of Wyoming and at Columbia University in New York.

After graduation from Wesleyan University, Elizabeth taught school in Nebraska and Texas, but most of her teaching career took place in Wyoming. She crossed Bird's Eye Pass by stagecoach in 1908 at the age of 20 to teach school in the Big Horn Basin of Wyoming. The wide blue sky, the white clouds, the red hills, green in spring and covered with larkspur, sego lilies and Indian paintbrush, were the same then as now; but the rest of the scene before ELizabeth's eyes was very different.

Her first schools were a one-room country school at Otto and one on South Flat near Worland, Wyoming. She walked to school some distance, and—as all Wyoming people still are—was accompanied on her way, in spring, by bird song and the sight of bluebirds, meadowlarks, rosy-capped finches, blackbirds and sometimes an eagle soaring high. In the winter she saw sparkling snow (sometimes blinding and blowing in the Wyoming wind), the gray sagebrush, brown prairie grass and bare cottonwoods, along the creek beds. In the fall, there was the warmth of later suns, golden aspen, blue haze on hills, and little busy creatures getting ready for winter.

The strength and beauty of the outdoors and nature became a part of Elizabeth's character as she grew older. She was a smiling person, happy and observant. Like all pioneer women she was realistic and capable. Long before the day of "Women's Lib," Elizabeth had liberated herself in the most effective way by assuming, and being equal to, responsibility.

While teaching at South Flat she met a young rancher, Garrett Russell, who was feeding sheep there. He was a promising young businessman and rancher with interests in Hot Springs and Fremont counties. In lieu of a fraternity pin, Mr. Russell gave Elizabeth his Woolgrowers' convention badge and, for a time, while Elizabeth taught at Owl Creek and Grand View schools on Owl Creek, their courtship continued. She married Garrett Russell on November 17, 1917, in Lincoln, Nebraska. They moved to Mr. Russell's ranch, one of the first in the Copper Mountain area. The new home was named "Stone-Dale" and still stands. Elizabeth took up a homestead which later on was added to the ranch. Their extensive ranch operation was eminently successful. Their brand was T—R connected, for both sheep and horses.

Elizabeth knew the experience of warming baby lambs behind the Home Comfort cookstove, or helping with the feeding of livestock during blizzards, of cooking for branding crews during the heat and flies (remember them?) of early ranch days.

Her joy was complete when two children, Kathleen and Virgil, were added to the family. Her steadfast love and high ideals are reflected in the successful lives of their children and grandchildren to this day.

The full life of a ranch woman added wisdom and strength to her character and rounded out her lifelong education. The schools of those days were well-furnished if a globe, a blackboard and an unabridged dictionary were available. The school board didn't count the sticks of wood furnished for the stove, as they did in the case of a pioneer teacher in Connecticut, but they **did** furnish the most unsplittable, unbreakable, tough cottonwood chunks for a teacher to turn into kindling! Coal was usually in a shed behind the schoolhouse. Water was pumped by the bucketful as needed, and the toilets (boys on the right, girls on the left) were outside. All grades were taught, and how lucky were the ones under Elizabeth's care, for she could so enrich and add to the knowledge found in the textbooks of that time.

After 10 short years of marriage Elizabeth's husband died of Rocky Mountain spotted fever. The sadness of his untimely death had to be bravely borne by his young wife. Two children to rear and the responsibility of carrying on the heavy ranch operation fell on her shoulders and left no time for idleness or tears. By this time, the Russells had purchased a house in Thermopolis in order to send their children to school, so the livestock was wintered on Kirby Creek and in summer taken to the range on Copper Mountain.

The Russell Sheep Company was not the only area of Elizabeth's work. She became county superintendent of schools of Hot Springs County in 1931. Under her leadership, the rural schools reached a higher standardization. Grass Creek School in Hot Springs County was the first rural school in Wyoming to be designated as a "superior school." Since the rural schools were widely separated, the duties of the county superintendent were to coordinate their curriculums, visit them twice a year (over all but impassable roads at times), organize spelling contests, choruses, track meets and give both standardized and final eighth-grade tests. Their work was invaluable and the teachers were given a backing, direction and loyalty from this source which really kept them going. They had to be resourceful in every way. At one time, Elizabeth, wishing to show an educational film at Holt School, hooked up to the motor of her Ford car in order to get electricity to show the film.

During these years, Elizabeth was given an assistantship at the University of Wyoming, where, with the state, she compiled and edited a course of study which is still in use. She was health director for the Wyoming Tuberculosis Association and a member of WEA, the DAR, the Rebekahs, and the Pioneer Association. The five-year National Educational Fellowship Thrust, into Wyoming, was financed from the estate of Mrs. Russell. She served as president of the Northwest District of WEA and shortly before retiring was honored by Hot Springs Teachers Association, naming her "Outstanding Pioneer Teacher."

Later on in her life, she traveled to Europe. While abroad, she especially enjoyed visiting the great cathedrals there. She was a loyal and devoted Christian all her life and when the new Methodist Church was built to replace the old wooden building in Thermopolis, the old bell was placed in the new tower. Above it gleamed a shining spire donated by Elizabeth. As the bell rings out on Sunday mornings we think of Elizabeth Russell with love and appreciation. She passed away in 1960 at the age of 72 years.

I recall the remarks made regarding Lucinda Matlock in SPOON-RIVER ANTHOLOGY by Edward Markham. They seem descriptive of Elizabeth, also.

"What is this I hear of sorrow and weariness, anger and discontent, and drooping hopes?

"Degenerate sons and daughters, life is too strong for you. It takes life to love life!"

— Iota Chapter

MAUDE S. RYAN

M rs. Maude Ryan began her teaching in a rural school north of Douglas, Wyoming, in 1925. She had just returned from two years at William Jewell College in Liberty, Missouri, when her father was burned very badly and had to be under the doctor's care for quite some time. That fall she could not return to William Jewell so she started to teach. The first school had 16 pupils, all grades but the fifth. This was a very new experience for her as she had never even attended a rural school. She often tells about that year and states she worked harder than any student she had. They were familiar with cattle, sheep and horses, but she had to learn, and often she will say she still wonders just how much the pupils learned.

The first certificate she held was a high school III, good for three years. She taught for those three years then she married John Ryan and helped raise seven children. She went back to teaching in 1954 at the South Grade in Douglas, teaching the second grade. She was there until she was elected to the office of county superintendent and that position she held until it was eliminated by the state Legislature. She earned her degree by going to school every summer and got that degree in 1962.

She said of the honors she has been awarded the most important are the NEA "Honor Award," given by the Douglas Classroom Teachers Association for her contribution to education; "Certificate of Merit," given by the state Board of Education for the 12 years of service to education; the membership to the Delta Kappa Gamma Society; and, of course, the wonderful honor the rural teachers gave her deputy and herself for their constant work and support. There are many others, personal thank-yous that mean so much to an office holder. She really thinks the most or maybe the biggest thrill is not what she has accomplished but the joy of seeing and knowing the things their families' have accomplished, the hurdles that she has helped many students jump, the ones that she helped by just talking them into staying in school and accomplishing a goal, these are the honors that Maude enjoys remembering.

— Nu Chapter

ESTHER RYDER

Thirty years devoted to classroom teaching, in three states—Wyoming, Washington and Colorado—comprise the varied teaching career of Mrs. Edward (Esther) Ryder of Douglas, Wyoming, who retired from the profession in May 1971.

Mrs. Ryder, a member of Nu Chapter, Delta Kappa Gamma, since that chapter's organization on May 4, 1968, continues to be active in education-related activities both in her home community of Douglas and also in nearby Glenrock, where she did her final years of teaching.

Foremost among Mrs. Ryder's current interests are several projects undertaken voluntarily on behalf of the public libraries in Douglas and in Glenrock, where for three years she served as local chairman of the National Library Week Committee.

Among her special interest areas is research in the field of Western Americana, particularly relating to the lives of pioneer residents in the Glenrock and Douglas areas. Mrs. Ryder is also currently working on a scrapbook and historical record for the Converse County Public Libraries. She is a charter member of the Wyoming Historical Society and a member of the Pioneer Association.

Esther Rose McCormick Ryder was born in Pierce County, Nebraska, October 13, 1907, the daughter of George W. and Nellie Ingalsbe McCormick. Her paternal grandparents, natives of New York state, migrated after their marriage to Green Bay, Wisconsin, the birthplace of Esther's father. Five years later the McCormick family moved to Missouri where they remained several years before settling in Nebraska. Here, young George grew to manhood and married, raising a family of seven children of which Esther was the youngest.

In the fall of 1908 George McCormick moved his family to western Nebraska where they settled on a homestead south of Harrison, in Sioux County.

Homestead years were lean ones for the McCormicks and their homesteading neighbors; there was never a surplus of food, but everyone kept busy and happy.

Esther's schooling began shortly before she was 5. She walked three-quarters of a mile to the country school of Summit, accompanied by her brothers and sisters.

When she was a fifth-grader, Esther's parents left the homestead to take up ranching on Nebraska's Niobrara River. School was no longer within walking distance, so for two years Esther had to forego formal classroom instruction. Her father then acquird a team and buggy, which enabled the three youngest McCormick children to drive the five miles to school. During the two years she was unable to attend school, she avidly devoured every book she could find to read and gathered the scraps of paper brought in by the west winds and lodged among the thistles along the fences.

"And," she says, "you would be surprised at how much my dolls could learn," as she lined them up for their school sessions. "Even Rosie, the tin-headed one, and the rag ones with tightly stuffed heads and the china one with the hole under its wig, all learned to read quite well but were never very proficient in arithmetic."

Upon completing the eighth grade, Esther entered Sioux County High School. After a little over a year, financial reverses again forced her to drop out of school—this time for a year. On re-entering school, she attended Wheatland (Wyoming) High School for two years, graduating in 1926. A month later she enrolled for the summer session at the University of Wyoming, in the field of elementary education, and in September took a position teaching a rural school near Glendo, at a salary of $85 per month.

"That first year of teaching resulted in many memorable experiences," recalls Esther. "On one occasion, I became so engrossed in working with my 10 pupils (grades one through eight) that I forgot to dismiss class!" Not until dusk began to fall, says Esther, did she think to check the time. "I was startled to discover it was nearly 6 o'clock!" she mused. "Not wanting to admit my grievous error, I hurriedly helped the children into their coats, warning them to go straight home . . . because the sun was setting early that evening!"

Esther's education at the college level stretched over a period of 31 years, by reason of her "taking time out" for marriage, and to begin a family. She received her BA degree in elementary education from UW in 1957, having taken nearly all of her courses either through extension work, by correspondence or during the university's summer sessions. She also enrolled for one fall quarter at Chadron State Teachers' College, Chadron, Nebraska.

Her teaching career, before marriage, began in 1926, and included four years spent in one-room schoolhouses, followed by a year in a two-teacher school.

In 1932 Esther married Edward Ryder. Due to economic conditions at that time, married women were not being hired in Wyoming. Esther, thus, devoted her time to homemaking, gardening, club work, Cub Scouts and various other civic projects. Two children, Gloria Kay and Edward Keith, were born to the Ryders.

At the advent of World War II, the family moved to Washington state where Mr. Ryder was employed in wartime construction. Due to the influx of workers, teachers were vitally needed.

"I really hadn't planned on working," commented Mrs. Ryder, "but I was suddenly 'drafted' into service through my daughter's response, when administrators—at the school she attended—asked the students if any of their mothers had teaching experience."

Kay reportedly waved a hand . . . and her Mom was promptly hired to teach fifth grade at Kennwick, where the Ryders were then residing. The family later moved to Shelton, where Esther taught second grade; and upon their next move to Woodland, she accepted a position teaching history and English in that community's junior high school.

After the war's end, the Ryders—in 1946—returned home to Wyoming. From 1948-50 Esther was involved in teaching a class of slow learners, comprised of first- and second-grade pupils. In 1950 a serious illness interrupted her classroom work, and for a time she traveled with her husband to various construction sites. But the schoolroom at last beckoned her back, and 1951 found her teaching in Colorado, at a little school in the shadow of KOA's towering radio transmitter in east Aurora, near Denver.

In 1952 Mrs. Ryder returned to Wyoming taking a position in the Glenrock school system, from which she retired in 1971. Although while teaching here she "commuted" to her home in Douglas every weekend (weather permitting), Esther devoted much of her time to Glenrock's weekday community activities, including the Book Club, Girl Scouts and the Federated Women's Club, in which she served as chairman of the local Book Club, Glenrock Women's Club president, state division chairman for Public Education (six years), state chairman for the Shell Oil Scholarship Program (four years), state chairman of American Heritage and Citizenship Division (one year), and president of the Central District of WFWC.

In connection with her teaching career, Mrs. Ryder has worked actively in the professional organizations at local and state levels, serving as vice president of Glenrock PTA; president of the Glenrock Education Association; president of the Central District of the Wyoming Education Association (WEA); and four years on the state board of the Department of Classroom Teachers, as director of the Central District of Wyoming.

In addition, she served two years on the WEA nominating committee; two years as Glenrock delegate to the WEA's Delegate Assembly; and as WEA delegate to the NEA conventions in Detroit and Dallas.

Upon her retirement Mrs. Ryder joined the Retired Teachers Association and helped found the local chapter in Converse County, serving as its first vice president and the year following, as president.

Since her interests have long centered around children and education she served for a short time on the board of directors for the Douglas Day Care Center.

Mrs. Ryder, who expresses the hope that she has "contributed in some small way to the betterment of society," resides in Douglas where she finds her retirement days full and rewarding.

— by Peg Layton Leonard, Nu Chapter
— Nu Chapter

Irene Meahl Shaffer

On March 12, 1902, on a farm in Jackson County, Indiana, a baby girl was born to John and Cora Meahl. Irene was welcomed into the family by two sisters and a brother. Later, two other sisters and another brother joined the family. Being the "tomboy" of the family, Irene preferred following her father around, helping him with his chores, to being in the house.

Irene has vivid memories of the first school she attended. It was only one-half mile from her home. The building sat in the center of a large grassy square which had huge beech trees scattered around it. She was particularly impressed by the size of the desks in the schoolroom. They were so big that two or three students shared each one.

Her second year Irene attended school in Vallonia, Indiana, a town four miles from the farm. The students were transported in a horse-drawn hack. Seats were placed along the hack's sides and the bed of the outfit was so narrow that the youngsters' knees bumped against those of the children opposite. The windows of the hack were made of isinglass and could be rolled up in cold weather. Roll-up curtains also added to the comfort of the rig. Sitting at the front of the hack, the driver controlled the team with lines through a slot in the front door. Heat was provided by charcoal foot-warmers or hot bricks wrapped in paper.

When she entered high school, a one-horse buggy was Irene's mode of transportation. The school was small and extra-curricular activities were limited, but Irene was able to play basketball.

She was also a member of the mandolin-guitar club. Irene could play both instruments and because the fingering for the violin was the same as that of the mandolin, she learned to play the violin also. Earlier she had learned to play the piano.

Despite the size of the school, all required subjects for college entrance were provided for the student. Upon graduation from high school, Irene attended Indiana State Normal School for 10 weeks in the summer of 1920. With that limited training, she taught one year in a one-room school near her home. It had all eight grades. The following year she decided to venture west. After teaching one year in a rural school near Springview, Nebraska, the "tomboy" spirit in Irene prevailed.

Adventuring even further west she and a high school friend accepted teaching positions in the 9-year-old county of Hot Springs in Wyoming. Barely out of the frontier stage, the county had many rural schools and it was in one of these that Irene first taught in the state.

The Padlock School was originally started in a home on one of the oldest ranches in the area. By Irene's time, however, a standard school had been built. But she had none of the amenities found in town schools. Her duties included carrying water, cleaning the schoolhouse and building fires in the pot-bellied stove. Not only did Irene's day start early and end late due to her chores, but she lived with families in the district. That meant that she had to walk to get to school. One of her most startling initiations into rural school teaching in the West was the day one of her older boys threw .22-caliber bullets into the stove. Irene soon had calm restored to her frightened charges. Mischief-makers among the students soon found out that it did no good to run away because she could outrun them all.

Besides her own pupils, grades one through eight, Irene was also given students from another school several miles away due to that teacher's quitting. One family of five youngsters traveled by stagecoach several miles down a mountain to attend the school.

After two years in Wyoming Irene returned to Indiana as head teacher in a two-room school. All of her summers during this time were spent in college. Then the West again called. When she returned to Thermopolis and Hot Springs County in 1927, she had obtained two years of college training.

Again she was placed in a rural school. It was 18 miles from town and she stayed with the only family who had children in school. They were a rowdy bunch and as had her predecessors at the school, Irene finally threw in the towel and resigned her job.

Romance had entered her life by that time and she gladly gave up her teaching career to become a farmer's wife. She married Roy A. Shaffer in December of 1927.

To this union were born three children, Bert, Peggy and Tommy. While turning her efforts to raising her family, Irene never lost her interest in education. She believed that parents should be involved in the educational process and was a staunch supporter of the PTA while living on the ranch. Later, she helped organize the PTA in Thermopolis. She served as president of that organization for one year and assisted it in various capacities during her years of membership.

During World War II, after 18 years' absence from the classroom, Irene was drafted to teach all eight grades in the Sunnyside School north of Thermopolis. She says, "Such a change from those early years when I taught—the curriculum, the books, the methods! When I taught before all of the tests were on an essay basis; now I had to learn to give multiple choice and true and false. Peggy, who was then in high school, was a great help to me in re-learning my teaching skills."

After two years at Sunnyside, Irene took a job in the Thermopolis school system, teaching from 1948 to 1956 in the fifth and sixth grades. Times were slim and the teachers often dipped into their own pockets to provide for the youngsters.

In 1956 Irene was promoted to the position of elementary school supervisor, a position she held until her retirement in 1968.

After her retirement from teaching, Irene was appointed to, and later was elected to, the office of Hot Springs County Superintendent of Schools. Since the state of Wyoming was closing out that office, Irene had the overwhelming job of disposing of all the materials that had accumulated from the time of the county's organization in 1913 to 1971.

During her years in the field of education, Irene was a very conscientious educator. She supported all aspects of the educational process. Being an accomplished musician herself, she felt music was a vital part of the curriculum. She often volunteered her assistance to the music department when special programs were being planned.

Irene was initiated into Iota Chapter, Delta Kappa Gamma, Alpha Xi State, May 12, 1956. She has served as secretary, first and second vice president, and president of that organization since her initiation.

Since her retirement from the world of work, Irene has devoted her time to being a homemaker and volunteer worker in various capacities. Her talents as a homemaker are equal to those as an educator. Despite her early "tomboyish" years, Irene became an expert seamstress and excels in the culinary arts, especially in the canning and preserving of meats, fruits and vegetables. She has taken many prizes at the local fair. Irene and Roy have successfully raised their children, who are holding positions of responsibility in their respective communities. Irene also has eight grandchildren and she and Roy have celebrated their 50th anniversary.

Early in her married life Irene became interested in extension clubs. Over the past 54 years she has given of her time and talents to these organizations. She was a charter member of the Hot Springs County Homemakers Council which was organized in 1932. During her term of office as president of that organization she was instrumental in organizing the Hot Springs County Farm Bureau. For many years she has assisted with the Hot Springs County Fair, many of those years serving as superintendent of the extension club division. Covering an area of five counties, Irene served as Northwest regional state director of homemakers' programs.

In 1969 Irene was selected as the Hot Springs County "Homemaker of the Year." One of her most prized possessions is the Quealy Award which was presented to her in 1970. This honor is given to a Wyoming woman who has shown outstanding leadership in the activities of the extension homemakers' program and in her community.

Following her deep-seated belief that religion plays an important part in a happy home, Irene has been a regular attendant at her church. As a member of the First Baptist Church she has participated in choir, served as pianist, was leader of the youth group for several years and acted as church clerk and as Sunday school secretary.

Besides using her musical abilities in education and in her church, Irene has given freely of her time playing for other groups. But, her talents for entertaining are not limited to the field of music. Her oral readings, particularly those written in dialect, have "brought down the house" on many occasions at various functions.

Despite poor health, at the age of 81, Irene continues to use her talents wisely and generously for family, education and society.

— Iota Chapter

LEORA B. SHIRLEY

Leora was born September 29, 1907, in Fairbanks, Oklahoma, to George and Ann Powell. She was the youngest daughter in a family of five girls and three boys.

Her father owned the General Mercantile Store in Fairbanks until 1913 when they moved to the family farm near Pollack, Missouri. It was here that Leora attended grade school and high school. She attended teachers' college for one year at Kirksville, Missouri.

Leora had accompanied her family on a trip to Yellowstone Park and liked Wyoming so well that she decided this was where she would like to live and teach.

She taught her first school in 1928 on Powder River near Sussex. The following year she taught the Wright School south of Gillette in Campbell County.

On June 7, 1930, she married James Reuben Everson, a cowboy rancher. Their first home was on the ZL Bar Ranch near Sussex; they later moved to the 4-Mile Country and lived on various places. In 1932 their first daughter, Ruby Ellen, was born, and in 1933, Audrey Joan arrived. In 1941 they bought the Byers place on Dry Creek, north of Kaycee, and lived there until 1948 when they sold it and moved to a place just north of Buffalo and Reuben became deputy sheriff.

Leora had started teaching again in 1939. She taught several different schools in Johnson County between 1939 and 1955; they were the 4-Mile School, Antelope Basin School, Highway School and Lower Johnson Creek School. In 1955 she moved to Newcastle where she continued to teach until the time of her death on April 25, 1970.

She received her bachelor's degree in education from Spearfish College in 1958. This was accomplished by taking many correspondence courses and attending summer school for several years.

In May of 1958 she married George Shirley of Pueblo, Colorado. They operated the Skelly Service Station at the northwest edge of Newcastle until the time of his death in 1962. Soon after this Leora moved into her own home in Newcastle.

Leora loved traveling and appreciated nature. In 1963 she went on a teachers' education tour to Canada, Alaska and north of the Arctic Circle. in 1965 she went on another tour which took her to the World's Fair in New York City, Washington, D.C., and on to the New England states and into Canada.

Since coming to Wyoming in 1928 she spent much of her time in the Big Horn Mountains of Wyoming and the Black Hills of South Dakota just roaming around, enjoying the scenery, visiting points of interest and being close to nature.

Leora is survived by her two daughters, Ruby (Mrs. Keith Ruby) of Buffalo, Wyoming; and Joan (Mrs. Richard Anderson) of Townsend, Montana. Also surviving are four sisters, two brothers, five granddaughters and four grandsons.

She was a member of the Rebekahs, Order of Eastern Star, Royal Neighbors, NEA, WEA, Wyoming Farm Bureau, Delta Kappa Gamma and Wyoming Historical Society.

Leora gave freely of her best, and the lives of the hundreds of pupils who came under her guidance are richer because of her. To the school and the community she left a real heritage.

— Lambda Chapter

GRETCH LOFTIN SMITH

Gretch Loftin was born August 17, 1886, in Hildreth, Illinois, to Melvin and Iola Loftin and was the third daughter of a family of four girls and one boy. The family moved several times in Gretch's younger years, and in about 1900 settled in Olney, Illinois, where she attended high school, graduating in 1904. She was mascot of the Olney High School football team in her junior and senior years, and president of her class in her senior year.

After graduating, Gretch clerked in a general store in Olney for $1.25 a week and worked until 9 in the evening. One day a friend of hers, who had come west and married a rancher at Casper, Wyoming, was visiting in Olney and suggested to Gretch that she come west and teach school. After getting her parents' permission (they didn't think she would get a school), she wrote to different school districts and accepted the first offer she got, which was for $40 a month.

Gretch bought a round-trip ticket on the train to Douglas, Wyoming, for $26, sat up in the day coach for three days and nights, and carried the lunch her mother had packed for her in a shoe box. This was in the fall of 1905.

The Ute Indians had left their reservation that fall and were camped just outside of Douglas. When the train Gretch was on came through Fort Robinson, Nebraska, they switched on three carloads of troops to escort the Indians back to the reservation.

On arriving in Douglas, Gretch had to wait several days to be taken to her school. While waiting at the hotel she became acquainted with Bill Barow, who was editor of the *Douglas Budget* and author and publisher of SAGEBRUSH PHILOSOPHY. He autographed one of these books and gave it to her. He also invited her to his home for supper and to meet his wife. Upon arriving in the Barow home she found everything in an uproar. The Barows had brought a Negro woman to Douglas as a cook and housekeeper, and just before Gretch reached the house that evening, the cook had gone into the kitchen just in time to find an Indian squaw scooping up some pies and bread the cook had baked for supper. Upon seeing the Indian in the house, the cook had started to pack her things and was going to leave on the next train for her home in the South.

Gretch arrived at her school in the mountains 85 miles west of Douglas on the sixth day of November and did not get out until the 25th of June the next spring, and they still had to shovel snow in places to get out with a team and wagon. She lived with the people whose children she taught, and saw only a few other people all winter, and did not get paid until she returned to Douglas in the spring.

When she got to her school, she found there were no books or school supplies of any kind. She made a blackboard from some flooring boards, painting them black and using pieces of starch for chalk. In those days starch came in small chunks and had to be dissolved in water before being used on clothes. The schoolhouse had been papered with old magazines and no care was taken to see whether the pages were right side up or not, so Gretch learned to read upside down just as fast as right side up.

The father of the family died in January, and Gretch helped to make his coffin and bury him in a snow bank, where they had to keep him for two weeks until the weather cleared so that the nearest neighbors (17 miles away) could take him to Little Medicine, Wyoming, for burial.

The next year Gretch taught on Boxelder Creek south of Glenrock, and two of her pupils were Charley and Frank Robins. Frank became world champion bronc rider and caught wild horses off the Red Desert. Gretch also became acquainted with Malcolm Campbell, the famous early day sheriff.

The following 10 years Gretch taught and went to school in Illinois and Indiana. She graduated from the Marion Normal School in Marion, Indiana, and also went to Indiana University for several years, but the call of the West was too strong for her and she returned to Wyoming in 1915, coming to Moorcroft to teach at the Kohns place, now the Jack Simpson place.

In 1916 "Tot" (Mrs. Hannum), Gretch's younger sister, came west and they took up adjoining homesteads and lived in their sod homestead shacks for several years and taught in that area until they proved up.

After proving up on their homesteads, they decided to go to California and purchase a private school with Mrs. Kohns. But neither Gretch nor Tot liked it there, so 1918 found Gretch back in Wyoming teaching in the coal camp of Oakley, non-existent now. She taught the first four grades there and had 54 pupils, of which only six were Americans. The rest were Italian and Japanese, some of whom couldn't speak English.

While she was at Oakley, the Japanese paymaster and his wife were murdered by someone trying to get the payroll. As Gretch lived in a miner's cabin by herself, she slept the rest of the year with a light on and a loaded revolver on a chair by her bed.

In 1919 she taught at Sussex, Wyoming, where she became acquainted with the "Hardwater" Davis family, with whom she was friends for the rest of her life. During the flu epidemic, while her school was closed because of it and after a bout with it herself, she went out to nurse other people, as whole families were down at the same time.

In 1920 she taught at Freland, Wyoming, in Bates Hole west of Casper, and a whole volume could be written about her experiences in all the places where she taught.

Gretch came to Gillette in 1921 to teach first grade in the Gillette schools. She continued in the grade school until 1923 when she went into the ranching business with her brother-in-law, Dr. M.J. Hannum Sr. She returned to teaching country schools when she moved to the ranch 22 miles southwest of Gillette and continued teaching in the country until about 1934.

Gretch married Jim Smith January 3, 1930, and continued to live at the ranch until 1937, when they moved to Gillette and built a greenhouse.

In 1934 a correspondence department was established in Gillette, in connection with the Campbell County High School and Gretch was chosen to take care of this department. At first she came to town two days a week but by 1937 the department had grown. Gretch taught several classes in the high school so that it became a full-time job.

Many a rancher will remember what a help the correspondence department was during the depression years when they couldn't afford to send their children to town to high school. At one time she had 126 students, some of them in Montana, enrolled in 23 different subjects and the university sent a man here to get copies of Gretch's outlines for the different subjects she taught to use in their correspondence department.

In 1945 Gretch resigned and moved with her husband to the Demps Luton place at Soda Wells, where she returned to teaching a country school.

In 1957 her health started to fail so they sold the ranch in 1960 and moved to Story, but she wasn't well there so they moved back to Gillette where she passed away November 16, 1965.

Gretch loved every minute of her teaching and every child she taught. Every one of them loved her, too, as is proven by the statements of many of them. One she had had in her first school visited her and told what a ray of sunshine she was in their home and how she had taught them more in that year, with nothing to teach with than any other teacher they had. Another told that of all the teachers she had had, Gretch was the only one she remembered.

Another student told how Gretch had bought his first suit of clothes during the Depression and another, in commenting about Gretch's ability as a teacher, said she taught you whether you wanted to learn or not.

I want to say that Gretch, as well as being a wonderful teacher, was the most wonderful wife and helpmate any man ever had.

— by Jim Smith
— Theta Chapter

VELMA VIOLA STECKLEY

I, Velma Viola Steckley, was born the fifth of a family of 13 children, to George and Jessie Phillips. I was born November 7, 1906, in a sod house near Rolf, a country post office located in the central part of the sand hills in Cherry County, Nebraska. I was raised on my father's cattle ranch in that sparsely populated area.

At the age of 7 I experienced my first day at school. With lunch pail in one hand, pencil and tablet in the other, perched on the spring seat of a lumber wagon, I began my first day of transportation to and from school. My eldest brother sat beside me to drive the team of horses. My other three brothers sat behind in the wagon box on top of a load of hay which served as feed for the horses during the school hours. We traveled seven miles, over trails and hills, to the one-room sod schoolhouse where I experienced my first three years of schooling.

Miss Webb, the teacher, was a motherly type of person. She wore a white blouse, black skirt, and a long white apron that tied around her waist with a big bow behind. Tucked into her apron band was an old cloth of some sort which she used to wipe tears from the pupils' eyes or to wipe running noses. If a child sniffed, Miss Webb was right there with her cloth. I told my mother as soon as I reached home about the cloth for all. That evening she made us hankies out of a batiste cloth she had bought for a blouse for herself.

Three years later a one-room frame schoolhoouse replaced the soddy. It was located several miles closer to home and we had a fairly good road to travel.

School terms were short, usually five to seven months a year. During the stormy days my four brothers rode double on horseback to school, leaving me at home. With a desire to learn and with help from my brothers, I managed to keep up with my studies. Acting as teacher I often played school with my younger brothers and sisters as students. It was at this early age that I had dreams of becoming a teacher.

I completed my first nine years of schooling in the rural schools which included the ninth grade. I attended high school in Alliance, Nebraska, the next three years, graduating with honors in 1929.

I took the state teacher's examination and received a third-grade certificate. Using my state normal school scholarship I attended Chadron State Normal School that summer and began my first term of teaching in September, 35 miles from home in Cherry County, Nebraska.

There were six boys and three girls enrolled in school. The white, one-room schoolhouse stood on a flat prairie surrounded by hills and blowouts. Inside the building were old battered desks, with the names of former students carved all over the tops. There was also a meager supply of textbooks, old and worn, a small slate blackboard, and a few scanty supplies. Water had to be hauled in. The outside surroundings were bare except for one homemade teeter-totter. Cattle often came next to the building for shade and protection. They would rub against it, shaking the building, and they would often furnish us with music with their bawlings. If they caused too much distraction, the children would go out and chase them away.

One afternoon in late autumn our first visitor knocked on the schoolhouse door. On opening it, I found an unfamiliar lady. She smiled, then tapping me on the shoulder, said, "Please tell your teacher that Mrs. Jackson, county superintendent of schools, is here to visit your school this afternoon."

My only lodging was with a very sweet elderly lady who lived two miles from school. My room was in the attic and when it rained the roof leaked. Room and board was $15 a month, and my salary was $75 a month. I walked to and from school. Occasionally during the coldest stormy weather a patron came by for me.

Distance, poor road conditions, and many gates to open and shut were factors which led me to apply for a school elsewhere. With luck I got one closer to home. The only drawback was that I had to ride horseback five miles to and from school.

It was at this time that I experienced a near tragedy. The schoolhouse was located near a large lake. Near the shoreline in front of the school building was an artesian well where the children got their drinks and water to use at school. Laid planks made a path leading to the well as the ground around it was wet and muddy. In the early spring the ice near the shoreline melted first, especially that near the flowing artesian well. One noon when class was dismissed we rushed to the well. A little first-grade girl had slipped on the wet planks and slid feet first into the icy water beyond. I grabbed the child only seconds before she would have disappeared under the ice, while the other screaming, horrified children watched. The next day a woven wire fence was installed around the well on three sides.

The next three years I taught in rural schools near Merriman, Nebraska. Many Saturdays were spent with the older students searching for arrowheads and other Indian artifacts along the Niobrara River. One day we made plans to ride horseback the coming Saturday to an old Indian hunting ground to search for Indian relics. The following day two sixth-grade boys got into a fight back of the schoolhouse. After discussing the situation with the two, I threatened to punish them by not allowing them to go along on the trip. One of the boys replied, "It doesn't matter. I'll take a horse and follow you." I learned a lesson I was never to forget. Threats seldom pay off as disciplinary measures.

It was while teaching near Merriman that I met and later married Lou Steckley on July 6, 1934.

On May 9, 1936, we moved to Wyoming and established our residence on my homestead 55 miles north of Douglas, which was then known as Verse Community. My brother had homesteaded the land in 1929 and had been living on the place prior to his death in 1932. Later that year I contested his homestead entry and applied for a homestead for the land in my name. It did not become final until January 1934. I was the last person to homestead in Wyoming. In 1934 the Taylor Grazing Act was passed, removing the government land from homestead entry.

We were blessed with an addition to our family two years later. Donald Eugene was born May 9, 1938. He shared our pioneer days on the homestead. He is now married and has two lovely daughters. They live in Douglas and Donald is an oil operator.

Our life on the homestead was a busy one, similar to that of the earliest pioneers. We first hauled water for drinking and household use 10 miles. We cared for our livestock, raised orphaned lambs to increase our herd, milked cows, and sold cream to the Douglas Creamery. The rural mailman usually delivered it. We raised a large garden, and canned vegetables, raised chickens and turkeys for market, churned butter for our own use, and made our own cheese.

During World War II I returned to teaching at mid-term in January 1943. I taught in the rural schools at Verse, Box Creek, Walker Creek and Pleasant Valley communities in Converse County. I taught for 13.5 years under County Superintendent Frankie Hern. I took my son with me and taught him his eight years in the elementary school.

The episode with the skunk when teaching at Box Creek stands apart in my life. It was a hot day so I had left the classroom door open. My only two students, a boy and my own boy, spied Mr. Skunk in the doorway. He leisurely strolled across the floor. Frightened, but cautiously and slowly some of the boys walked along the opposite wall and out the door. The boys ran for help and I kept track of the visitor. A sheepherder nearby heard their yells and came at once to our rescue. He coaxed the animal outside and away from the building before disposing of him. It was quite an exciting incidental experience. The man discovered the skunk was old and blind and was unaware he had trodden on private property.

School incidents I remember were the fun we had putting on parties and programs for parents and other people living in the community. These especially were the Halloween parties, Christmas programs and plays, Valentine parties, pie suppers, box socials and the last-day-of-school picnic. Usually after the entertainment, if space was available, desks were pushed aside or carried outside and everyone danced to the tune of a fiddle, guitar or organ until late hours in early morn.

The last-day-of-school picnic was a big event. The pupils and parents brought well filled baskets of lunch to a grove of trees near a river or lake, for all to share. Usually homemade ice cream was the delight of all. After lunch were the foot races, sack races, three-legged races, egg races, ball throwing and, if time permitted, a baseball game with the men, women and children participating. Before they departed for home, most of the food was devoured.

Box socials attended by parents, students and people of the area were exciting times. Box suppers were sold by auction. The purchaser of the box was privileged to eat with the young lady who had prepared the "good eats" and decorated the box. The name of the girl who brought the box supper was not told so the bidder had to guess the owner. Rivalry was keen at times when the bidders thought a man wanted to get a certain lady's box; they would run the bidder very high to "make him pay" for the privilege of eating with his girlfriend. The money from the sales was used for the much needed supplies and equipment for the school.

A teacher in the rural school not only taught, but was janitor, nurse, doctor and parent at all times. It was not uncommon for an older brother or sister to burst through the schoolhouse door leading a little one in one hand, a bag in the other, uttering words of explanation that Mother and Father are on their way to town. The little one was the teacher's responsibility.

I began teaching the fourth grade in the elementary school of Glenrock, Wyoming, in the fall of 1956. I continued to serve that school for 17 years and retired from there on June 1, 1973.

I attended the University of Wyoming during the summer sessions, continued with extension and correspondence courses during the school year. I received my bachelor of arts degree from the University of Wyoming in 1959. To keep up with trends, I continued with my education, earning 26 hours of graduate credits beyond my degree.

What a wonderful career has been mine, touching so many lives through teaching. Many fellow teachers have often told me I was a dedicated and encouraging educator. I always explored new plans and ideas to promote interest, happiness and learning to students.

My work covers a span of 35.5 years and in the teaching profession, all of them in Converse County.

Besides being interested in professional organizations, I sponsored Future Teachers, was a leader of Girl Scouts, a leader of a 4-H club, a member of the Teckla Ladies' Club, Sunday school teacher in rural areas and a member of the Dry Creek Ladies' Club.

I now live in Douglas, Wyoming. I am a member of our local Converse County Retired Teachers Association, having served as vice president one year and president one year. I am a member of WEA, NRTA and Delta Kappa Gamma Society in which I served eight years as treasurer and two years as president. I enjoy working with 4-H members and continue with reading and educational courses. I sew, knit, crochet, make quilts, do arts and crafts, and enjoy canning and gardening besides my housework.

Beautiful and memorable years.

— Nu Chapter

Marjorie Lynn Thomas

Marjorie Lynn, pioneer teacher, was born to Oweta and Wilber Lynn July 4, 1906, in Shenandoah, Iowa. She was raised on a farm, attended a one-room school, and graduated from Shenandoah High School in 1924. She taught in a rural school in Iowa for two years before attending Peru State Teachers College in Peru, Nebraska. At Peru she met and married Craig E. Thomas. In 1927 they moved to the land of cowboys and Indians—Cody, Wyoming. Quite an exciting adventure for an Iowa farm girl.

Marge's husband, Craig, was principal of Cody High School for several years. Marge taught fifth grade for two years before their children, Lynn and Lyle, arrived on the scene. In 1938 they bought a tourist resort near Yellowstone Park, but Marge returned to teaching in a rural school for three years and in the Cody elementary schools for another seven years. Marjorie became a charter member of Gamma Chapter of Delta Kappa Gamma in 1949 and was also active in Eastern Star and the Cody Methodist Church. That same year she was nominated for "Teacher of the Year" in a national contest.

Marge and Craig spent their winters in California for several years before retiring to the beautiful little sea coast community of San Clemente, in 1958. Although Craig passed away in 1975, Marge continues to live in California. She belongs to Eastern Star and the World War I Auxiliary. She is a very active member of the United Methodist Church where she is most famous for the dozens of aprons she makes every year for their bazaar. She is also involved as a hospital auxiliary volunteer at San Clemente General. As an Orange Aide she has earned over 1,000 hours.

Marge's daughter and son are both graduates of the University of Wyoming. Craig Lyle is the general manager of the Wyoming Rural Electric Association, headquartered in Casper. Lynn is a fifth-grade teacher in Laramie. She is a member of Zeta Chapter of Delta Kappa Gamma. A granddaughter Margie and grandson Terry are also teachers in Wyoming schools.

Marge has eight grandchildren and one great-grandchild, and she enjoys spending part of the year visiting them in Wyoming. She continues to pursue her hobby of sewing and needlecraft and enjoys her rose garden. Many of her hours are spent calling on the ill and caring for those who are alone, much as she cared for and helped children in the classroom so many years ago.

— written by Lynn Thomas Martin, Zeta Chapter
— Pi Chapter

159

WINNIE THOMAS

I was born June 15, 1892, in the town of Carbondale (near Topeka), Kansas. Our household consisted of my mother and father, my father's father, his younger brother and his sister.

About 18 months after I was born a sister joined our group, and soon my teaching career started as I struggled in vain to teach her to use standard English instead of baby talk. As I observed that adults seemed to admire and were entertained by her talk, I tried using that myself but was scolded rather than admired.

Before I started to school we had moved to South Dakota and at that time were in Elk Creek. I was 8 years old when I started. We had only summer terms and progressed at individual speeds so it was possible to make a grade in a term, it seems. In the little school we had our own assignments and were kept quite busy. We looked forward to doing what the more advanced pupils were doing and were reviewed as we observed the work with lower grades. It was an experience for me when I went to Deadwood, South Dakota, for a short time. I was supposed to be in second grade but, since I had attended school such a short time, I was tried in first grade. When given an assignment I prepared it, raised my hand and said that I knew my lesson, and then had to learn what others knew—that you keep step and move with the others. Anyway, next day I was put into second grade. I was not entirely happy there as I had to be in the lower section as I couldn't do long division.

Most of my elementary school education was in rural schools near Roubaix, South Dakota. We went to school in a log schoolhouse crowded with eight grades; we had school in the Miners' Union Hall with only upper grades; we went to our new two-room school building and had two teachers for the building. By the time I was in eighth grade we were again taught by one teacher for the eight grades. We had to work hard and do much independently. It seems to me we had good teachers. I recall the joy of learning fractions in fifth grade. Our mother, I believe, thought "grammar" was being neglected in sixth grade, and a sister and I were sent for tutoring to a retired teacher for a time. However, I recall some of the things we learned in that grade. We prepared a school newspaper, we learned to conduct meetings and to participate, and to write minutes. And somewhere in the grades we must have become acquainted with debate and rules of debate.

My high school years took me to Colorado Springs, Colorado, to Deadwood, South Dakota, to Spearfish Normal School at Spearfish and finally to Effingham, Kansas, where my sister nearest me in age and I graduated. This was a normal training high school so I graduated in Latin, normal training and commercial. My college work was done in Spearfish and in Greeley, Colorado. In Greeley I received the bachelor of arts and master of arts degrees. I took some special work in Washington University at St. Louis, Missouri. I have some extension credit from the Chicago University, and some from the University of Minnesota.

In important learnings, I go back to the home with its many opportunities for learning. There were many people in our home—almost always an aunt or an uncle or both. Mother's twin sister lived with us from before I started to school until she passed away at 88 years of age. The twins were very close and sympathetic and talkative. I heard discussions and evaluations. Father's sister had a piano and gave music lessons. Both she and my father loved to read. Our home still has many of the beautiful books Papa collected. We had a big music box, and I had a hand organ before school age.

In the early home I can recall pulling basting threads for the women sewing and of trying to piece a little quilt. Aunt Sarah helped me learn crocheting—and we all made hairpin work. I crocheted a hood before I started to school.

We didn't have to have babysitters at our house, and there was always someone to take us when an event was one we might attend. I recall going to neighborhood Bible study or prayer group when I was probably 6 or 7 years of age. I got to see the cornerstone laid in a church in Deadwood and to see the documents put into it I was one of the first members of the Sunday school established in Roubaix (Perry then) in 1901, and still at this late date get to teach in it.

It seems we were really fortunate in not having television and radio in those days. They might have made us miss many valuable experiences. Radio became real in our group when our younger brother began building a set and maybe late at night might call out to Mother that he was hearing music on the little cigar box set that he tuned by opening and closing the lid.

A third girl in our family came when I was 7, and I had the chance to help in caring for a younger one. Our one brother was born when I was 11; I was ready to appreciate a new baby and to learn much from observation and participation in child care and training.

After graduating from high school I taught my first school. I had 35 pupils in eight grades and taught in the school from which I had graduated from the eighth grade. Some of my pupils knew little English. Of course, besides the teaching there was janitor work. But since I was teaching near home my father did a lot of that work. The family helped me understand and handle many situations which might have been difficult without the sympathetic interpretation the maturer minds could supply. I taught two years before going to college. My methods courses had more meaning than they would have had before my teaching experience.

In my own teaching experience and my preparation for it I am glad I didn't start to school too young. I appreciate the amount of individual instruction and the association with people of varying ages I had in the rural school. I was helped and taught and strengthened by the continued nearness and help of immediate family and other near relatives. I value the community experiences from early childhood to church and in business and in recreation in which I was able to participate with the family. Cooperative pupils and students all along the way have brought joy. Fellow teachers brought challenge and inspiration. It was my privilege to go to school when Dr. F.L. Cook was president of the school that is now Black Hills State College and to teach under him and later under Dr. E.C. Woodburn and then under Dr. R.E. Jonas.

I started teaching in 1911 and closed my teaching in May of 1969. I taught rural schools, was principal of a town school, was county superintendent of schools in Lawrence County, South Dakota, did county institute work, was a supervising teacher and later principal of the Laboratory School at Black Hills Teachers College, was a college instructor in various areas including method courses, and taught special education and remedial reading there and in Upton, Wyoming. In the years between 1911 and 1969, besides in teaching, my time was spent in going to school and helping in the store and post office. Most of my professional work was done in an area not more than a hundred miles from where I started teaching in my home town of Roubaix, South Dakota, in 1911.

In a class once I asked, "What do you think of teaching?" "It's hard work." "It's fun." "It's a tremendous responsibility." They were earnestly conscious of the challenge. To me it has seemed good to be a teacher.

After retirement I live in Spearfish. I became a member of Lambda Chapter of Delta Kappa Gamma in April 1963.

— Lambda Chapter

WYNONA EWOLDT THOMPSON

Wynona Ewoldt was born in Oakland, Iowa, in 1911. She received her high school education there and graduated from Grinnell College, Grinnell, Iowa, in 1933, with a BA degree in English and drama.

She taught fourth grade and high school in Oakland and Logan, Iowa, for five years before she married Max M. Thompson in 1938. They moved to Cody where they continued to live. Wynona taught English, speech and drama in Cody High School for 30 years, from 1943 to 1973, directing 60 major play productions as well as supervising one-act plays and the Readers' Theater and presenting speech and interpretive events for local, district and state speech meets. She also was the director of the permanent stage crew for the auditorium.

She became one of the charter members of Gamma Chapter, Delta Kappa Gamma, in 1949. She served as president of the Cody Classroom Teachers Association, of the Big Horn Basin Speech Association, and of the Wyoming State Speech Association.

Mrs. Thompson was chosen "Teacher of the Year" for school District 6 in 1966. She received awards from school District 6, the state Speech Association, and from Cody VFW Post for "Voice of Democracy" sponsorship. She was especially honored in 1973 when the Cody High School auditorium was named the Wynona Thompson Auditorium.

She retired from teaching in May 1973.

— Pi (Gamma) Chapter

Isabella Schramel Thrasher

What a long road Isabella has traveled since November 18, 1905, when she entered this world and saw the light of day from the window of her grandmother's sod house near Herndon, Kansas.

Isabella's parents were Theresia Leitner Schramel and John Schramel. Both maternal and paternal grandparents came from Golz, Austria-Hungary. They endured the usual hardships of European emigrants homesteading in a strange land, including economic and language difficulties.

When still very young, Isabella moved with her parents and sister to a tiny town near Lincoln, Nebraska. She attended elementary school in a country school under the direction of a teacher who managed all eight grades and up to 60 children in one term. In spite of it all the children managed to assimilate a goodly smattering of the basic "three R's."

From here Isabella graduated to what her class thought was the ultimate in school buildings, a new consolidated high school which combined three rural districts. What a wealth of activities she felt she was permitted to have here! No one could have appreciated to a greater degree the advantages offered in this small community school, where she completed the work in three years.

Isabella immediately enrolled in summer school at the University of Wyoming. That same fall, 1925, she began her career as a teacher. She taught a small country school north of Keeline, Wyoming, for three years. The first year was a liberal education in itself as she taught all grades including beginners up to 15 years of age. It was necessary to assume the role of advisor, supervisor, friend, janitor and doctor as well as teacher. There were many ups and downs and many times Isabella felt discouraged enough to call it "quits," but after borrowing money to attend the university there was no backing out and running home. Then, too, her parents were the kind that were not in sympathy with one's not completing a task once begun.

Isabella boarded two miles from school and since all the pupils rode horseback, she thought she should learn to ride in order not to be labeled a "greenhorn." Learning to ride was a real challenge when all she knew about a horse was that it had four legs, a front and a back.

Isabella was married to Harold Thrasher in 1927. A son, Paul, came to bless their home in 1928. Harold passed away in 1939. Isabella returned to teaching in 1941.

Isabella taught all eight grades in Jay Em, Wyoming, for four years and grade five in Lingle, Wyoming, two years. She taught grade four in Torrington, Wyoming, from 1947 to 1970, totaling 31 years.

Isabella received her BA degree from the University of Wyoming in 1953 and completed one year above her BA degree.

Isabella has traveled to 41 states. In 1966 she went to Hawaii on a geography trip through Chadron College. Other trips were to historic spots in the southern and eastern USA and four trips to Canada.

Isabella kept active in many areas. She is a charter member of Epsilon Chapter (1950). She has held the offices of president, vice president and corresponding secretary as well as serving on numerous committees.

She held memberships in national, state and local educational associations, Kappa Delta Pi, Business and Professional Women, state Historical Society, Presbyterian Women's Circle, and served as vice president of the local Classroom Teachers Association.

One of her articles, "Teachers Accept Challenge and Teach Without Textbooks," was published by Arthur C. Croft Publications.

Isabella's hobbies include gardening, painting, reading, embroidering, crocheting and tatting.

Having taught for 11 years in fourth grade with Isabella, I found her to be a master teacher in all subject areas. She was a very devoted teacher who placed the welfare and learning of children first. She was always ready and willing to help her co-workers and carried more than her share of the load on any task to be done.

Isabella often said, "In some small degree may I have been a good influence on most of my pupils." Many of her pupils would testify that she definitely was to a great degree, a good influence on their lives.

— by Geri Wood
— Epsilon Chapter

Loretta Booth Updike

My mother raised six children, four boys and two girls. She had graduated with honors in music and literature from Dushane College, Omaha, Nebraska. Father, Frank M. Booth, was a graduate in dentistry from Union College and the University of Nebraska where he taught dentistry at the dental college. He later opened an office in Lincoln and my parents separated. He finally became a dentist in Lovell, Wyoming, and later died at Missoula, Montana.

Mother provided for us. Our grandfather had proved up on what was called a "Walnut Claim" on Stevens Creek in Lancaster County, Nebraska. After the Civil War he planted three groves there. The 340 acres now belong to my two brothers. The other boys chose to work at other professions. My sister, Alice, and my mother are no longer with us.

I was born August 16, 1902, in Lancaster County, Walton, Nebraska. I attended District 6 (my grandfather had given a portion of his land for a school) for a part of my schooling and the remainder at St. Theresa's Catholic School in Lincoln.

We children drove a horse six miles to College View where we took a street car for another six miles to school daily. That was when we kids met William Jennings Bryan. He called us little "devils," but we liked his attentions. Some days were so very cold that we almost froze trying to reach the street car. By this time Mother was alone and she wanted us to be well grounded in our Catholic faith. I completed grade school and two years of high school with the sisters.

Money was scarce and I had about one good dress. I wanted to work and teaching was my first choice. At the ripe age of 16 I quit high school, late in October of 1917. I went to Lincoln and talked to the state superintendent of public instruction who gave me two names and addresses. I wrote to one and received a school—at Cherry in Cherry County, Nebraska. When my mother heard of it, she was shocked, but she said, "You got yourself into this, so you will **follow through** with it."

After corresponding with the director of Cherry School, I found I would have to go to Mullen, Nebraska, where someone would meet me. He was five hours late and didn't arrive until nearly evening. We stayed that night at a ranch only halfway to Cherry. The driver had car trouble and the roads were very sandy. It would be easy to lose one's way at night. Mother had bought my ticket, but she had given me only $5 so I didn't have enough to go home.

I tried to keep my age a secret since I was a year younger than two of my boy pupils. One was very unhappy over the fact, but we resolved the difficulties and I still correspond with them.

In April of the term I was offered a three-month school deeper in Cherry County. I received $5 more—the princely sum of $60 for 20 days! Mother wrote that when the term was over I was expected home. There I taught the Marshall School, a family school which had several families enrolled. They had no winter school as it was too isolated. Following this I taught one term three miles east of home. By then I knew that I needed more schooling.

The next summer and fall I went to the teachers' college high school, completing junior and senior years in one and a part of summer school, giving me university credits. After completing two more years of college, I taught at Anselmo, Nebraska, to stay there for 13 years.

While at Anselmo I met Jesse Updike who was to become my husband. We celetrated our 50th wedding anniversary recently with an open house. Jesse's father, Samuel, had been his teacher and a very stern one, too. Jesse says he had to sell books in order to get money to go to college and his pay was very low.

We moved to Riverton, Wyoming, in 1939. At that time no married woman was allowed to teach in the city schools. In 1939 and 1940 I taught the Miles Family School. I taught sixth grade part-time during the following term. The year after that I substituted all but 19 days. Then I was taken in as first-grade teacher.

While at Riverton I took extension courses and attended summer schools at Laramie, receiving my BA degree from the University of Wyoming and earning over 45 hours since that time.

I taught kindergarten five years after I retired from the Cody public schools in 1965. Our kindergarten was given an "excellent" rating from the state Department of Education.

We left Cody about 1971 and purchased a home in Mesa, Arizona, an area known as "Apache Wells Resort and Retirement Country Club." The summers are HOT and the winters cool, with an occasional rainy spell.

At the University of Nebraska I belonged to the Theta Phi Alpha Catholic Sorority which I had helped to organize and which I served as first president. I have been president of the Anselmo Community Women's Club. In college and at the community level I have acted in many plays.

I am a member of the Business and Professional Women's Club, took part in a play to raise scholarship funds, and portrayed "Niki, the Winged Serf" on the July 4th float.

I was classroom teacher organizer in Riverton and president of that organization for two years.

I belonged to the Toastmistress Club at Cody, Wyoming, and was its president for one term, acting as judge for the Toastmasters on occasion. I also served as president of the Cody Altar Society.

I was a charter member of Gamma Chapter of Delta Kappa Gamma, international honorary society of women educators, in 1949, held several offices at the local level and was chairman of several of the state committees of Alpha Xi State.

I've done some oil painting and am learning some new stitches in needlepoint. When in Cody I was director of duplicate bridge—I became a master player. I play bridge, ride a bicycle, swim when the weather permits, and walk daily, besides caring for my invalid husband who is in and out of the hospital.

— Pi Chapter

166

MARTHA WALLIS

My parents were Noah and Jane Trewartha Wallis. My father had stopped in Laramie on his way back to Wisconsin from a trip to Montana in 1868 and decided to locate there. In 1873 he returned to Wisconsin and the next year my mother, as a bride, came with him to Laramie where they made their home.

I arrived December 28, 1882, to join two brothers and a sister. By the time I started to school the furnace and restrooms of the junior high school building, which had been built in 1878, were in a one-story brick building on the west side of the main building. When I started to school, I waited on the corner for Mrs. Betsy Whiting, my teacher. For several years our reports were printed in colors. Blue was for the best grades, red for the next best, and black for lower grades. I believe it was an incentive to work.

Laramie's school system went only through the 10th grade and we continued at Prep. My university work was indeed mixed up. I started in normal work but switched to business courses hoping to go to work sooner and help pay bills from my long illness. My professor remarked to me that I was in the wrong work. I knew it, as I loved my teaching in Sunday school. The next fall I checked credits and went back to normal. I had worked in an office part of the year before and spent part of two years at the ranch. YWCA and Mandolin Club were the activities I enjoyed most.

In June 1909 I received my normal diploma. In September I registered with the idea of having a degree but a position opened up and I decided to apply for it. In late November of that year I began with a mixed class of third- and fourth-graders. The next year observation classes in public schools for student teachers were started. The children really enjoyed them more than the teachers—sometimes.

One year Mr. Wright, pastor of the Methodist Church, talked to us about Lincoln. He said Mr. Lincoln would surely have enjoyed reading a sign that Mr. Wright had seen above the entrance to a basement cafe. The sign read, "A cup of coffee and a roll downstairs for 10 cents." For the rest of the day there were sudden bursts of laughter.

Eastside attendance had increased so the cloak rooms had been made into classrooms, and St. Paul's Lutheran Church was used for a second grade for a few years. My next move was to the southwest corner of the main floor with first grade. I enjoyed fourth grade, but first grade was more rewarding for me. Our room enrollment was usually about 30 to 35, occasionally more.

I recall the late Smart Glenn as a first-grader. I would call him Glenn instead of Smart. Not long before his illness, we met and laughed at my error.

About 1912 Mrs. Emma Howell Knight invited our room to give a lesson in phonics for county institute during her term as county superintendent of schools. We used Miss Adsit's plan of word families, new words from a story in Reader and several long words for syllable accent. The children liked to bring words they had figured out at home.

Grace Peabody, our music supervisor, and I retired June 1919 and it closed 10 years of enjoyable work for me. I now had time for the church activities I had always enjoyed.

Since the deaths of my parents, one brother and a sister, my brother, Bert, and I have lived in Laramie where from 1934 to 1944 we had roomers. The two of us had trips into the mountains, where Bert trailed cattle for years. We motored to other places also.

I remember severe winters during my childhood, with blizzards that caused loss of stock some years. Many times the men going to the barns would tie a rope to the door of the house to guide them back. Mother said she often stood on the crusted snow to hang the clothes. The summers were as lovely as now, with the prairie colorful with wildflowers.

Early Laramie was unusual as we had running water in small ditches on both sides of the street to irrigate the trees and give pleasure to the children. In the beginning each street, or sometimes two streets, would form a water company. As a house was built, the owner joined the water company, paid his assessment, and then connected with the main line. Later, as the town grew and repairs were needed, the city took over all mains. For years Laramie had so-called "free" water, for the upkeep was part of the general tax, with restrictions on hours and days.

After the depression of 1893, Father rented ranch property or contracted to put up hay. Mother and I did the cooking. The water was in pails, our cupboards were makeshift, there were lamps to clean and fill, and one year there was a leaky roof which meant several times moving the table already set for dinner. However, when the work was done, we would walk to the field near the house and watch the men cutting, raking and stacking the hay. All work was done by horsepower.

Since the home ranch was sold in 1946, Bert and I have lived in Laramie. We have spent a few summers in the cabin on the Little Laramie River. There I often sit on the steps in the evening, thinking how people miss the beauty of the sky when living in town.

— by Martha Wallis, April 24, 1961,
"Some Early Laramie Reflections"
— Zeta Chapter

Anna Marie Weinlick

Anna Marie Weinlick was an unforgettable teacher. Thirty-five years since she left Sheridan, Wyoming, where she taught for 16 years, she is still spoken of often and warmly by former students and others who knew her. When her name is mentioned in a group, there is a lift of voices and an eagerness that shows how close they feel to her. She returns occasionally for a visit and is welcomed as a beloved friend. She has forgotten no one, and she listens with pride and sympathy to the stories she hears from many adults who were once her junior high school age students. Her understanding and encouragement have restored hope and self-confidence in many troubled persons.

Anna Marie was born in Bethel, Alaska, to the Rev. and Mrs. Joseph Weinlick who were missionaries to the Eskimos. Her father was Austrian by birth and her mother was born in South Germany. Eskimo children were her first playmates, and she was often the only white child on the station. She enjoyed these early companions and the stories she heard from them. I once heard her tell this true story that she had heard many times from her parents:

"Once, in traveling with my parents when I was 1½ years old, we were drawn in a dogsled. The dogs spied a rabbit and took chase and in passing some brush, the sled overturned. It was necessary when this happened to have the sled righted immediately. I was on my mother's lap covered with fur robes. When the sled overturned, my mother quickly did her part in retrieving blankets. Then the sled went on. After a quarter mile of travel, Mother said, "**Where** is Anna? I can't find her!" Nothing would do but to turn around. Imagine the relief when I was found unharmed on the snow, not even crying! Needless to say, there was much rejoicing."

When Anna Marie was about 8 years old, her parents returned to the states to put the little girl in a suitable school. They planned to go back to Alaska but due to circumstances, they remained and Mr. Weinlick served in various places as minister in Moravian churches. Other children were born who, in later years, had distinguished careers in the fields of education, social welfare and the Christian ministry.

Anna Marie graduated from the St. Charles, Minnesota, High School in 1917, from Winona Teachers College in 1922, and from the University of Minnesota in 1938. Before coming to Sheridan, Wyoming in 1925, she taught in Minnesota.

Miss Weinlick was an exceptional teacher. When a colleague and friend of the Sheridan years was asked about her recently, she had this to say:

"Miss Weinlick had such fundamental qualities as intelligence, training, scholarship, personality, character, personal appearance, intellectual honesty and common sense, along with such traits as sincerity of purpose and the genuine interest in the life of each pupil. She radiated enthusiasm and taught not only the importance of the essential tools of learning, but awakened the desire to apply them in life's situations. Beyond and above this, education became the enrichment of life itself. Her warmth of personal friendship showed each student how to meet his/her difficulties with determiniation and helped them to build bridges over the obstructions that beset each one in order to reach the desired goal."

While in Wyoming Miss Weinlick was selected to become a state charter member of Alpha Xi, Delta Kappa Gamma, and in 1940, along with 35 other women, she was initiated by Annie Webb Blanton, the founder of the society. At that time, she was principal of Hill School in Sheridan. Other organizations that she belongs to are PTA, PEO, ADG, the Wisconsin Historical Society and the Women's Fellowship of Church.

In 1941, Anna Marie left Wyoming to be nearer her ailing parents who lived in DeForest, Wisconsin. Her going was a great loss to the people of Sheridan whose lives she had so enriched. But her good work in school, church and community continued. She taught in Baraboo 1941-1942, Morristown 1952-1956 and DeForest 1942-1952; 1956-1965, all in Wisconsin. She retired in 1965 and continues to live in DeForest where she is active in the work of her church. The people of her area of Wisconsin have shown their love and appreciation of her by honoring her on several occasions.

Among her special interests are literature, music and travel. But her life has shown that above these, she loves her fellow man.

Anna Marie Weinlick was a wise and dedicated teacher, and her far-reaching influence for good cannot be measured.

— by Martha M. Wyland, Kappa Chapter

— Kappa Chapter

Gertrude Wenande

Gertrude Wenande was born on December 14, 1897, in Sundance, Wyoming. Her childhood was spent in Sundance and she attended grades one through 12 there.

Upon graduation from high school, Gertrude decided to apply for a teaching certificate. At that time a person could take an exam on eight subjects and acquire a first- or second-class certificate to teach for one or two school terms. A person could teach for four terms if she successfully passed an exam which included 12 subjects. For a life-time certificate, a person could take a test that included six college subjects. To keep her certificate a person had to take a test on two subjects every year and also go six weeks to summer school. Gertrude never went to college, but did take the exams to keep her teaching certificate. She did take a few correspondence courses.

In 1915 Gertrude started her teaching career at the Rifle Pit School near Beulah, Wyoming. She taught there for one term. In 1916 she was assigned to the Lone Tree School in Campbell County and taught there for one school term. She then taught for three years at the Horse Creek School. She also spent a half term at the New Haven School. She had teaching experience in grades one through eight.

In 1919 she was married to William Wenande at Mitchell, South Dakota. After her marriage, Gertrude taught three years at the Stroner School north of Moorcroft. William and Gertrude had two children, Mrs. Sonny Moore of Moorcroft, Wyoming, and Bob Wenande of Oshoto, Wyoming.

They lived near Moorcroft at Stroner for many years. In fact Gertrude was appointed postmaster at Stroner and held the position for 40 years. Her husband was engaged in cattle raising and they purchased the Dickey Ranch, which was located 40 miles north of Moorcroft. William and Gertrude also operated a grocery store at Stroner for 15 years.

After her husband's death in 1961, Gertrude discontinued her job at the post office. She then moved to Gillette in the '60s and sold their ranch to her son. She bought a house in Gillette and later moved to the Pioneer Apartments.

Gertrude had many interests which included hospital auxiliary work, volunteer work and bridge clubs. She also enjoyed handcrafts and helping neighborhood children with homework. One of her main interests was church work, and she taught Catholic religion classes for 17 years.

Gertrude is proud of her five grandchildren and six great-grandchildren. Although she taught only three years after she was married, she did enjoy teaching very much and still shows a definite interest in children.

— Theta Chapter

CLARICE WHITTENBURG
Professor Emeritus of Elementary Education
University of Wyoming

Clarice Whittenburg did indeed "blaze a trail where none was made before." She was inspirational and outstanding as a teacher of children, a college instructor, advisor to students and as a supervisor of student teachers. She was an educational leader at state, regional and national levels. She gave much time to research and writing and has probably done more on Wyoming history for the elementary child than any other person. She was active in and a leader in many community and educational organizations. She was an active participant in numerous committee assignments at the University of Wyoming, and as she did not hesitate to speak out on her convictions, her influence and guidance in committee roles were always most effective.

She served on the President's Advisory Committee, University Curriculum Committee, University Library Council, the 75th Anniversary Committee, and on many College of Education committees concerned with curriculum development, promotion and tenure, self-evaluation and graduate programs. She was highly respected by her colleagues and her advice and counsel were solicited by them and by students. She was known throughout Wyoming as an exemplary teacher who took a deep personal interest in each of her students. Former student teachers received regular bulletins of ideas for use in their classes.

Clarice was born April 12, 1899, in Marshfield, Missouri. She was a graduate of Central Missouri State Teachers College, received the master of arts degree at the University of Chicago, and did additional graduate work at the University of Southern California, Ohio State University, the University of Texas and the University of Wyoming. She taught in the public schools in Missouri, prior to joining the faculty at the University of Wyoming in 1930. During the academic year of 1949-50 she served as visiting professor of elementary education at the University of New Mexico and during the summer of 1959 at the University of Connecticut. Many times she was encouraged to accept regular college teaching assignments or an administrative position at the University of Wyoming, but she felt that her influence was greater as an elementary classroom teacher, and in that capacity she dedicated her efforts to the high quality teaching for which she became known and respected in local, state and national circles.

Clarice gave much time and effort to research and will be long remembered for her articles on methodology especially in the area of arithmetic which appeared in such magazines as the *Instructor, Grade Teacher, Educational Forum* and *Wyoming Education News*. Altogether, she authored approximately 50 articles and book reviews published in national journals. She wrote a section of "Wyoming" for the Britannica Junior Encyclopedias. Her book, WYOMING'S PEOPLE, written for fourth-grade children, is a classic in its field.

In recognition of her professional achievements, Clarice was the recipient of many honors and awards. She was a member of Kappa Delta Pi, education honorary, and was awarded their "Honor Key" for service to education. She was elected to membership in Pi Lambda Theta; the Delta Kappa Gamma Society; and became an honorary member of Mortar Board—a service organization on the campus at the University of Wyoming. In 1963 the Wyoming Education Association presented her the "Golden Key Award" for outstanding professional leadership and contributions to the building of the profession of teaching. In 1958 she had received state awards from the Wyoming Historical Society and from the Wyoming Press Women for her book, WYOMING'S PEOPLE.

Clarice was especially interested in state and Western historical writings and was an associate member of Western Writers of America. She was an active member of both the Albany County Historical Society and the Wyoming Historical Society. She received special recognition from the Wyoming State Historical Society for her research of Wyoming.

Prior to her demise she gave a collection of children's books on Western history to the Wyoming University School Library, a collection of Western books to the William Robertson Coe Library and her files of photographs, pictures and her research papers to the University of Wyoming Archives.

After her retirement, Clarice continued her research of Wyoming and regional history and her many community activities. She presented a series of radio programs for the 100th anniversary celebration of the Union Pacific Railroad coming to Wyoming. She prepared a publication for the Wyoming Travel Commission which is treasured by many people in the state. She gave much pleasure and information to various groups in the state as a speaker on topics related to Wyoming and Laramie history. Recipients of her unique Christmas cards depicting Wyoming history and those who have autographed copies of WYOMING'S PEOPLE feel that they have a part of a priceless heritage from a remarkable woman and a true friend.

Clarice retired from active teaching in 1964. She passed away in Laramie, Wyoming, May 11, 1971.

Henry Books Adams said: "A teacher affects eternity; he can never tell where his influence stops." Clarice Whittenburg was, indeed, a great teacher, devoted to her profession.

— by Edith W. Watters

— Zeta Chapter

JENNIE WILLIAMS

No matter now interesting your life may have been to you, what events in it will interest others? I'm sure that my history has seemed very orthodox to the outsider. My father was a rancher, my mother a school teacher—the usual combination that helped populate Wyoming in the '90s. At the age of 18, my father reached Wyoming from Nova Scotia, becoming a "bull whacker" for the first eight years, then homesteading on Piney Creek in 1883. My mother doubled her salary as an Iowa teacher by coming to Wyoming in 1890. They met at a beef round-up that fall. Also, according to Western tradition, they married the following April and spent the rest of their lives on the ranch which my father added to from time to time by buying or leasing more land.

I was the middle one of the three children, arriving in May of 1894. The house I was born in was a seven-room log house, boasting an upstairs (a vanity in that era), which my father had built with the help of neighbors. We soon moved into a spacious stone house built of the native sandstone. The neighborhood schoolhouse was also of that material, the first in the district which also included Story.

I started to school before I was 5, shocking the entire neighborhood. My mother's reason for letting me attend was sound. She said I might as well sit around at school and read as to do it at home. So I've spent a good many hours sitting around in classrooms and thoroughly enjoyed most of them.

As to further education, after graduation from Sheridan High School, I had a year and a half at Grinnell College in Iowa; two years and a summer term at the University of Colorado in Boulder, where I received an AB degree; one summer term at Berkeley; and then took my MA from Denver University.

I am occasionally introduced by local friends as a rural school teacher, but my country school teaching lasted just three years. Since that time I have done everything in the teaching field from nursery school, which I set up for the state of Colorado, to junior college instruction in Idaho and Wyoming.

Between jobs in the teaching field, I have had a number of unrelated jobs—from rural mail carrier and book agent to being office secretary to the Colorado Mental Hygiene Society. This was a private enterprise, organized by individuals who saw the need for something of the sort long before our benign government was conscious of the need. I spent four years with the state Department of Education in Cheyenne as state high school inspector, which gave me the opportunity to visit every town in Wyoming which sported a high school and a number of rural schools which gave ninth-grade work in addition to the usual eight years—a job that recharged my enthusiasm for my native state.

Another strenuous diversion was membership in home extension work, everything from membership in the first extension club to be organized in Wyoming, to national president of the organization. That, incidentally, was one of the surprise honors that came along the way. Other surprises were not so gratifying; such as, being told by your boss on Saturday noon not to return to work on Monday morning, or opening your wallet and finding only the $1 bill you had carefully wrapped around your month's pay.

It was while I was neck-deep in extension work, serving at the time as secretary to the state organization that I made my first trip abroad to Copenhagen to attend the international meeting of the Associated Country Women of the World. I was official representative of the U.S. national organization. Other tours have been to Rhodesia and South Africa, the only countries on that continent that are ruling the native Africans justly and beneficially. Another delightful trip was to Australia and New Zealand with the Fijis thrown in for an accent of flavor. I have also gotten acquainted with many of the Caribbean islands, thanks to a nephew who was stationed on various ones as part of his very interesting career. I have visited most of the provinces of Canada and all but two of our states.

One of my other interests has been politics. My interest in that began with the assassination of President McKinley. From that time on I was an ardent Republican, which eventually climaxed in another unexpected honor. I went as a delegate to San Francisco in 1964 to the National Republican Convention.

I consider that I have had a most varied and interesting (to me) life. Lately, I seem determined to share certain anecdotes from it with anyone who can be induced to listen.

I shall always feel that my one outstanding achievement was that I managed to be born into the right century. Nothing could have been finer than the last decade of the 19th century in which to get one's start in life.

— Alpha Chapter

Alice Williamson

Alice, one of three daughters of David H. Williamson and Jessie Seaver Williamson, was born in Independence, Iowa, November 27, 1884.

She graduated from the University of Colorado in 1910 and did graduate work two summers at Columbia University and one at the University of Wyoming.

Her first teaching experience was at Victor, Colorado. She often walked the two miles from Victor to Cripple Creek to play bridge with Keturah Fleischli, a lifelong friend, who also made Cheyenne her home for many years.

In 1914 Alice moved to Cheyenne, Wyoming, where she taught for one year at Corlett Elementary School. Then she transferred to Central High School where she taught mathematics until her official retirement July 1, 1950. However, Alice taught two more years at Central, substituted at Central, and did tutoring at F.E. Warren Air Force Base.

Alice traveled extensively. She took many bus tours all over the United States and to Lake Louise in Canada. Edna Stolt of the state Department of Education accompanied Alice on several trips. Her first trip to Europe was in 1930 by ship and included the United Kingdom and most of the continent. She went to Hawaii twice, once renting an apartment for a two-month visit. In order to travel, Alice put aside a certain amount from each paycheck.

Alice had many hobbies in addition to traveling and playing bridge. She was an avid reader on a broad scope of topics which made her a most interesting and knowledgeable conversationalist. She maintained her interest in reading until her eyesight diminished at age 94. She also enjoyed doing crossword and jigsaw puzzles. Her family, however, was her greatest source of pleasure. She adored her nephew's children and spent much time at the family cabin near Centennial, Wyoming, with this family and her sister. Alice always made herself useful there. She even helped oil the cabin logs! Alice's greatest hobby was people—all ages and all types.

Alice Williamson became a member of Delta Kappa Gamma May 11, 1929, and helped co-found the organization in Cheyenne and in Wyoming where she was the first president of Alpha Chapter and served as the first Wyoming state president.

She became a member of the DAR on January 29, 1924, and later served as regent. In 1932 she was elected to membership in Chapter C of the PEO Sisterhood. She was also an active member of the Presbyterian Church. She belonged to professional organizations and was a member of the Retired Teachers Association.

Alice was a very little (in size only) person who was well-groomed and well-dressed. She always wore earrings—even when oiling the logs—and never wore oxfords, "old ladies' shoes."

Of the many honors she received, one especially pleased her. On Curt Gowdy Day in Cheyenne, dedicating the park named for him, Curt, who had attended school in Cheyenne, extended a personal invitation to Alice to attend the dinner in his honor. There Curt asked her to stand and said she was the one teacher he remembered, the person who had influenced him most. (Curt left Cheyenne years before and had become one of the best-known sportscasters on television.)

Alice Williamson died January 11, 1981, at age 96—mentally alert and enjoying people to the end. As a final tribute a number of those attending the funeral service were ex-students honoring "the best teacher and friend" they had had.

A quotation sent to Alice May 16, 1966, honoring her as the first president of Delta Kappa Gamma, summarizes best: "A rose for her two qualities that make life so wonderfully worth living. No matter what the task, she put forth her best efforts and being helpful to others gave her special satisfaction."

— Alpha Chapter

LEAH MAY WINDER

"Rattlesnakes—the sage-covered prairies were full of them and I was terribly afraid of them out on our homestead north of Orin Junction in the spring of 1919. But you have to face up to life and make the best of it. When I found a rattler in my garden I made myself kill it with a hoe."

Thus, Leah May Winder recalls her early days in Wyoming. Her statement, ". . . you have to face up to life . . ." typifies her personality, but she should have added, ". . . with a sense of humor and a song in your heart."

Leah May Lindley was born May 8, 1895, on a small farm near Sharpsburg, Iowa. Her parents, Henry M. and Nancy Jane Gray Lindley, had five children, Albert, Laura, Clifford, Leah and Fern. They sold this farm and bought another one near a rural school north of Bedford, Iowa. Leah started at this school when she was only 4 years old and went there for eight years. Then she drove a horse and buggy to Bedford High School. History, English and science were her favorite subjects.

After finishing high school and taking a state examination, Leah went to teaching a rural school for $54 a month. In those early rural schools the teacher was her own janitor and taught all grades. One group of students was called up to recite their lessons while the others stayed at their desks and studied. It was a tight schedule working in many classes on different subjects from beginners to eighth-graders. The most discouraging part was that in early spring farmers took their sons out of school to plow. In five years Leah taught in three different schools in Taylor County, Iowa. Her last school was rated as one of the top two schools in the county.

On Christmas day 1918 Leah married John Winder, a livestock feeder. Then for half a year she served as assistant county superintendent. Her brother, Clifford, had homesteaded near Orin, Wyoming, and encouraged them to come west. So, in the spring of 1919 John shipped his three horses, machinery and household goods out in an emigrant car and Leah came by train to Orin. Orin was named for Orin Hughitt, uncle of the president of the Chicago and Northwestern Railroad and was a flourishing town with two stores, a saloon, hotel, depot, other businesses and a number of residences.

John Winder filed on a homestead and an additional homestead two and a half miles north of Orin. He started to build a two-room cement block house but did not have it finished by the time the hard winter of 1919 broke. Texas steers that roamed the prairies without feed or shelter died like flies in the cold storms.

Leah was busy that winter teaching the Fisher School on Shawnee Creek. The schoolhouse was a large log cabin at an old sheep-shearing camp and the pupils were children of homesteaders. John, who worked on the railroad section crew, walked to the schoolhouse on his way to work, built a fire and the schoolhouse was warm by the time Leah and the children arrived. Most of that winter the Winders lived in an old freight car to which they had moved from the brother's homestead shack.

In the spring John finished their house on the homestead, dug a well by hand, broke land and planted cane, corn and potatoes. Leah put in a large garden. At last they were home, after having moved seven times during their first year in Wyoming. Next winter John was helping build a bridge across the Platte River at Orin Junction and came home only on weekends. So Leah stayed home to care for the livestock and chickens.

That winter a horse, Queen, fell into the root cellar and had to stay there for several days until John came home and made a large enough opening to get her out. The young settlers helped one another and considered many things, like getting Queen out of the cellar, to be lots of fun.

In 1924 Leah started teaching in the Platte Valley school five miles southeast of Orin. She taught there four years and stayed at the Jim Shaw ranch. Then the Winders moved to Orin and Leah taught the primary grades in Orin's three-room schoolhouse for two years. Orin was dwindling in population and the number of teachers was reduced. So the third year Leah had 29 pupils in the primary and upper grades. She taught in Orin for six years until all married teachers in Wyoming were dismissed.

In the Depression year of 1934 Leah was a case worker in the eastern and southern parts of Converse County. Driving a 1928 Chevy that she bought for $100, she visited ranch homes often following dim trails to isolated ranches to gather needed information. Leah says this was the most exciting year of her life. She resigned her job on December 1 and Christmas Day, on their 16th wedding anniversary, their first child, John, was born. Laura Jo was born in February 1938. Leah turned down all offers to teach. She was too busy and happy raising her own children, who eventually went by bus to school in Douglas. Husband John passed away with a heart attack in December 1946.

Leah started taking correspondence courses from the University of Wyoming as early as 1924. In 1947 she attended summer school at Laramie. That fall she moved to Lusk and started teaching the second grade, which she continued to do for 17 years. During some summers Leah continued her education at the University of Wyoming until she had a full three years of credit. At a final summer school in Chadron, Nebraska, she received a BS degree with a major in primary education and minors in history and English. She graduated magna cum laude. Leah retired in 1964 after 33 years of teaching.

In rural schools Leah played outdoor games with the children. She was one of them but she always kept their respect. Her eyes both flashed with determination and softened with fondness as she remembered one boy who would not obey or get his lessons. That day he was sent home from school to chop wood for his mother. Next day he was taken into the basement and given a firm talking-to. Leah told him she was ready to help him all she could, but that his life was what HE made it. Now the boy, a successful man, always remembers her birthday.

When children became restless and bored in school, Leah told how she gave them a change; told them to go out and run around the swing three times and come back in; sing a song and clap hands; imagine themselves as sacks of meal and lie down flat on their desks and relax while the meal ran out of all four corners of the sack. She made going to school a challenge for their abilities and made life fun to live.

Now Leah's hobbies are visiting her children and four grandchildren, and music. Once she taught all children in Orin to play her piano which she still has and plays. She belongs to Delta Kappa Gamma, Kappa Delta Phi, Sigma Delta Nu, National and Wyoming's Retired Teachers Associations, Eastern Star, Congregational Church and Circle, Niobrara Hospital Auxiliary, Republican Women's Club, Federated Women's Clubs, and is past president of Lusk Business and Professional Women's Club. Leah is still a very busy and happy person.

— by Mae Urbanek, Epsilon Chapter

— Epsilon Chapter

PEARL WRIGHT

I was born in Broken Bow, Nebraska, on the homestead of my grandfather, Jacob Mauk. This town was named many years after my grandfather homesteaded there. My brother, sister and I were raised on this farm on which my mother, Mary (Mauk) Wright, and father, Charley Wright, remained during all their married lives.

I was unable to finish high school, due to illness, so went to a college and took a business course. At this college I served as secretary for the registrar for a number of years. However, I wanted to be a teacher, and started teaching in my early 20s. My first teaching was in my home town, a fifth grade, with 47 students. The next year I was advanced with my class to the sixth grade, where I was grade principal for several years.

In the early '30s, when I received enough credits to be a high school teacher, I came to Wyoming and taught in a rural consolidated school at Morrisey, Wyoming. I have many fond memories of my patrons who were mostly homesteaders. From there I moved to another Wyoming town where I was a business teacher and became principal there.

I have life certificates in Wyoming, Nebraska, Colorado and South Dakota, and was high school principal in three of these states.

I received my college credits mostly in summer schools, and received my BA degree in Nebraska and my master's in Colorado. Most of it came through summer school work, but I enjoyed my vacations in Colorado, California and Nebraska while I was getting these degrees.

I have been high school principal in Wyoming, Colorado and South Dakota. I completed my teaching at Lingle, Wyoming, and have many wonderful friends among both students and patrons there. It has been a joy to teach seniors and juniors for 25 years of my 41 years of teaching. I am now retired, but miss the association with my young people very much. I learned the problems of life with them.

After the severe illness of my father in the 1940s, I took over the business of the farm, and learned many things which were of value to me in my later years. I taught in my home town, Broken Bow, while helping my father carry on his farm work.

On an occasion during my teaching of seniors, the farm topic of milking came up. I remarked that I had done such work while on the farm. One of my senior boys laughingly remarked, "A teacher knows how to milk?" I answered, "Yes, a teacher who knows how to milk." Some time later I was invited to dinner in that farm home. During the evening this boy came in from his chores, planted a bucket by my side and remarked, "Show me." I went with him to the barn, took the bucket and started milking. He stood in amazement and finally said, "Goodness, you can milk, can't you!" I wasn't questioned about a farm after that.

— Epsilon Chapter

179

FLORENCE E. WOGOMAN

Florence was born on May 14, 1898, in Garden City, Kansas. She was left an orphan when very small and various relatives took care of her. When she was 17, she came to Powell to make her home with Dr. and Mrs. Mills. Mrs. Mills encouraged her to continue her education until she became a well-qualified teacher. She taught in Park County for about 33 years.

Her first year of teaching was at the Marquette School, a one-room school about 15 miles west of Cody. It had cross lighting, a big, pot-bellied coal stove for heating, no electricity and no indoor plumbing. Her course in normal training had emphasized the importance of making the schoolroom attractive, so she set about blackening the stove and hanging sash curtains at the windows.

Florence boarded at the nearby ranch of Andy Martin, where she enjoyed the family of young people. One of her pupils, Sylvester Martin, built fires for her at the schoolhouse so the room would be warm when the pupils arrived.

Florence was paid $65 a month for nine months. Board and room sliced off quite a sum, but she felt rich and indulged in a record player with her first available funds. The highlight of her recreation was to travel by horseback or team to dances—sometimes 20 miles away—where everyone danced until dawn.

In 1918-1919 she taught the Fairview School near Powell. In 1919 she taught first grade in Powell, but she resigned at the end of the year intending to try the Kansas schools. She could not forget Wyoming, and she returned to teach the Dick Creek School above Meeteetse, Wyoming.

Florence married Bryan Wogoman, a Sunlight rancher, in 1926. She loved their ranch, and they lived there until the early 1940s when they sold out and bought a home in Cody.

In the meantime, since ranching didn't bring in much money, she continued to teach—first at Paint Creek, then at Pat O'Hara, Clark, Sunlight, and back to Clark. After moving to Cody, Florence taught at Oregon Basin and finally in Cody where she remained until 1950, making a total of 33 years as an elementary teacher.

In 1950 the death of the Park County Superintendent, Amy Irwin, a Delta Kappa Gamma member, left a vacancy to be filled. The county commissioners knew of Florence's fine work and asked her to fill that vacancy. Her memory went back to the 1930s and to one school in particular, where there was constant quarreling and guns were brought to district meetings. The county superintendent had to be brought in to try to restore peace and calm. At that time Florence said to herself, "I'd never want to be a county superintendent!" But the persuasive tongue of Mildred McKelvy, a good friend, caused her to change her mind, and she became Florence Wogoman, Park County Superintendent of Schools.

In preparation for her position, she had her college degree from the University of Wyoming as well as her many years of experience. Never one to sit back and rest on past achievements, she visited Old Mexico with Margaret Dempster one Christmas vacation. She was constantly anxious to give more and more services to her rural schools. She always took a good movie to show when visiting, or a new record. She compiled a boolet of well-known poems to be used by students and had a combined program every year in Cody for students to give original stories, poems and songs. Every spring, Florence planned a track meet, either in Cody or some school where the grounds were adequate. The school winning the most points was given a very fine trophy to exhibit in their school. Florence kept a cherished collection of original poems, compositions and funny sayings of her pupils. Pictures of rural schools and a year-by-year account of teachers and pupils are among her souvenirs.

180

After almost 53 years of service to Park County, Florence retired January 1, 1971. Her many friends and fellow workers of the Park County Courthouse held a very lovely reception in her honor. It was attended by people of all the school districts. The group gave her a lovely photograph of the Sunlight area, taken in color by Jack Richards. This gift was really appreciated by Florence and her husband, Bryan.

May D. Shoemaker, retired superintendent of Big Horn County schools in Greybull, shares her recollections with us:

Florence was an active member of the International Educational Organization for Women Educators, namely Delta Kappa Gamma Society. She was also a devout member of the Christian Science Church.

Because I was county superintendent of schools of a neighboring county, Big Horn, Florence and I were brought together on many occasions of mutual and professional interest. Frequently she invited me to share her car as we traveled to various meetings. Needless to say, we soon became fast friends.

Aside from the many short trips we made together by car, we took several distant ones by plane. Just to mention a few of these, we went to Washington, D.C.; Miami, Florida, extending into the Everglades; then turning westward visiting in all the states bordering the Gulf of Mexico; then north through Texas to Wyoming and home. An enjoyable trip!!

Perhaps the most interesting trip that we ever made together was the one made following the honor we both had received of being appointed goodwill delegates to Russia in conjunction with President Eisenhower's "People to People" program. It was on this memorable tour in 1959 that Florence and I became the very best of friends day by day, as we shared the same room or were seatmates, as the case might be, on this three-week journey.

In addition to spending more than a week behind the Iron Curtain in Russia, East Berlin and Czechoslovakia, we visited six other countries, namely: Finland, Sweden, the Netherlands, West Berlin, Belgium and France. This was a never-to-be-forgotten journey to which we often referred in our conversations of later years.

Florence and her husband lived happily in their comfortable and attractive home in Cody after his retirement from the U.S. Forest Service. The last few winters were spent in the pleasant climate of Arizona following Florence's retirement.

Florence's sudden death on April 2, 1975, came as a shock to her numerous friends and associates. We all, however, find comfort as we recall the useful and upright life she lived, the pleasant memories of time spent in her company, and the assurance that all is well with her now.

— by Margaret Dempster and May Dot Shoemaker

— Pi Chapter

MARGARET FRANCINA WYMORE

M argaret Francina Wymore was born on November 16, 1902, in Laramie, Wyoming. Her father was A.J. Wymore, who came to Laramie City, Wyoming Territory, from Iowa. Her mother was Elizabeth Smith Wymore from Illinois. Both arrived in the Laramie territory in May of 1890.

Francina relates the following story about her life:

Mother was a school teacher. Father was a plasterer and cement man by trade. He and his brother, Saul, kept all the Union Pacific buildings in repair between Ogden, Utah, and Sidney, Nebraska, before 1900. One brother, who is a retired body and fender repair man, lives in Santa Maria, California.

I went to school through grade seven in rural schools in Albany County. After several years on the ranch I decided to make whatever sacrifices were necessary to obtain an education. At age 14 I went to Laramie to work for my board, room, tuition and books to go to school. I graduated from the state training preparatory school at the University of Wyoming in 1924. Among my classmates, and president of my high school graduating class, was Jack Stephen Bugas, now widely known for his vice presidency of Ford Motor Company and administrative work in various field of endeavor.

My master's degree was awarded in 1940. My majors were sociology and economics. I had enough in each field to go on for a doctorate. My thesis, "A Sociology and Economic Study of Laramie, Wyoming," is preserved in the archives of the Wyoming university. It can be used only under supervision for research on Laramie.

I taught my first school, Lakeside School, in Albany County for the year 1924-1925. I received $100 a month for this assignment. From June 1925 to August of 1926 I attended the University of Wyoming where I worked for all my expenses. In 1926-1927 I taught in a rural school in Niobrara County. From 1927 to 1931 I taught in Campbell County schools. The last three years there were spent as a high school teacher. In 1928 I graduated from the University of Wyoming with a normal diploma from the College of Education. In 1931 I received a BA degree from the College of Liberal Arts at the University of Wyoming. In 1931-1932 I taught the two-year high school at Fort Fred Steele, Wyoming. In 1932-1933 I taught English at Fort Laramie in the high school. During 1933-1934 I taught the Snodgrass School in Natrona County and in 1934-1935 I taught grade school at Kaycee, Wyoming. In 1936 from January to June, I taught grade 11 at the Nellie Iles School in Laramie, Wyoming. From September of 1936 until June of 1947 I taught English and government in Laramie High School. From 1948 to 1964 I taught the physically handicapped children of Laramie. This program had the most students of this kind, per population, of any town in the United States. Several of those students graduated from high school and the University of Wyoming.

Organizations and offices which I have held are:

Past chief of Pythian Sisters in Laramie, Wyoming; past secretary of American Association of University Women; chairman of the Wyoming History Group for 13 years; charter member of Daughters of Union Veterans of the Civil War; secretary for two years of the Women's Relief Corps (the auxiliary of the Union Veterans of the Civil War); past secretary and past chairman of International Affairs and programs for the Laramie Business and Professional Women; charter member and first secretary of Laramie Citizens for Good Government; and charter member and tour guide for Laramie Plains Museum Association.

I have written a brief history of Laramie for the Laramie Plains Hotel, Motel Association brochure. I have also written the story of the Laramie Plains Museum. Both of these articles have been accepted for publication. Through the last several years, letters I have written have been published in the *Boomerang* column entitled, "The People Speak."

On February 19, 1981, I addressed the Lambda Delta Sigma national sorority on the subject of "service." I was awarded the honorary recognition for exemplary life and the contribution in promoting the ideals of Lambda Delta Sigma.

Delta Kappa Gamma came to Wyoming on June 1, 1940. That first meeting was held at the Plains Hotel in Cheyenne. It was a dinner meeting. Dr. Annie Webb Blanton presided at the meeting and installed the group as a state chapter. It is now Alpha Chapter. I was elected its first secretary. I was named one of the state founders, an honor I hold more deeply than any other I have received. My

40 years with Delta Kappa Gamma have been ones of development, happiness, growth and enjoyment, but most of all of thanksgiving that I could become associated with such a noteworthy organization. "Thank you, Delta Kappa Gamma, for all the kindnesses and help you have given me. It has certainly been worth the effort to have been selected by Annie Webb Blanton to become one of your group."

At the Alpha Xi State convention in Cheyenne on April 25, 1981, Francina Wymore was recognized and presented with a founder's pin by the president of Alpha Chapter, Janet Laughlin. Francina accepted the pin with great joy, stating that it was one of the great moments in her life. She has truly been a faithful and dedicated member of Delta Kappa Gamma.

— Alpha Chapter